The Debt Dilemma
of Developing
Nations

Recent Titles from QUORUM BOOKS

Disaster Management: Warning Response and Community Relocation
Ronald W. Perry and Alvin H. Mushkatel

The Savings and Loan Industry: Current Problems and Possible Solutions
Walter J. Woerheide

Mechatronics
Mick McLean, Editor

Establishing and Building Employee Assistance Programs
Donald W. Myers

The Adversary Economy: Business Responses to Changing Government Requirements
Alfred A. Marcus

Microeconomic Concepts for Attorneys: A Reference Guide
Wayne C. Curtis

Beyond Dumping: New Strategies for Controlling Toxic Contamination
Bruce Piasecki, Editor

Payments in the Financial Services Industry of the 1980s: Conference Proceedings
Federal Reserve Bank of Atlanta, Sponsor

Japanese Business Law and the Legal System
Elliott J. Hahn

YOUTHJOBS: Toward a Private/Public Partnership
David Bresnick

State Government Export Promotion: An Exporter's Guide
Alan R. Posner

Principles for Electric Power Policy
Technology Futures, Inc. and Scientific Foresight, Inc.

The Debt Dilemma of Developing Nations

ISSUES
AND CASES

Chris C. Carvounis

Quorum Books
WESTPORT, CONNECTICUT

Library of Congress Cataloging in Publication Data

Carvounis, Chris C.
  The debt dilemma of developing nations.

  Bibliography: p.
  Includes index.
  1. Debts, External—Developing countries. 2. Debts,
External—Developing countries—Case studies. I. Title.
HJ8899.C37 1984   336.3′435′091724   84-1981
ISBN 0-89930-062-6 (lib. bdg.)

Library of Congress Catalog Card Number: 84-1981
ISBN: 0-89930-062-6

First published in 1984 by Quorum Books

Greenwood Press
A division of Congressional Information Service, Inc.
88 Post Road West, Westport, Connecticut 06881

Printed in the United States of America

10 9 8 7 6 5 4 3 2 1

To Willie and Nicky

CONTENTS

TABLES

ACKNOWLEDGEMENTS

A generous measure of thanks must be accorded to the researchers and writers whose reportage, conceptualizations and commentaries have provided the substantive basis of this book. They are to be especially commended for their broad and timely response to a crucial topic having universal implications.

I wish to extend my gratitude to my colleagues at St. John's University, especially to Drs. Francis Lees, Maximo Eng, Anthony Angelini and Chaman Lal Jain, for their guidance in this project, and to Professors Terrence Brady, Edward Downe, Valerie Englander, Adrian Fitzsimons, Arlene Furfero, Stephen Kagann, Stanley Lawson, Geoffrey Poitras, John Alexion, Lee L. Lattimer, Ann Bynoe, Frederick D. Schmidt, LeRoy E. Pagano, Joel J. Sokoloff, Angelos Tsaklanganos, Thaddeus Tuleja, Raymond Kudla, and Peter Charanis for their valuable insight. Appreciation is also due to the staff of St. John's Loretto Memorial Library, particularly Francine Russo, Eugene Hunt, Joseph Lipari, William Stone and Rose Leonardi. Most of all I thank my assistant Roger Fields, whose expertise in research and editing proved invaluable in all stages of my work and without whom this volume would never have been realized.

ABBREVIATIONS

ALFA: Groupo Industrial Alfa, a privately held, Mexican conglomerate

BIS: Bank for International Settlements, a multilateral, balance-of-payments adjustment institution

CCC: Commodity Credit Corporation, a trade-credit agency of the United States government

CMEA: Council of Mutual Economic Assistance, an economic support alliance among Warsaw Pact nations, similar in form to the EEC

COC: Comptroller of Currency, a regulatory agency of the United States government

COMECON: Alternative acronym for CMEA

CTLD: Convertible Lira Deposit Scheme, a foreign exchange acquisition program instituted by the Turkish government in the mid-1970s

DAC: Development Assistance Committee, a multilateral body of industrialized nations concerned with global development

DSR: Debt-Service Ratio, a rough index of debt service capacity

EEC: European Economic Community, also known as the Common Market, a mutual economic support alliance among West European nations

FDIC: Federal Deposit Insurance Corporation, an official regulatory and underwriting agency of the United States government

GDP: Gross Domestic Product

GNP: Gross National Product

IBRD: International Bank for Reconstruction and Development, the parent and largest organization within the World Bank Group, a multilateral lending organization

IDA: International Development Association, an organization within the World Bank Group for extending concessional credit to developing countries

IFC: International Finance Corporation, an organization within the World Bank Group similar to the IDA

IMF: International Monetary Fund, the central, multilateral balance of payments institution

JP: Justice Party, a Turkish political party

LDC: Less-Developed Country

LIBOR: London Interbank Offered Rate, the interest rate or cost of funds to prime borrowers in the Eurocredit market

MDB: Multilateral Development Bank, a term covering the IBRD and its regional banks for an organization using funds from a number of nations to support economic development

MNC: Multinational Corporation

NIC: Newly Industrialized Country, an advance LDC

ODA: Official Development Assistance, covers both bilateral and multilateral foreign aid in the form of grants or concessional loans

OECD: Organization for Economic Cooperation and Development, a multilateral economic support and development alliance of the industrialized nations

OPEC: Organization of Petroleum Exporting Countries, an energy cartel dominated by the nations of the Middle East

PEMEX: Petroleos Mexicanos, Mexico's state-owned petroleum production monopoly

PLO: Palestine Liberation Organization, a group representing Palestinian refugees

PRI: Institutional Revolutionary Party, Mexico's largest political party

PT: Worker's Party, a Brazilian political party

RPP: Republican People's Party, a Turkish political party

SAL: Structural Adjustment Loan, a loan extended by both the IBRD and the IMF to help nations adjust to external shocks, e.g., the oil price hikes of the 1970s

SDRs: Special Drawing Rights, a form of "currency" issued by the IMF as a means of redistributing balance of payments surpluses

SEE: State Economic Enterprise, a government-owned enterprise common in the Turkish economy

SIFT: Statement of International Financial Transactions

SNI: Brazil's national security agency

UMS: United Mexican States, official abbreviation for the Mexican government

The Debt Dilemma
of Developing
Nations

Chapter 1

INTRODUCTION

Purpose

This book presents both a unified framework for conceptualizing the current external debt dilemma faced by major borrower nations of the developing world, and a set of country case studies geared to this interpretive model. Taken together, the issues and cases set forth in this volume will provide the reader with a multiple perspective on the present developing nation, or less-developed country (LDC), debt crisis and with substantive examples of developing countries having heavy foreign debt-service burdens. The work has its origin in a perceived gap within the body of LDC debt literature as it now exists. Treatments of the Third World debt quandary tend to be of two kinds. On the one hand, there are the scholarly texts and articles devoted to the topic. Frequently written under the aegis of major multilateral institutions, for example, the World Bank, these studies typically feature a broad chronological scope, and while they usually include reference to specific events and trends, their orientation is generally theoretical. On the other hand, there are the professional pieces, such as those which appear in the pages of financial journals and business magazines. These items offer a wealth of detail on the topical aspects of Third World debt, but unless they are followed on an ongoing basis, they tend to be piecemeal and to have no explicit connection to a consistent analytical model. By incorporating elements of both genres, this study seeks a cross-fertilization between theory and practice, affording the reader a more cogent and complete view of the LDC debt problem as a whole.

Scope

It is apparent that a comprehensive explanation of the current LDC debt crisis cannot be contained within a single volume, and so this study's scope of inquiry is squarely focused on the most timely and important areas of the topic.

The developing Third World consists of over one hundred nations with extremely diverse economic, political and social characteristics; most of these countries are net international debtors. The debt and development difficulties of the neediest Low-Income LDCs may be even more pressing in vital, human terms than those of the countries considered in this book, especially in light of what Cyrus Vance has called the "disgraceful" performance of the United States in reducing official aid and loans to these lands over the past five years.[1] My examination is concentrated, however, on developing nations with investable economies. Designated Hi-Income, Non-OPEC LDCs in developmental jargon, these are the nations that have been able to tap commercial credit markets and now find themselves pressed to restructure their official and commercial repayment schedules. Because it is this class of nations that is at the center of my discussion, a major portion of this text will zero in on the most troublesome component of their external debt problems: commercial, floating-interest Euroloans contracted from international banks over the past decade. A Euroloan is, most broadly, a loan granted in a currency, usually $US, other than that of the lender's nation or the site from which the loan is issued. Narrowly defined, it is a loan from a European lender denominated in $US. The definition has broadened since inception of the Euromarket. Among the Hi-Income, Non-OPEC LDCs, this mode of lending is the largest element in their accumulated debt stocks, outweighing official bilateral and multilateral obligations. It is also the costliest form of credit extended by suppliers of autonomous capital to LDC borrowers, and the large proportion of such debt due in the near term is presently the greatest onus on the annual debt service of these countries. In short, while this book cannot address the LDC debt crisis in its entirety, it does aim at the heart of the matter by centering on major developing nation debtors who have encountered serious problems in meeting foreign loan servicings.

All of the "issue" portion of this book and the bulk of its case material pertain to the period 1971 to end–1982. To be sure, both an expansion of the Euroloan market and Third World borrowings occurred in the 1960s, but external loan flows to borrowers in developing countries did not reach significant proportions until the 1970s. As important, the entire global financial environment has been irrevocably altered since 1971. Foreign exchange rates now float, international rates vary, the real cost of OPEC oil has quadrupled, commodity exports have gone up and down erratically in volume and price, and all of these innovations have had a profound impact on developing nations in contracting and servicing foreign debt. In 1982–1983, major LDC debtor nations found themselves on the cusp of an equally significant change in the pattern of cross-border capital movements. According to one projection, even with a resumption of bank lending in the mid–1980s to levels approximating those of 1979–1981, there will be a net resource transfer back from developing nation borrowers to commercial lenders, so that "in the five years 1982/1986 banks would receive a net inflow from developing countries averaging $12 billion a year."[2] Indeed, for some heavily indebted developing countries, like Mexico and Brazil, this historic switch in the direction of resource transfers is already under way. Clearly, the next few years will be a critical hurdle for major LDC debtors, and now is the time when concerted attention must be paid to their difficulties.

As the aggregate external debt of the developing nations approached $1 trillion, the year 1983 was one of limbo in international lending to the Third World. The question of whether these major debtor nations of the developing world would reschedule was answered in the affirmative during 1982, so that the "first stage" of the present LDC-debt dilemma has been completed. The second stage, hopefully ending in a successful solution to the problem, or, more pessimistically, ending in a series of debt moratoria or repudiations by the borrower, has not yet been reached. Lenders continue to pare down their loans to heavily indebted LDCs, but the largest among them (the "money-center banks") continue to be pressured by the International Monetary Fund (IMF) and their own governments to extend fresh monies to these countries. Thus, when the Mexican government announced on 8 December, 1983 that it was seeking a $4 billion "jumbo" loan from commercial creditors, international bankers with high exposure in Mexico blanched at the prospect of IMF arm-twisting in support of this request.

The impact of IMF austerity programs in debt-burdened LDCs has been mixed. The Brazilian austerity package with the IMF included a 70 percent devaluation, but inflation continues at over 100 percent within Brazil. Austerity measures and IMF suasion contributed to a $6.5 billion syndicated loan from 700 foreign commercial banks approved on 28 January, 1984, most of it to be used in repayment of Brazil's $90 billion official external debt. Austerity measures, however, have evoked popular discontent in Brazil and elsewhere: Carlos Langoni resigned his position as president of Brazil's central bank in September, 1983, in response to the "socially punitive" effects of the IMF austerity package imposed on Brazil.

Politically, 1983 was a fairly positive year for relations between the industrialized nations and the major debtors of the developing world. Looking specifically at U.S. relations with the five case countries examined here, the ascension of Turgut Ozal as head of the new civilian government in Turkey, based on the electoral victory of his Motherland Party in 1983, is both a political plus for the United States and a positive sign for Turkey's creditors and potential lenders, as is the recent round of conciliatory gestures transmitted between Turkey and Greece over the Cyprus question. Mexico's President, Miguel de la Madrid Hurtado, has encountered political scandal concerning the pocket-lining activities of officials in the Lopez-Portillo Administration, almost all of whom were members of de la Madrid's own PRI party; but the Mexican President has sought closer relations with the Reagan Administration, and this is a welcome sign for Mexico's external creditors. In Brazil, *abertura* continue to progress, this political "opening" helping to offset unpopular austerity measures mandated by the IMF. In Argentina, the return to civilian government and the installation of moderate Raul Ricardo Alfonsin at its head bodes well in terms of an improvement in the the stability of the Argentine polity. While Alfonsin's debt and development policies stressing continued investment expansion and higher levels of current consumption will not calm the fears of Argentina's international creditors, the consensus is that Alfonsin will soon adopt more orthodox adjustment policies as a means of improving his country's debt-service capacity and securing conditional IMF loans. Although the domestic situation in Poland remains volatile, the Reagan Administration has moved in the direction of a thaw with the Wojciech Jaruzelski regime, rejoining other Western governments in reorganization of Poland's official debt.

In brief, the LDC external debt situation in early 1984 remains essentially the same as it stood in January, 1983, with improvements outweighing downturn by a slim margin. Having entered into official and commercial reschedulings within the framework of IMF adjustment programs, major LDC debtors face a year-by-year round of reschedulings into the late 1980s. Loans reorganized in 1982 and 1983 will continue to be restructured through 1984, 1985, 1986 and 1987 given (1) the need to amortize short-term loans contracted in the 1981–1982 period along with principal payments on medium-term loans extended in the late 1970s; (2) depressed commodity markets and continuing protectionist regimes in OECD nations, an externality that hampers LDC debt repayment capacity despite improvements in both energy costs and international interest rates; and (3) the *ad hoc*, informal, short-horizon characteristics of the rescheduling process for both Paris Club restructurings and bank workouts. The reader should be warned, however, that the potential for a drastic event that would transform the situation overnight, such as a unilateral moratorium on external debt repayment by one or more prominent borrowers, looms large.

Structure

Structurally, this work is divided into two parts which must be considered in conjunction with each other. The first half deals with general issues related to LDC debt. The artificial separation of parties into borrowers, lenders and negotiators is a gross simplification given the overlaps among these groups, (for example, the lenders of the Paris Club negotiating body and the IMF as an international creditor). It does represent the clearest breakdown of the participants in the fundamental sense that the roles of borrower, lender and negotiator are functionally distinct. Chapters 2 through 4 focus upon the position of one of the interested parties. The positions of the borrowers and lenders have been approached as a four-part series of parallel issues: (1) Why engage in international borrowing/lending? (2) From whom to borrow/to whom to lend? (3) Who is responsible for the present predicament in LDC debt service? (4) What is to be done about the situation as it now stands? It becomes plain that while borrowers and lenders face virtually identical issues, they do so from divergent viewpoints, with very different criteria and objectives. Chapter 4 examines the negotiators: the IMF, the Paris Club and the bank cartels which have served as forums for the reorganization of LDC foreign debts. Here the issues are inherent in the mechanisms of debt restructuring within each stage of the negotiating process and the linkages among these mechanisms.

The case portion of the book (chapters 5–9) examines the accumulation and handling of foreign debt by five major LDC borrowers: Turkey, Mexico, Brazil, Argentina and Poland. With the exception of Poland, each case is subdivided into two parts: a chronology giving background information on the case country, and a commentary section presenting analysis of key debt-related matters. While there are variations in the commentary/analysis segments of the cases, they commonly consider the points of national economic development strategy in handling of economic sectors; the orchestration of internal and external economies; the role of the central government as an investor and regulator; and domestic and foreign political factors pertinent to the country's external debts. In some cases, the commentary will also include an account of lender behavior before and during the nation's rescheduling of foreign commercial borrowings.

The overall structure of the book dictates its sequence of presentation. Chapters 2, 3 and 4 deal respectively with borrowers, lenders and negotiators, the borrowers given the "lead-off" position so that a popular misconception concerning their profligacy can be remedied from the outset. The case countries have been selected because (1) they are major debtors among Third World nations, (2) they have entered into large-scale, multilateral rescheduling exercises, and (3) they are different enough from each other to constitute a reasonable cross-section. In the broadest sense, the cases are arranged along a spectrum of certainty, moving from conditions of comparative certainty in the resolution of present debt problems to conditions that make such resolution dubious. Turkey has been chosen as the first case as it was the first nation to initiate rescheduling in the present era, and its debt restructuring has been all but successfully completed. Mexico and Brazil are examples of countries that have rescheduled official and commercial debts but have not yet reached a stage of resolution in their reorganization equivalent to that of Turkey. Argentina is further down the list, its potential for political upheaval casting doubts on the lasting impact of its latest (1982) restructuring rounds. Finally, Poland is accorded the last position because its official creditors reject any negotiations with the martial law regime now in power.

Method

The theoretical and empirical bases of this book have been derived from three sources: recent scholarly texts and articles; pieces appearing in business and financial journals; and official government and international studies, e.g., monographs and reports from the IMF, the International Bank for Reconstruction and Development (IBRD) and the Organization for Economic Cooperation and Development (OECD). This range of sources is a necessary result of the work's twofold organization, its multiple perspective and its inclusion of non-economic factors.

The reader will notice that, unlike many other studies in the field, this book presents a minimal amount of statistical and quantified analysis. There are a number of reasons why the author has elected to dismiss extensive statistical treatments in preference to a rough and generalized approach to the data. Despite advances in the reporting of debt-related information, the mountain of figures issued from international reporting systems is far from adequate as a precise descriptor or predictor of present and future trends. LDC debt figures are not comprehensive; variations in definitions and coverage make cross-country comparisons extremely difficult. Some calculations of international debts discard short-term loans; others exclude non-guaranteed private debt; still others cover only disbursed, not committed, debts; and finally, some register gross indebtedness, which may be a far cry from net figures. The accuracy of the inputs into national account data has been improving of late, but some country reporting systems, for instance, that of Poland, remain suspect. In combination with variations in definitions and coverages, this imprecision has led to situations such as that of Mexico in 1981 when "three Mexican departments issued what should have been the same set of figures, but they differed by several billion pesos."[3] There is often a substantial time lag between the occurrence of a debt-related event and its inclusion in official accounts, an interim of two years being standard for World Bank statements. As Marilyn Seiber summarizes:

> With these several systems operating, it is not surprising that the inconsistencies in data, overlaps in information, double counting, varying the number of countries included in the "developing country" category, and statistical imperfections occur. In addition, short-term debt is not included and there is no satisfactory way of calculating its magnitude. These conditions make precision in debt analysis nearly impossible.[4]

Thus the first reason for downplaying the role of the numbers here is that they are not completely reliable indicators of actual performance.

Part and parcel with these objections, an overemphasis on quantification, rationality and the quest for certainty has led to some highly unfortunate consequences. Speaking of delays in World Bank project planning, Bettina Hurni has said of the problem of statistical pretensions: "It often seems as if the World Bank's elaborate appraisal methods are too sophisticated, contain too many 'stylized facts,' and place too great an emphasis on economics in an environment where sociological and anthropological factors are at least as important as economic ones."[5] Intricate number-crunching exercises do display impressive feats of conceptual and mathematical gymnastics. Unfortunately, these statistical pyrotechnics have only a frail hold on reality. Two central reasons for the non-conformity of quantitative analysis to the actualities of LDC debt are (1) the failure to include subjective factors, and (2) artificial limits on the unit of analysis.

As to the first of these shortcomings, Anthony Sampson has remarked on the distance between lending behavior and abstract economic analysis, observing from the banker's side that "down in the marketplace itself there are real people trying to impress and persuade other people, worrying about their bank's balance sheet and writing off bad debts."[6] The rows of figures produced in national accounts and bank ledgers do not move themselves from column to column automatically: real people do real things of which the data are but pale reflections. At bottom, "credit is behavioral, not mechanistic."[7] The IMF's "seal of approval" argument is a primary example illustrating the subjective considerations of international lending. The Fund contends that the seal of approval accompanying successful adjustment by a debtor nation using a conditional IMF loan restores the confidence of commercial lenders in the creditworthiness of the borrowing country. Spokesmen from developing nations counter that going to the IMF and receiving the Fund's seal does not guarantee a renewal of bank lending, and in fact serves as a signal to lenders of dire economic/financial circumstances, prompting them to reduce or cut off commercial credits. The point here is that both lines of argument hinge on the subjective perception of lender confidence, and the degree of subjectivity entailed can be measured as the difference between their respective conclusions.

The second drawback of a "sophisticated" quantitative orientation toward debt is systemic in nature. Country risk models often portray nations as if they were somehow hermetically sealed off from external influences. As the IBRD has stated in its 1982 *World Development Report*: "For much of the past thirty years growing interdependence—through trade, capital movement and migration—strengthened the forces of economic expansion and spread them around the world. But as recent events have illustrated, these links can transmit problems from country to country just as surely as benefits.[8] Without moving too far ahead, the "externalities" that have undermined the debt-service capacities of many heavily borrowed LDCs have originated outside their borders, have been beyond their ability to command or influence, and have come about as the result of conscious decisions taken by others, primarily the leaderships of the industrialized nations and the member states of the Organization of Petroleum Exporting Countries (OPEC) cartel. As a final example of the inadequacy of country-by-country analysis in an era of growing global economic integration, suppose that the banking community has two potential LDC borrowers requesting loans, A and B, and that A and B are major trading partners. Assume further that all commercial lenders determine that A is creditworthy, while B is not. Cash is funneled into A to increase its productive capacity, but when A tries to sell its exports in B's markets, B, having been neglected by international lenders, cannot pay for these goods. The result is that the creditworthy A, experiencing a balance of trade shortfall, becomes an indirect victim of the lending policies that favored it above B, and may have difficulty in servicing its foreign loans as a consequence. For better or worse, the world's economy is becoming more and more unified, so that simply estimating a nation's credit without consideration of outside forces that can affect its future performance is an exercise in self-deception and futility.

Political Context

While this study does not adopt a full-blown interdisciplinary approach, political and social considerations are taken into account in the course of its analysis. Domestic and foreign political factors affect the salient issues involved in international debt, and social conditions within borrower nations deeply influence decisions concerning foreign loans. The country risk models used by commercial lenders explicitly acknowledge the role of political and social forces in determining a nation's capacity and willingness to repay external borrowings. Among the countries examined here, Foreign debt has played a major part in the rise and fall of civilian governments in Turkey, Argentina and Poland, while both the Mexican and Brazilian regimes have responded to and against political/social pressures in assuming debt, undertaking adjustment within the context of indebtedness and entering into debt restructuring.

In terms of foreign relations, the external debt of Third World countries is a meaningful element within the framework of the two power axes that divide the nations of the world. The most obvious global power context in which LDC debt is an active agency is the North/South dialogue between the industrialized countries of North America, Western Europe and Japan, on the one hand, and the developing nations of Latin America, Asia and Africa, on the other. "The debt relief negotiating process," for example, "is part of a larger political-economic process, the North-South debate on the creation of a New International Economic Order."[9] Seen from a non-Marxist dialectical perspective, the current LDC debt problem is a restatement, at a higher level of organization, of a pre-existing contradiction—the wealth and income disparities between the "have" and "have-not" countries, and the inefficiencies which they generate from the standpoint of worldwide needs optimization. Much of the North/South dialogue has been devoted to the crucial needs of the world's most abject economies, but, as Hi-Income LDCs undergo the strains of external debt repayment, they have become increasingly willing to cast their lot with the rest of the non-aligned world and to call for some form of orderly, generalized debt relief.

While the world has moved toward a more polycentric distribution of power, strategic nuclear arms have maintained the basic East/West bipolarity in force since the late 1940s. This second power axis also affects Third World debt. Contemplating the prospect of a direct, unilateral repudiation of debt by a principal LDC borrower, David Gisselquist concludes that only a shift in allegiance from the capitalist to the communist world or from the Eastern to the Western camp would permit such an action, citing Cuba (1959–1960) as an example of the former and Indonesia (1965–1966) as an instance of the latter.[10] Among the case countries surveyed in this volume, Mexico, Brazil, Argentina and, to a lesser extent, Turkey have all shifted their policy axis away from continued dependence on the West, while Poland briefly attempted to move out of the Soviet sphere and increase its Western contacts. The relationship between changes in foreign policy and external debt is reciprocally interactive: onerous debt-service burdens prompt a search for greater economic and political independence, while policy shifts permit new debtor options in the repayment of foreign loans. Should major snags arise in the restructuring of a developing country's debt, this, in turn, could affect such wide-ranging areas as trade between debtor and creditor countries, direct investment in debtor nations and political/military influence of creditor nations on the borrower government. Even more likely, an intra-bloc fracture among the nations of the NATO/OECD alliance could erupt as various industrial regimes pursue their own special interests in disbursing and collecting repayment of LDC credits.

Significance

No analyst has the definitive view on the risks involved in the current LDC debt crisis, in terms of either their form or their magnitude. At the beginning of 1982, the most significant question was whether major developing nation debtors would initiate a reorganization of their official and commercial loans. As of this writing, the question has been answered, since virtually every debtor country in trouble at the start of 1982 has been compelled to undergo rescheduling. With this unknown resolved, the possibility of a debt moratorium, repudiation and/or declaration of default has become more prominent in the minds of Third World debt analysts. However, as was previously the case with rescheduling, there remain "conflicting views on the seriousness of the debt situation and disagreement on the implication of the debt for the future stability of the international financial system."[11]

Unlike the physical sciences, economics cannot replicate objects and conditions of study within a controlled experimental setting. As with all social sciences, economics must rely on the unsatisfactory arrangement of looking to the past to describe the present and forecast the future. The use of cross-country, time-series data as the basis for country risk appraisals is a prime example of a "technique that assumes that history repeats itself, so that a good explanation of past events produces a good—or the same explanation of future events."[12] Searching for a historical analogy to the present debt dilemma of developing nations and their creditors, some analysts have cited failed speculative loans to Latin America in the nineteenth century or the collapse of the international bond market during the Great Depression of the 1930s as evidence of an impending LDC debt disaster. Others, however, point to the use of external credit by the United States in the nineteenth century and by Western Europe in the post–World War II era as instances of nations assuming heavy foreign loan obligations and successfully transforming them into productive investments. All of this is simply nonsense. The post–1971 world economic/financial environment is just too different from the past to allow alleged historical parallels to remain valid in discussions of the present circumstances. Moreover, today's developing countries face a unique challenge in the sense that they must develop their economies while competing with previously industrialized states.

One need not delve into the remote past to cull evidence in support of a given LDC debt prediction. As the reader may recall, there was talk of an imminent Third World debt crisis after the first oil shock of 1973–1974, so that, from a sanguine viewpoint, it may be argued that the world will solve (or respond adequately to) the present problem since a similar debt crisis has already been overcome. More realistic thinkers identify the inherent fallacy behind this line of reasoning. Federal Reserve Board Chairman Paul Volcker recently observed that, "in a sense, we muddled through the post–1973 period without really dealing effectively with the problems, and we lost some of the sense of urgency for doing so because no disasters occurred."[13] With gross LDC indebtedness approaching $1 trillion, unsupportably high debt-service ratios becoming commonplace and official assistance following a makeshift, erratic pattern, doomsayers have more than enough data to support their apocalyptic conclusions. Other observers assert that these ballpark figures must be put into perspective, one international banker commenting in 1982 that Mexico, Brazil and Argentina "are only suffering from liquidity problems" and that even Poland can reverse its present situation given its economic potential.[14] In its *World Development Report* for 1982, the World Bank, using a single global model of economic/financial activity, projects two scenarios, derived respectively from High case and Low case assumptions and inputs. The IBRD's High case scenario sees a successful handling of LDC foreign indebtedness, resting largely upon a 4 percent annual growth rate in the developed world, which would lead to expanded LDC exports, credits and aid, allowing Third World countries to "sustain growth at least at their 1970–80 rates."[15] Under Low case assumptions, declining growth in the industrial world, accompanied by increased protectionism, inhibits LDC exports, credit and aid, making the pace of progress achieved by developing countries in the 1970s unattainable in the 1980s. Noting that the World Bank forecast presumes no variation in the future lending behavior of commercial creditors, it is evident that even the most informed and astute world body cannot come to a single, firm prediction of the course of Third World debt over the next ten years.

Short of any definitive forecast of the future evolution of Third World debt, the question arises: Are there common characteristics shared by a set of deeply troubled countries which form a sharp enough pattern to serve as an indicator of potential foreign debt problems among other LDCs? The answer is a qualified yes. The factors inventoried below are manifest in each of the countries examined in the case section of this book, and while a direct cause-and-effect relationship between their presence and serious debt-service problems cannot be confirmed, these factors have influenced debtor countries in their assumption of foreign loans and their repayment performances.

Turkey, Mexico, Brazil, Argentina and Poland share these characteristics:

A. Criteria used in their selection for study
  1. Comparatively high levels of per capita income (in excess of $2,000).
  2. Comparatively rich natural resources, developed markets and skilled labor forces.
  3. Large outstanding net external debts, significant annual debt-service obligations, and initiation of official and commercial debt restructurings between 1977 and 1982.
B. Role of the central government
  1. Active and extensive involvement in the planning and implementation of national economic policy by the central government.
  2. Relatively large shares of total investment by the central government in productive activities.
  3. Tolerance of high levels of deficit spending in support of investment, consumption and debt repayment.
  4. Strong regulation of internal and external economies by the state.
  5. Periodic efforts to divest government from a portion of its ownership/regulatory roles in favor of private sector ownership and open market mechanisms, creating a "stop-and-go" pattern.
C. Basic development strategy
  1. Initial adoption of the "engine of growth" capital-intensive approach to national economic development, favoring industrial and infrastructural modernization while bypassing rural, traditional sectors.
  2. Maintenance of high levels of current consumption in combination with expansionary investment, including subsidization of domestic producers and social welfare programs.
  3. Continued high levels of investment and consumption despite external shocks, which are made more serious by the capital-, material- and energy-intensive orientation of national development.
D. Integration of internal and external economies
  1. Prolonged periods of protectionism, import-substitution and isolation of the domestic economy from competitive external influences.
  2. Periodic efforts to open the economy to external forces by lowering protectionism and promoting exports, again leading to a stop-and-go pattern.
E. Borrowing policy
  1. With the exception of Poland, previous reschedulings in the 1960s.
  2. Reliance on commercial Euroloans at high-nominal, variable interest rates.
  3. With the exception of Brazil, resorting to short-term credits as commercial lenders deny long- and medium-maturity loans.
  4. Use of foreign borrowings to compensate for delays in adjustment to external shocks.
F. Domestic and foreign politics
  1. Periods of military or one-party rule between 1977 and 1982, most continuing without civilian government.
  2. Widespread social discontent, partially as a result of growing disparities in the distribution of incomes and wealth.
  3. Central government promises of greater democratization which have either been postponed or rescinded in response to reactionary pressures, another stop-and-go pattern.

4. Well-established national identities which emerged long before the post World-War II liberation of colonial holdings.
5. Signs of pursuing greater economic/political independence from a major world power, that is, the United States or the Soviet Union.

Among the five case countries studied, the following differences stand out:

1. Variations in resource mixes, balance of trade positions, export composition, degree of multinational corporate activity in the domestic economy and the role of worker remittances from abroad.
2. Variations in population size and growth, social homogeneity and the spatial distribution of populations.
3. Poland's special situation as a non-member of the International Monetary Fund.

The reader is left to draw his own conclusion on whether the similarities outweigh the differences among these countries, but in the author's opinion there are enough common characteristics to sketch an outline of a debt/development syndrome based upon the shared features of these nations. Starting with the borrowers, we find heavily centralized control by the government over all facets of national economic and financial life. This control is typically exercised in a stop-and-go manner as regimes with different ideological outlooks successively assume power. Uncertainties surrounding the government's policies in key areas inhibit private sector investments, distort the operation of markets and generate political frustration. As external shocks interact with wavering policies, sovereign borrowers employ foreign loans to delay adjustments and placate their publics. This behavior on the part of the borrowers is both abetted and undermined by the lending policies currently followed by commerical creditors. Banks extend large sums to sovereign LDC borrowers without scrutinizing their purpose or payback potential, thereby permitting the debtor to postpone necessary policy changes. It is only when external debt service leads to a liquidity crisis on the part of the borrower that lenders begin to exercise prudence. Unfortunately, the banker's newfound caution results in a drastic reduction of commerical loan flows, exacerbating the debtor's foreign exchange shortages. By the time the negotiators appear on the scene, the borrower's predicament has already reached the emergency stage. The short-term, *ad hoc* character of the rescheduling process as a whole cannot address the debtor's problems in any lasting way, i.e., within the context of its developmental needs, and a series of year-by-year restructurings is the inevitable outcome. Unless there is a basic alteration in the attitudes of all interested parties, this syndrome is likely to recur, and so, in the absence of such revision, one can only conclude that the present LDC debt dilemma is extremely grave.

Notes

1. Roger S. Leeds, "External Financing of Development—Challenges and Concerns," *Journal of International Affairs*, Spring/Summer, 1980, p.23.

2. John Calverley, "How the Cash Flow Crisis Floored the LDCs," *Euromoney*, August, 1982, p.23.

3. Alan Robinson, "How Latin America's Economies Are Under Pressure," *Euromoney*, April, 1982, p.9.

4. Marilyn J. Seiber, *International Borrowing by Developing Countries* (New York: Pergamon, 1982), p.34.

5. Bettina S. Hurni, *The Lending Policy of the World Bank in the 1970s: Analysis and Evaluation* (Boulder, Colorado: Westview, 1980), p.107.

6. Anthony Sampson, *The Money Lenders: Bankers and a World of Turmoil* (New York: Viking Press, 1981), p.16.

7. P. Henry Mueller, "A Conspectus for Offshore Lenders," in *Offshore Lending by U.S. Commercial Banks*, ed. F. John Mathis (Washington: Banker's Association for Foreign Trade, 1981), p.32.

8. *World Development Report: International Bank for Reconstruction and Development (IBRD), 1982* (New York: Oxford University Press, 1982), p.1.

9. Stephen D. Cohen, "Forgiving Poverty: The Political Economy of International Debt Relief Negotiations," *International Affairs*, Winter/Spring, 1981–1982, p.70.

10. David Gisselquist, *The Political Economy of International Bank Lending* (New York: Praeger, 1981), p.177.

11. Seiber, *International Borrowing*, p.xiii.

12. J.N. Robinson, "Is It Possible to Assess Country Risk?" *The Banker*, January, 1981, p.27.

13. Leeds, p.21.

14. Charles Grant, "The Stuffees Have Left, the Stuffers Remain," *Euromoney*, November, 1982, p.35.

15. IBRD, *World Development Report*, pp.31–32.

Chapter 2

THE BORROWERS

The Crux of the Dilemma

An understanding of the dilemma that major LDC borrowers face begins with consideration of the gaps that have emerged between development theory as it was originally formulated in the early 1950s and its applied results to date. Anticipating an era of greater global integration, Western theorists and policy-makers sought means of modernizing markets, increasing productivity and improving living conditions in the post-World War II economies of Latin America, Asia and Africa. The approach which eventually received widespread endorsement and served as the basis for practical policy decisions rested upon a straightforward and plausible premise: via direct investment, aid and credit, external resources could be effectively used to advance Third World economies, and these advances would ultimately allow LDC borrowers to repay their industrial country benefactors, both directly and indirectly. The central mechanism of the chosen model was also comparatively simple and reasonable. Capital and technology would be selectively channeled to the modern sector of a given developing country's economy, especially to its infrastructure and industry. This enrichment, in turn, would transform the modern sector into an "engine of growth," which would "push" or "pull" the initially neglected traditional, rural sector upwards, so that the benefits of the process would "trickle down" to the populace at large, and balanced, self-sustaining progress would be set in motion. Once this concentrated but short-lived stimulus of external inputs occurred, it was thought that national economic development would naturally unfold according to distinct, linear stages.

Consensus on the utility of this model eroded rapidly as snags, slippages. and gaps appeared in its implementation. While the basic strategy worked well in certain cases (e.g., Israel, Hong Kong, South Korea), in others the expected linkages between the enhanced modern sectors and their traditional, rural counterparts did not take place, and a relatively permanent dual economy was the outcome. Subsequently, as greater emphasis was extended to the agrarian sectors of LDC lands (the "Green Revolution" of the early 1960s), the trickle-down phenomenon still did not materialize, leading welfare economists to cite inherent contradictions between the goals of economic growth, expressed in gross national product (GNP), capital-output ratios, etc., and the reality of vital human needs, expressed in stagnating or declining living standards. Finally, while concentrated investment in industry and infrastructure virtually assured productivity gains, it did not guarantee the acquisition of sufficient foreign exchange receipts to service obligations to developed nation investors and to purchase imports to support continued growth.[1]

As the evidence has mounted over the course of three decades, the underlying reasons for the mixed and often erratic performance of the original approach became more and more apparent. First, the empirical foundation of the "take-off" paradigm was found to be inadequate because, despite the legacy of nineteenth century Western development and the more recent achievements of the Marshall Plan in rebuilding Western Europe and Japan, there was, in fact, no historical parallel to the circumstances that Third World countries confronted at mid-twentieth century. Secondly, the notion of a universal blueprint for development ran directly counter to the wide variations in baseline endowments, political structures, social systems and cultural backgrounds among the underdeveloped nations. Finally, the quantitative, deterministic, rational, problem-solving orientation implicit in the "take-off" design could not serve as a decision-making guide for LDC leaderships compelled to take qualitative, probabilistic and non-economic factors into account in the ongoing execution of their development plans.[2] When these leaders came to grapple with issues related to the use of foreign resources in the development process, they did not have a proven conceptual framework on which to base their responses, for while the critics of the initial approach had clearly identified its pitfalls, they had not been able to construct a viable alternative, and development theory itself became more diffuse and fragmented.

The central point is that there is currently no general agreement concerning the value or function of foreign inputs (e.g., external funds) in the process of national economic development. It is not that the leaders of the heavily indebted LDCs have somehow failed to learn the ABCs of development, or, having learned them, willfully deviated from the orthodox course; it is, rather, that definitive solutions to questions about whether and how to use external funds are just not available. Uncertainty regarding such problems has been magnified by the turbulent global environment of the past decade, as LDCs find themselves strongly affected by devastating externalities while trying to move forward in a purposeful, coherent way. Moreover, the "answers" that developing country governments can endorse are severely limited by the political necessity of balancing demands from powerful and diverse domestic interests (including the government apparatus itself), all of whom have a stake in how foreign borrowing is handled. It is not surprising, then, that policies related to external debt as part of overall development planning typically elicit a stop-and-go pattern from decision-makers, a "flip-flop" sequence inimical to the intensive and long-term requirements of development, with these turnabouts being made all the more frequent by fluctuations in the availability and terms of external borrowings. At bottom, since Third World leaders cannot wait for development theory to perfect itself, they are forced to improvise, to "wing it," in their treatments of debt/development problems, as they encounter a series of issues revolving around transnational resource transfers which comprise the core of the present LDC debt crisis.

Issue 1: Whether to Use External Funds

As a rule, external funds provide only a small portion of the monies invested within developing economies, usually less than 5 percent of the total, with the remainder formed from domestic sources.[3] The first issue that potential LDC borrowers face is whether public and private bodies can effectively use foreign financial flows to increase investment and/or consumption beyond that which is available from domestic savings, i.e., whether or not a "savings gap" exists.[4] In many cases, particularly among the poorest of the developing nations, the answer is a flat no, simply because the absorptive capacities of their economies do not permit the use of foreign flows as the basis for profitable, long-range growth and modernization. If a given economy can absorb additional funds in a balanced manner, foreign capital can be employed not only to bridge the savings gap, but also to overcome the foreign exchange or trade gap arising from shortfalls in foreign currencies necessary to purchase imports and fulfill previously contracted obligations. External borrowings fill these tandem gaps in the ability of a nation's productive capacity to meet a variety of domestic expenditures—broadly speaking, those of investment and current consumption—by augmenting domestic resources.

As Seiber has observed, if a developing nation government is conceived as a "utility maximizing entity" (an assumption which contains its own rationalist bias), then that government and its guaranteed agencies ought to accept external loans "to the point where marginal social benefits equal marginal social costs."[5] Apart from the difficulties involved in defining and quantifying social benefits and social costs (Whose benefits? Whose costs?), the borrower's capacity to predict and monitor how external funds contribute to diverse projects, programs and plans is far from complete. There are few reliable empirical studies in which the marginal benefits of capital borrowed from abroad to finance (or more usually, partially finance) an investment, social program, balance of payments objective, etc., have been isolated and measured,[6] there is an even greater paucity of instances in which foreign financing can be directly related to "a net increment in the exchange receipts or exchange savings of the borrower,"[7] receipts which must be used in part to service debt issuing from these loans.

Consequently, any effort to calculate and weigh the advantages of external funds against their drawbacks is necessarily an imprecise and piecemeal undertaking. As to the positive effects of foreign funds, they can be reduced to three broad categories.[8] First, there is the "investment effect," as external monies allow LDC economies to raise rates of capital formation for investment purposes above those attainable by exclusive reliance on domestic sources. Monies channeled into productive investment cause growth in GNP, capital-output ratios and, on the whole, per capita income. International markets often permit borrowing at a total "cost" below that available from within, especially when these flows come from official bilateral or multilateral sources on concessionary terms and/or when they contain a grant/aid component. A second advantage of external borrowings comes in the form of trade opportunities, with foreign capital providing means for expanding imports that can be consumed, invested in productive capacity for domestic markets and/or used to facilitate the expansion of exports. Finally, external funds can assist a country in building up its reserves of foreign exchange, to support balance of payments deficits due to remediable structural inefficiencies, and to meet temporary, short-term deficits in current national accounts.[9]

Offsetting these positive effects are a wide range of negative consequences that can ensue in the wake of external loans. First and foremost, debt problems occur not in the process of borrowing monies, but as part of the obligatory process of paying them back. Debt contracted must be serviced in the form of payments on amortization, interest and fees, these outflows compelling the borrower to forego some alternative investment and consumption throughout the life of the loan. Debt service is "a contractually fixed charge on real income and savings," manifesting itself as a "rigidity" in a developing nation's balance of payments.[10] This burden is both economic and financial because debt denominated in the currency of the lender usually requires repayment in that currency, generating a need for "sufficient foreign exchange to carry debt on an ongoing basis."[11] To avoid a liquidity crisis caused by external debt, developing countries may find themselves constrained to adjust their balance of payments positions by limiting imports, encouraging exports or borrowing additional sums. If this adjustment does not occur or is postponed for too long a time, a liquidity crisis leads to a failure in meeting debt service as originally contracted and the need for some form of debt restructuring.

Foreign capital can function as a tool for achieving self-sustained development, but it can also serve as a crutch, enabling LDC governments to delay necessary balance of payments adjustments and continue expansionary investment and/or high levels of current consumption despite the long-term negative consequences of such tactics. Operating from a deficit position, LDC borrowers may have recourse to foreign loans, serving to worsen that position further as time goes on. When foreign investment is narrowly targeted to distinct areas within an LDC economy (e.g., capital-intensive sectors) and withheld from others (e.g., labor-intensive sectors), reform of existing wealth and income disparities is impeded, and, again, a dual economy results. By favoring the status quo, the "investable" or creditworthy segments of the economy having access to foreign resources, external funds frequently abet status quo conservative authoritarian regimes at the expense of democratic reform movements. Part and parcel of this crutch inhibiting reforms is the atrophy of domestic capabilities as borrowed funds replace, rather than supplement, internal resources. For example, it has been noted that "foreign savings tend to supplant rather than supplement domestic savings."[12] Whether this "displacement effect" is a pat cause-and-effect relation is highly questionable,[13] but the flow of foreign funds into a developing economy is usually accompanied by a decline in domestic savings.

A number of economic inefficiencies are frequently engendered by strong dependence on foreign loans. Inflationary forces are unleashed by any new infusion of liquidity into LDC economies, often resulting in an overvalued exchange rate and the consequent deterioration of export competitiveness in international markets. Funds from foreign nations, particularly in the case of official, government-to-government loans, are often tied to the procurement of goods from the lending country, as in the extension of export or supplier credits. Since these goods are usually more expensive than comparable items from other suppliers, the actual cost of such a loan is significantly greater than that reflected in the repayment schedule.

Finally, drawing upon all of the arguments against the use of foreign loans, grants and investments, *dependencia* critics charge that an external presence in national economies delays both economic and political independence. Debt-servicing obligations yoke the borrower to the lender, making the former dependent on the latter for necessary imports and a continuing supply of funds. Given the use of official loans to further political purposes, and the influence that developed country governments exercise over their private lenders, these funds (and their continued disbursement) may be made provisional on the LDC borrower's following, or at least not interfering with, the foreign policy aims of the lending government. Thus, foreign loans can and are used by developed nations to reward or punish the borrowers for their foreign and even their domestic policies, comprising a blatant incursion on national sovereignty and the perceived legitimacy of the administration in power.

Issue 2: From Whom to Borrow

Having evaluated the advantages and disadvantages of using external funds and found the benefits outweighing the drawbacks, a second set of questions arises for developing nation borrowers: From whom and on what terms should foreign capital be sought? There are basically four sources of external financing available to creditworthy LDCs: (1) direct investment through multinational corporations; (2) official, government-to-government bilateral flows; (3) official multilateral flows, primarily from multilateral development banks (MDBs), such as those of the World Bank Group; and (4) what is, in the end, the critical component of the present LDC debt quandary: commercial loans. Not only do the terms typically offered by these four classes of funding sources vary from soft (low interest, long maturity, generous grace period) to hard (high interest, short maturity, stringent grace period); the conditions under which they can be obtained diverge widely as well. The first three sources will be dealt with at this juncture; the role of MDBs will be discussed in detail in Chapter 3.

Extensive reference to the role of direct investment through multinational or transnational corporations (MNCs) rarely surfaces in discussions of the current LDC debt problem. Having stood for more than a decade at the center of global economic controversy, the MNCs have kept a remarkably low profile with regard to developing country indebtedness. One reason for keeping MNCs out of the analysis of present LDC debt considerations is that while profit remittances from subsidiaries in the Third World to parent firms headquartered in advanced nations "also fall within the category of funds required to service foreign obligations,"[14] they do not occur according to a fixed repayment schedule and can be stretched out over a fairly long period of time. Even though the economic and financial burdens accompanying multinational activities in developing economies are "thin," that is, spread over many years, many international corporations have achieved substantial penetration of key industries within developing economies, particularly among the countries of Latin America. Radical critics rail against "unholy alliances" between corporate executives and LDC officials, but, more often, developing country governments are affected in their behavior by the threat of growing MNC activity within their borders, as in the sequence in which their public sectors expand to counterbalance the power and flexibility of their MNC guests.

While multinational corporations continue to have an appreciable impact on LDC economies, their relative invisibility in today's debt picture is partially a product of a decline in net inflows of direct investment to underdeveloped countries in comparison with flows from other sources. During the 1960s, direct investment was the dominant form of external capital in most LDCs, while autonomous capital flows remained at fairly low levels.[15] United States direct investment alone rose elevenfold from 1950, when it totaled $12 billion, to 1976, when it reached $140 billion.[16] However, between 1970 and 1977 "direct foreign investment declined in relative terms from 13 percent to 8 percent of total capital flows from external sources to non-oil LDCs."[17] There are some signs that direct investment by multinational corporations will again increase in the 1980s, due, in part, to LDC dissatisfaction with the results of foreign loans and the simultaneous reduction of credit to sovereign borrowers, but clearly this source of funding reached a plateau in the early 1970s and has since leveled out in volume while shrinking in relative share of total flows to LDCs.[18]

Why have MNC flows to LDCs declined in relation to other types of external funding? Recession in Western economies where MNCs are based provides a partial explanation, but the high rates of return for MNC investments in developing nations, with yields averaging 18 percent to 21 percent over the period 1950 to 1976, compared to an average 9 percent to 11 percent return for MNC investments in the industrialized nations,[19] makes it difficult to understand a decline in purely economic terms. In fact, mutual dissatisfactions have arisen between the multinationals and their former LDC partners in progress. The MNCs, on the one hand, have come to fear LDC regulations and potential expropriations, especially within the context of waning Western government power in the Third World. For their part, calculated exploitation of cross-border factor flows, transfer pricing, corruption and a host of other distasteful multinational practices have evoked outrage among LDC leaders, causing them to seek alternative sources of capital and to institute regulations concerning ownership, source of inputs and profit remittance by MNCs.

A similar situation holds in official bilateral flows from the governments of the industrialized nations to the governments of the LDCs, the bulk of these funds issuing from the members of the Development Assistance Committee (DAC) and the Organization for Economic Cooperation and Development (OECD). At first glance, loans from official sources appear attractive to LDCs since they usually carry softer terms than commercial credit from the international banks. However, from 1970 to 1973 expensive, high-cost bank lending to LDCs more than doubled in dollar terms,[20] while the ratio of non-concessional debt to concessional debt owed by middle- and high-income developing countries climbed dramatically from 1.7:1.0 in 1971 to 3.8:1.0 at the end of 1982.[21]

On the supply side, the major motives behind the expansion of commercial bank lending to LDCs will be examined in the next chapter. As to the reduction of official bilateral flows to the Third World, recession in the industrialized nations has played a part in this decline, as has the acknowledgement that simply dispensing low-cost funds to selected LDCs is not an effective means of influencing their foreign and domestic policies. Some of the funds that previously went directly from developed nation governments to public borrowers in the Third World have been rerouted and transmuted into guarantees to private lenders offering trade-related loans to LDC entities.[22] Finally, although the terms attached to official bilateral loans are still more favorable to the borrower than those extended in the open market, they have stiffened somewhat, thereby lessening their appeal to potential developing country borrowers.

The principal cause of the decline of bilateral flows to the Third World resides on the demand side of the ledger. LDC governments often prefer hard, expensive loans from commercial banks to soft, inexpensive credits from official sources. In order to comprehend this seemingly irrational borrowing pattern, it must be recognized that borrowing sources can be arranged not only in a hierarchy of terms, but also in a hierarchy of conditions.[23] In essence, LDC preference for costly bank money over cheaper official funds is derived from their desire to maintain freedom and flexibility in controlling their use.[24] Whether explicitly or implicitly, official credits are almost invariably tied to economic *and* political conditions, and the continued flow of these funds depends upon the borrower's performance in meeting these specific provisions and tacit understandings. By way of contrast, loans from commercial sources, e.g., banks, are normally granted on the sole provision that the borrower is deemed creditworthy by the lender.[25] Ironically, banks, being politically neutral (or least "more neutral" than their official counterparts), are viewed by LDC borrowers as far more reliable than foreign governments in supplying ready capital. Bank lending policy is based primarily on the objective criteria of profit and growth, so that if a potential LDC borrower can contribute to these objectives by meeting its contracted debt service, the banks are willing to "lend money for no specific project, with no political strings, and with far less delay" than official sources.[26]

Bank lending to LDC borrowers takes numerous forms. The loan recipient may be (1) the sovereign government itself, (2) a "guaranteed" entity of either the public or the private sector having the "full faith and credit" of the government behind it, or (3) a private body or individual. The first two categories comprise public debt, while the last is classified as private debt. Bank loans differ, according to their maturities and ostensible purposes, from short-term credits to support trade and balance of payments adjustments to long-term financing of large industrial and infrastructural projects. Regardless of the maturity or purpose, most international commercial loans to LDCs have been obtained on the Euromarket in the form of syndicated loans at variable rates of interest based on the cost of funds to the banks, plus a margin and fees representing the banks' profits. Eurolending will be discussed further in the following chapter, but at this juncture the point which needs to be emphasized is the one catch to reliance on commercial funds: the borrower must maintain a favorable credit rating in the market to be eligible for these loans. What this translates into in practice is that only a small number of LDCs can tap the Euromarket, most developing countries being judged too risky and too poor to use external borrowings in a manner that allows for any degree of certainty regarding their repayment. Several notches above these nations are LDC borrowers who can obtain limited funding from the international banks, but who must pay a premium above that paid by prime candidates, this surcharge coming as higher spreads and fees to compensate the banks for the greater risks involved in such loans. (The spread is the difference between the cost of funds to the lender on the interbank market and the cost of funds to the borrower; i.e., the lender's gross profit.) A final hitch in bank lending to LDCs is that the borrower's credit standing is subject to change without notice. An LDC borrower whose credit has deteriorated will find that he must pay higher margins for loans to obtain fresh funds, and, if the downgrading is serious, he may be denied any new credit altogether.

One of the factors that has had a profound impact on Third World debt is the growing volume of Euroloans offered under the institutional innovation of floating or variable interest rates. In contrast to fixed-interest loans, in which interest rates are set for the entire term, floating-interest loans have their interest rates recalculated periodically to reflect rises or falls in the cost of funds to the lender on the interbank market, usually by pegging them to the London Interbank Offered Rate (LIBOR) or the U.S. prime rate, with spreads and fees remaining constant. The spreads or margins on new funds fluctuate greatly from time to time and from borrower to borrower. For example, in 1981 Non-OPEC developing nations paid spreads averaging twice those granted to industrial country borrowers.[27] While such disparities in bank profits are a source of vexation to the LDCs, it is the volatility and rise of floating interest rates that has affected them most greatly. Variations in spreads affect only "new" funds, but changes in the floating rate affect not only fresh loans, but also the existing stock of debt contracted under floating rates.[28]

In 1972, fixed, official interest rates for all borrowers averaged 4 $1/2$ percent moving to 5 percent by 1981. Over the same period, variable interest rates to all borrowers skyrocketed from 5 $1/2$ percent to 17 percent.[29] Even more disturbing, fixed interest rates for LDC borrowers averaged 5.0 percent until 1977 and rose to 7.9 percent at end-year 1982, but floating interest rates to LDCs mushroomed from 7.8 percent to 17.5 percent.[30] To fully appreciate the significance of these trends it is necessary to view these figures in relation to changing rates of inflation. If inflation rates are higher than interest rates over the course of a loan, then the net interest rate is negative and there is a real transfer of resources from the creditor to the borrower. With fixed interest rates, then, unanticipated inflation results in a debt bargain for the debtor. In contrast, variable interest rates contain a safeguard against the deterioration of the loan value due to inflation[31] because, over time, interest rates which serve as the basis of LIBOR tend to adjust to inflation rates.[32] However, this "automatic" adjustment can be delayed, as when dominant financial powers, such as the United States, institute fiscal and monetary policies that curtail inflation while allowing interest rates to remain high. Quite obviously, if inflation rates are lower than interest rates, a net transfer of resources from the debtor to the creditor occurs as the "real" rate of interest becomes positive.

During the 1970s, rates of inflation were, on average, well above prevailing interest rates on both fixed and floating loans. Regardless of the deflator used, debt was a "bargain" throughout the decade,[33] since real interest rates averaged −2 percent,[34] meaning that there was a real transfer of capital from creditors to borrowers.[35] Now, however, a very different situation prevails because nominal interest rates have risen more than is needed to compensate for inflation, with interest rates high in nominal terms and positive in real terms.[36] The upshot of this change is that the net resource flow has been reversed to the advantage of the lender and to the detriment of the debtor.[37] Since loans contracted under variable interest rates reflect this altered relationship between floating interest levels and inflation, all of the debt contracted by LDC borrowers at LIBOR currently carries a positive real rate of interest.

How great is the impact of the interest component on variable-rate loans to the developing nations? According to one study, each 1 percent rise in interest rates results in a $4 billion increase in the current account deficits for Non-Oil LDCs.[38] For nations with a large portion of their total debt contracted at variable interest rates from commercial sources (virtually all of the major borrowers), the effect is especially powerful. A 1 percent rise in LIBOR adds a total of almost $1.41 billion to the annual debt service of just four nations, Mexico ($593 million), Brazil ($455 million), Argentina ($205 million), and South Korea ($155 million).[39]

Debt service consists of payments on the amortization of principal and interest charges, so that the maturity structure of loans owed in a stock of debt has an integral role in determining yearly debt-service burdens. In the recent past, there has been a noticeable shift in maturities granted by commercial lenders to LDCs. Trying to limit their long-term exposure, the banks have switched from offering medium- and long-term loans to granting only short-term credits. Unable to obtain lengthier maturities, many developing nations have resorted to "rolling over" short-term credits, which thus "become the equivalent of a high-cost, medium-term source of finance."[40] Combined with variations in loan demand during the 1970s (e.g., increased LDC need for financing after the first oil shock of 1974–1975), the compression of amortization that has occurred as a consequence of the shift to short-term maturities has resulted in a sharp "bunching" of debt-service payments due in the early and mid–1980s. Because of the rush to borrow in the wake of the first energy price hike and the accompanying global recession during the mid–1970s, a disproportionate amount of medium-term debt is due in the early 1980s.[41] In conjunction with the increased volume of short-term commercial lending, this bunching of maturities means that one-half of the total debt of all developing nations is due to be repaid between 1982 and 1987.[42] Taken in aggregate, the rise of net interest rates, the large portion of debt contracted at variable interest rates, and the bunching of maturities, along with an increased volume of total lending to developing countries, have led to annual LDC debt service obligations which are astronomical in comparison to the burdens of the early 1970s. Table 1 illustrates the impact of this confluence of factors on the annual debt-service requirements for all LDCs and for Non-Oil LDCs.

As Table 1 reveals, total annual debt service for all developing countries has multiplied tenfold in a little more than ten years, with non-concessional debt service (mostly owing to commercial banks) increasing 1,337 percent and interest charges nearly equaling amortization payments. For Non-Oil LDCs, debt service has also increased more than tenfold, non-concessional debt growing 1,140 percent and the interest element currently exceeding amortization of principal. Because external debt must normally be serviced in currencies other than that of the borrower, the ratio of annual debt service to yearly export receipts (debt-service ratio, or DSR) provides a rough yardstick of a nation's capacity to meet current debt obligations. In 1970, major debtors of the newly industrialized countries (NICs) had to target 15 percent of their total foreign exchange export earnings to service external debt, giving them an average DSR of 15. By 1982, this ratio had risen to a mean of 24 for the NICs.[43] By mid–1982, the debt-service ratios for major Latin American debtors (Brazil, Mexico, Argentina) had reached 100 and above, so that, even if all the foreign exchange receipts of these nations could be marshalled to service external debt

Table 1
Annual Debt Service for All LDCs and Non-Oil LDCs, 1971–1982

(in $ billion)

All LDCs	1971	1982
Total Debt Service	11.0	131.0
Interest	3.3	60.1
Amortization	7.7	71.2
Non-concessional	9.3	124.4
Concessional	1.7	6.9
Non-Oil LDCs		
Total Debt Service	9.5	98.3
Interest	2.6	49.7
Amortization	6.9	48.6
Non-concessional	8.0	92.2
Concessional	1.5	6.1

Source: Adapted from Organization for Economic Cooperation and Development (OECD), *External Debt of Developing Countries: 1982 Survey* (New York: OECD, 1982), pp. 27, 29.

(and, for practical purposes, they cannot), these countries would still be unable to meet their international debt schedules without a fresh infusion of funds from the original lenders or elsewhere. Under such circumstances, debt restructuring becomes a virtual arithmetical inevitability.

Issue 3: Who Is to Blame

The preceding account of the deterioration of LDC debt profiles and the resultant gravity of their debt service burdens leads naturally to a third issue which heavily indebted LDCs have had to address, specifically, the knotty question of who is responsible for the current developing nation debt crisis. From one angle, ultimate responsibility for the quandary which ensnares major LDC borrowers rests squarely with the debtors themselves. No one overtly forced these countries to take on external loans, and, as will become evident in succeeding chapters, the policies adopted by the borrowing nations frequently exacerbated their debt problems. However, the rise in interest charges in floating-rate loans was clearly beyond the capacity of the borrowers to control, or even to predict. While LDC imprudence certainly contributed to the present debt crisis, externalities, largely unforeseen factors beyond the debtors' command, must share part of the blame. The persistence of high real interest rates above inflation, especially for loans denominated in U.S. dollars, is the last in a series of external trends which have hamstrung LDC policy-makers in their efforts to simultaneously finance national economic development and meet payments owing on external debt. Three other major externalities created pressure on major LDC borrowers over the last decade:

1. The change from par-value to floating exchange rates accompanying the 1971 United States announcement of the inconvertibility of the dollar into gold.

2. Two major petroleum price hikes by OPEC, precipitating the two oil shocks of 1974–1975 and 1980–1981.

3. Deterioration of terms of trade, particularly commodity export prices and rising import costs for manufactured goods, along with a slowed growth in LDC exports due, in part, to recession and protectionism in the markets of North America, Western Europe and Japan.

The impact of these external factors was twofold: they created pressures on LDCs to increase the volume of their borrowing to meet balance of payments requirements and fund development, and they made it all the more difficult for the developing countries to generate export earnings to service external debt.

"Under the fixed-exchange system of 1946–1971, the value of a currency was fixed relative to other currencies with very limited flexibility."[44] In 1971, the fixed par-value exchange rate system, mandated at Bretton Woods in 1944, fell apart. Repeated waves of speculation against the U.S. dollar prompted American officials to unilaterally declare the inconvertibility of the dollar into gold. This was followed in the same year by a 7.8 percent devaluation of the dollar and, in 1973, by a further official depreciation of 10 percent.[45] These actions spawned a regime of floating exchange rates with wider bands in the movements of relative currency values, allowing nations to shield themselves from undesired international liquidity creation.[46] The Jamaica Agreement of 1976 gave the floating exchange system *de jure* status, but in fact variable exchange had become a permanent feature of the world's financial system by 1973.

The immediate reaction of the developing nations to the freeing of exchange rates was decidedly negative.[47] While the devaluation of the dollar created an export windfall for nations with currencies tied to it, the depreciation caused a loss of reserves for nations with foreign exchange cushions consisting mainly of U.S. dollars and a rise in real costs of LDC imports from Western Europe and Japan. Many LDCs themselves shifted to quasi-flexible, managed exchange rates, the so-called crawling peg and trotting peg mechanisms. The floating exchange rate system had a remedial benefit for LDCs suffering from chronic overvaluation under the fixed rate system, and, given the volatility of inflation, interest rates and energy prices, continuing with a par-value system through the 1970s would have certainly caused major disruptions in the world economy.[48] At the same time, floating exchange rates created new sources of uncertainty concerning import costs, competitive export pricing and the real value of foreign exchange receipts.

As Richard Flamson has observed, floating exchange values, theoretically determined purely by market forces, can be manipulated through policy intervention, so that "as nations came to realize the close connection between exchange rate movements and domestic inflation, the leaders of the world's industrialized economies continued to adjust interest rates in an attempt to influence capital movements and thereby inhibit exchange rate fluctuations."[49] In the early 1980s, with Paul Volcker heading the Federal Reserve, a monetarist stress on "whipping inflation" and stemming the expansion of credit, combined with continued Federal deficits, resulted in a rise of U.S. interest rates *and* a sharp appreciation of the dollar.[50] U.S. interest rates, of course, have a substantial influence on international interest levels, so that upswings in U.S. rates cause a significant increase in debt-service claims against LDC borrowers. Some four-fifths of the bank debt owed by the ten largest LDC debtors is denominated in U.S. dollars,[51] and, consequently, LDCs must now meet even greater real debt burdens while watching import prices rise and export earnings fall, as terms of trade deteriorate without a corresponding shift in debt service.[52] For LDCs with currencies tied to the dollar, the difficulty of this task is compounded because their now-overvalued currencies make their exports less competitive on international markets.

If the activities of monetary authorities in developed nations have hindered LDC debtors, the pricing policies of the OPEC cartel have been equally debilitating. With several major LDC borrowers committed to energy-intensive development plans, the first oil price hike of 1973–1974 added $11 billion to the oil bills for non-oil developing countries.[53] The effects of this first OPEC fiat began to subside in the late 1970s, with oil prices holding steady as a result of decreased global demand. A second oil shock was in the offing, however, as events in the Middle East, particularly in Iran, were used as a pretext for another OPEC decree leading to a 138 percent petroleum price rise from $13 a barrel in January, 1979 to $31 a barrel in May, 1980.[54] It has been estimated that every $1 rise in the per barrel price of oil generates a $2 billion increase in LDC import costs,[55] making the aggregate oil bill for developing countries in year–1980 amount to somewhere between $50 billion and $55 billion.[56]

OPEC members have publicly acknowledged the LDC energy plight, for which they are chiefly accountable, and occasionally more enlightened cartel members have attempted to partially alleviate this additional pressure on Third World development. But the amount of assistance offered by OPEC is fairly small in relation to the excess burden placed upon Non-Oil LDCs, and most direct aid from OPEC nations has been funneled into a handful of Muslim lands.[57] For their part, the leaders of the developing countries have generally refrained from criticizing OPEC,[58] being careful not to alienate potential allies and funding sources, and sharing a certain common interest in the establishment of Third World cartels counter to the longstanding dominance of the developed world.[59]

Although the first oil shock fueled high rates of domestic inflation within the economies of major LDC debtors,[60] it did not cause a major deterioration in their balance sheets, and, on the whole, these nations adjusted well to the first shock. The total impact of the second oil shock on the developing nations is somewhat more difficult to evaluate because all the repercussions have not yet been assessed. The World Bank anticipates a better adjustment to the second oil shock by the LDCs than was the case with the first price hike, citing the continuing implementation of energy-conservation programs initiated by the LDCs after the first shock and the creation of "more resilient economic structures" within developing nations as the basis for its optimism.[61] Other, less sanguine, analysts paint a different picture of the prospects for successful adjustment to the second shock, noting the failure of some LDCs to fully recover from the first price rise,[62] the resumption and continuation of expansionary policies in the mid–1970s and through the present,[63] and the interaction of the second shock with inflation, interest rates and terms of trade.[64] There appears to be some relief on the horizon for Non-Oil LDCs, with global petroleum prices remaining constant and even declining in 1982. As new Non-OPEC sources of oil and gas come on-line, the cartel's grip on world energy needs loosens: currently, OPEC controls less than one-half of the world's oil supplies.[65] However, even if OPEC's hold has been weakened, there is no reason to believe that alternative suppliers will not support high prices for their petroleum exports in the future.

The rise in dollar interest rates, exchange rate volatility and growing oil import costs for most LDCs are all contributing factors to their worsening balance of trade positions in terms of volumes and relative prices. As the developing countries were bearing the brunt of the first oil shock, they were subjected to another harmful externality in the form of a 40 percent increase in the price of manufactured imports over the period 1973 to 1975.[66] From 1973 to 1979, unit prices on all LDC imports increased 124 percent.[67] These increases were largely the product of stagflation in the industrialized nations, brought about mainly by rising world energy prices. Continued recession in developed countries, moreover, has inhibited demand for LDC exports, driving most commodity prices other than oil to their lowest levels since World War II.[68] While advanced LDCs have boosted their share of manufactured exports to total exports in the past decade, their "bread and butter" exports remain agricultural and mineral commodities. In 1981 alone, coffee, cocoa, sugar, copper and tin prices dropped from 15 percent to 40 percent on world markets.[69]

While recession and stagflation are part of the reason for decreased LDC export demand in North America, Western Europe and Japan, a much more controversial role has been played by a rash of developed country protectionist measures. It is not the budding volume of manufactured goods from the Third World that has suffered from these barriers. Having a low absolute weight amounting to only 1.3 percent of aggregate developed country gross domestic products (GDPs), manufactured exports from LDCs have been allowed comparative freedom of movement into the markets of the "First World."[70] It is primarily in the area of agricultural exports from LDCs that U.S., Common Market and Japanese trade defenses have been erected. The list of U.S. import duties on LDC exports includes a 69 percent tariff on avocado pears, and duties of 25 percent for textiles and 57.7 percent for rum. That of the European Economic Community (EEC) contains tarrifs of 20 percent on meat, 25 percent on fish, 50 percent on grapes and 27 percent on chocolate, while Japanese duties run from 50 percent on grapes to 335 percent on tobacco and a 712 percent duty on wine.[71] Additionally, a variety of non-tariff protectionist measures has been established by the developed nations including quotas, voluntary restraint, anti-dumping legislation, and subsidies for exporters and import-substituting enterprises.

Looking at all of these externalities together, it is plain that they are not matters of mere chance which have accidentally befallen heavily indebted LDCs. Instead, these hammer blows from the external environment have resulted from the conscious and purposeful activities of others, namely the leaderships of the industrialized nations and the OPEC cartel. Seen in this light, the responsibility for the present LDC debt problem must clearly be apportioned between debtor and creditor nations, a point which will become all the more apparent when we consider the part played by the lenders in bringing about the current LDC dilemma.

Issue 4: What Is to Be Done

Fundamentally, the debt problems of developing nations are balance of payments problems. "A country's current account position may deteriorate because of expansionary financial policies, a deterioration in terms of trade, price distortions, high debt service," or, as in the case of leading LDC debtors, "a combination of these factors."[72] The fourth issue facing major LDC debtors, then, is what is to be done about the situation in which they find themselves as a result of contracting external debt. This question, in turn, can be restated as one of how to improve balance of payments positions, of which debt service is a contractually fixed element.

According to the World Bank, there are four basic ways for LDC nations to adjust to a current account balance of payments deficit which in response to the externalities they have encountered:

1. By slowing growth and reducing import demand.
2. By switching production toward additional exports and import substitutes.
3. By external borrowing providing resources for structural adjustment.
4. By postponing adjustment and meeting the deficit through a drawdown on reserves.[73]

Surveying the alternatives, we find that the fourth course can offer only a temporary respite, while the third deepens the problems of LDCs who are already in external debt difficulties. The topic of slowing growth will be dealt with in Chapter 4 as part of a discussion of the International Monetary Fund's approach to adjustment. In practice, given the foreign exchange burden entailed in meeting external debt service, major LDC borrowers must focus on measures

for improving their balance of trade.[74] In order to meet their foreign debt obligations, LDCs follow an adjustment process which "basically consists of policies to expand the volume of [LDC], "exports and to restrain the volume of
imports," including the importation of capital via foreign credit.[75] This adjustment process, then, is broadly analogous to a fundamental choice involved in
the selection of an overall national development strategy, whether to follow an
import-reduction/import-substitution path or an export-promotion one. These two
tactics are not mutually exclusive and in fact some LDCs seeking rapid adjustment of their balance of payments and debts position have attempted to follow
both; but because expansion and increased efficiency in the production of tradeables usually involve some importation of factors of production from abroad,
there is an inherent antagonism between the two courses. As one analogy has
it, import-substitution can be conceptualized as travelling "up the staircase" in
the sense that it generally results in high domestic costs per unit of foreign exchange saved, while export-promotion can be thought of as moving "down the
staircase" since it usually results in low domestic cost per unit of foreign exchange saved.[76]

Import-substitution—the promotion of domestic production of goods and services formerly purchased from others (or comparable items)—is a politically
favored adjustment route for LDC governments. Domestic producers, usually
more numerous and powerful than exporters, advocate this course since it usually involves subsidies to their interests and protection against foreign competitors.[77] Governments are also attracted to this adjustment method since its real
costs emerge only after a substantial time lag.[78] Nevertheless, there are several
serious disadvantages characteristic of this road to adjustment. First, while restricting imports limits foreign exchange outflows, it does not restore value to
exports, and export inflows are requisite to debt service.[79] Secondly, costly
import-substitution schemes are frequently initiated when import costs are high,
only to become unnecessary and inefficient ventures when import prices drop.[80]
Protection of import-substitution industries effectively raises consumer prices
on these goods, fuels inflation, cuts current consumption and eliminates products from the market which cannot be replicated domestically.[81] A final objection to import-substitution stratagems (one stressed by the IMF) is that not only
are they ineffective in the long run at the country level; on a transnational or
systems level they are highly disruptive for, in effect, they impose an unwarranted penalty on competitors[82] and may lead to counter-restrictions against a
country's exports.

Given this inventory of drawbacks associated with import-substitution, it is
not surprising to find that an export-promotion approach to balance of payments
adjustments, debt-service adjustments and overall development strategy is currently favored by free-market economists. Promoting exports—through subsidies, tax incentives, realistic exchange rates and the lowering of protectionist
barriers for imports essential to production of tradeables—permits a nation to
reap greater amounts of foreign exchange. It avoids the inflationary effects of

import restrictions, allows higher levels of consumption of imports, and contributes to a "fair" and theoretically efficient free-market global economy. The World Bank strongly recommends an outward-oriented adjustment policy,[83] noting that, despite the fact that "open" economies are more vulnerable to external shocks—such as price increases on essential imports—they are more successful in overcoming these externalities[84] and more effective in their efforts to control inflation.[85] Unfortunately, one cannot export without demand in foreign markets, and, therefore, in the context of global recession, increased protectionism and the worsening of terms of trade for LDC commodity exports, there are profound constraints on the ability of developing nations to implement this best of all possible adjustment approaches.

While the IMF opposes competitive rounds of devaluation among its member nations, it recommends, and indeed often insists upon, an official devaluation of the currency of an LDC experiencing severe or chronic balance of payments deficits. As an adjustment technique, devaluation is a means of stimulating exports and reducing domestic demand for imports. Devaluation enhances the profitability of exports, making them less costly and more competitive in foreign markets relative to similar products from alternative suppliers "without reducing foreign exchange reserves or public sector savings."[86] Because imports are made "more expensive" through currency depreciation, devaluation cuts excess domestic demand for these goods. In conjunction with reductions in public deficit spending and restraint on credit creation, devaluation is a comparatively effective and mechanically simple means of improving a country's balance of payments position, and hence its capacity to service external debt.

In practice, however, LDC governments are subject to strong and diverse pressures against official devaluation, there being an entire set of countries for whom devaluation is anathema.[87] Nations committed to rapid economic development, among whom major LDC debtors are most prominent, are especially mindful of the negative consequences that a devaluation of their currency against a strong foreign currency (e.g., the U.S. dollar) can engender.[88] Devaluation is both a "contraction" and a "confiscation." Its general effect is recessionary in nature, leading to reduced GNP and GDP growth rates, real rises in the cost of living and wholesale unemployment.[89] Wage earners tend to feel these effects most strongly, as they are hit by a combination of a decline in real wages, unemployment and a reduction of government goods and services.[90] In turn, while the government can proclaim an official devaluation, whether it will stick remains problematical. A "devaluation will usually be partially" or even wholly "eroded through defensive wage increases,"[91] as workers try to offset the negative impact of devaluation upon them. Recognizing this fact of life, LDC leaders frequently devalue further than necessary,[92] hoping to hit the target through a process of give and take. What may occur is that even a correctly calculated target is missed, setting off further rounds of devaluation and an inflation-devaluation spiral.[93] This circumstance not only works against the devaluing country itself; it also prompts major trading partners to follow suit and institute their own devaluation.[94] Instead of functioning as a curative to be used sparingly in countering severe balance of payments difficulties, massive devaluation can become a habitual recurrence, and it can "contaminate" exchange rate policies of other LDC economies with a like syndrome.

The Present Position

In 1969, total LDC external debt amounted to $60.88 billion.[95] According to one study, this figure reached $517 billion in 1981,[96] while another source places the total at $629 billion at end-year 1981.[97] The aggregate LDC foreign debt is not as pressing as the high proportion of this total owed by a group of some twenty Hi-Income, Non-Oil LDCs.[98] The "Hi-Income" status of these countries has enabled them to tap commercial credit markets, while their "Non-Oil" designation results from large energy-import bills. OECD statistics place total outstanding debt for all LDCs at $629 billion, of which Non-OPEC LDCs owe $520 billion or about 83.7 percent.[99] "Ballpark" debt figures must be approached with caution, and here it is important to note that there is a sizeable difference between gross figures, such as those presented above, and net debt. In particular, Hi-Income, Non-Oil LDC borrowers (both public and private) are themselves major depositors with international financial bodies; they lend monies to other LDCs; and their banks purchase government-issued instruments on the Euromarket. Therefore, when dealing with countries of this group, it is essential to keep in mind that net debt may actually be less than one-half of the gross outstanding debt.[100]

Third World external debt is concentrated among Hi-Income, Non-Oil developing nations, but an even greater concentration of external debt is evident among a subgroup within this category: the newly industrialized countries (NICs). A recent study shows that in 1982 just four nations—Mexico, Brazil, Argentina and South Korea—had a composite external debt of $249 billion (exclusive of short-term obligations), and a total of 84 percent of all LDC net floating-interest debt, with Brazil and Mexico alone accounting for 26 percent of total LDC debt service.[101] In other words, LDC external debt is centered in Hi-Income, Non-Oil nations who have continued expansionary development strategies, including the use of foreign borrowings to finance industrial modernization, in spite of the powerful externalities that they have encountered over the past decade.

The issues that major LDC debtors have confronted serve as the basis for their official positions on the predicament in which they now find themselves. Should these countries have used foreign monies to increase the pace of national economic development? LDCs answer that, on the one hand, Western theorists argued for such borrowings, industrialized governments supported the process and international banks were eager to expand their loan portfolios with the addition of claims against LDC borrowers. On the other hand, rapid growth, increased productivity and improving living standards could not possibly have been realized in most LDCs through exclusive reliance on domestic resources. Without such development, the vast majority of LDC debtors would not have been able to meet pressing needs for consumption and employment of their growing populations. Should the LDCs have tapped commercial credit markets on hard terms? Again, the major debtors argue yes, because other sources of external flows had been reduced, and because commercial loans allowed them to circumvent the strings attached to official borrowings. Who is to blame for the current crisis? While acknowledging some past policy errors, particularly those of previous administrations, the LDCs point to the combined effects of externalities,[102] especially the three hammer blows of high U.S. dollar interest rates, increased energy costs and worsening terms of trade.[103] These exogenous factors were beyond the capacity of the borrowers to anticipate or influence, and they were brought about by the collective actions of others, notably the industrialized nations and OPEC.[104] What is to be done? The external debt problems of the Third World are viewed by developing countries as a common problem requiring a common, orderly solution, i.e., debt relief from lenders on a regular and partly automatic basis. LDC governments, then, make no distinctions between debt relief and balance of payments assistance,[105] nor do they distinguish between debt relief and development assistance.[106] As will be detailed shortly, this platform stands in sharp contrast to the stated positions of both lenders and negotiators, who frame the current crisis in terms of the issues that they confront and arrive at decidedly different conclusions.

Notes

1. Hurni, pp.14–15.

2. Seiber, *International Borrowing,* p.5.

3. Hurni, p.117.

4. Everett E. Hagen, *The Economics of Development,* 3rd ed. (Homewood, Illinois: Richard D. Irwin, 1980), pp.290–294.

5. Seiber, *International Borrowing,* p.51.

6. David Roberts, "The LDC Debt Burden," *Federal Reserve Bank of New York,* Spring, 1981, p.34.

7. Henry J. Bitterman, *The Refunding of International Debt* (Durham, North Carolina: Duke University, 1973), p.38.

8. Seiber, *International Borrowing,* pp.10–12.

9. Ibid., p.12.

10. Ibid.

11. Roberts, p.36.

12. Seiber, *International Borrowing,* p.6.

13. Hagen, pp.289–290.

14. Millard Long and Frank Veneroso, "The Debt-Related Problems of Non-Oil Less Developed Countries," *Economic Development and Cultural Change,* April, 1981, p.503.

15. Albert Fishlow, "Latin American External Debt: The Case of Uncertain Development," in *Trade, Stability, Technology and Equity in Latin America,* ed. Moshe Syrquin and Simon Teitel (New York: Academic Press, 1982), p.143.

16. Anthony Angelini, Maximo Eng and Francis A. Lees, *International Lending, Risk and the Euromarket* (New York: John Wiley, 1979), p.14.

17. Leeds, "External Financing," p.22.

18. IBRD, *World Development Report,* p.35.

19. Angelini, Eng and Lees, p.14.

20. David P.Dod, "Bank Lending to Developing Countries: Recent Developments in Historical Perspective," *Federal Reserve Bulletin*, September 1981, p.648.

21. Organization for Economic Cooperation and Development (OECD), *External Debt of Developing Countries: 1982 Survey* (New York: OECD, 1982), p.10.

22. Dod, p.647.

23. OECD, p.11.

24. Leeds, "External Financing," p.25.

25. Michael DaCosta, "How Bank Lending Helps the LDCs," *The Banker*, October, 1980, p.49.

26. Sampson, p.144.

27. OECD, p.20.

28. IBRD, *World Development Report,* p.18.

29. G. Russell Kincaid, "Inflation and the External Debt of Developing Countries," *Finance and Development*, December, 1981, p.45.

30. OECD. p.11.

31. Bahram Nowzad, "Debt in Developing Countries: Some Issues for the 1980s," *Finance and Development*, March, 1982, p.16.

32. Roberts, p.35.

33. Fishlow, "Latin American External Debt," p.152.

34. Roberts, p.40.

35. Kincaid, p.45.

36. Ibid., p.48.

37. "LDC Debt: Vital U.S. Role," *The Banker*, February, 1981, p.79.

38. Laurie Goodman and Nancy Worth, "The Future of Commercial Banks in LDC Financing, " *The Banker's Magazine*, November/December, 1981, p.79.

39. OECD, p.14.

40. Bahram Nowzad and Richard C. Williams, *External Indebtedness of Developing Countries*. IMF Occasional Paper No.3 (Washington: International Monetary Fund, 1981), p.3.

41. Tim Anderson, "The Year of Rescheduling," *Euromoney*, August, 1982, p.19.

42. Chandra Hardy, "Rescheduling Developing Country Debts," *The Banker*, July, 1981, p.33.

43. OECD, p.17.

44. Angelini, Eng and Lees, pp.20–21.

45. Ibid., p.21.

46. Group of Thirty, *Risks in International Bank Lending* (New York: Group of Thirty, 1982), p.100.

47. William R. Cline, *International Monetary Reform and the Developing Countries* (Washington: Brookings Institution, 1976), pp.5–6.

48. Ibid., pp.8–10.

49. Richard J. Flamson, "How Structural Distortions Hamper World Recovery," *Euromoney*, September, 1982, p.167.

50. Lamberto Dini, "Financial Strains in the World Economy," *Banco Nazionale del Lavoro: Quarterly Review*, March, 1983, p.54.

51. Dod, p.652.

52. IBRD, *World Development Report,* p.18.

53. Hagen, p.297.

54. Tony Killick, "Euromarket Recycling of OPEC Surpluses: Fact or Myth?" *The Banker,* January, 1981, p.21.

55. Seiber, *International Borrowing* p.94.

56. Ibid., p.79.

57. Killick, *International Borrowing,* p.16.

58. Seiber, *International Borrowing,* p.97.

59. Deepak Lal, *A Liberal International Economic Order: The International Monetary System and Economic Development,* Essays in International Finance No. 139 (Princeton: Princeton University, 1980), p.9.

60. OECD, p.5.

61. IBRD, *World Development Report,* p.7.

62. Seiber, *International Borrowing,* p.99.

63. Dod, p.648.

64. OECD, p.5.

65. Bluford H. Putnam and Lee Thomas, "Oil Might Soon Be $25 a Barrel or Less," *Euromoney,* February, 1983, p.103.

66. Killick, p.15.

67. Ibid., p.19.

68. Pedro-Pablo Kuczynski, "Action Steps After Cancun," *Foreign Affairs,* Summer, 1982, p.1022.

69. International Bank for Reconstruction and Development (IBRD) *The World Bank Annual Report: 1982* (Washington: World Bank, 1982), p.89.

70. IBRD *World Development Report,* p.12.

71. Alan Robinson, "The End of Illusion in Latin America," *Euromoney,* September, 1982, p.77.

72. Karim Nashashibi, "Devaluation in Developing Countries: Difficult Choices," *Finance and Development,* March, 1983, p.14.

73. IBRD, *World Development Report,* p.7.

74. Alexander McW. Wolfe, "International Lending Risks: Country Risk," in *Offshore Lending by U.S. Commerical Banks,* ed. F. John Mathis (Washington: Banker's Association for Foreign Trade, 1981), p.44.

75. Dod, p.648.

76. Bela Balassa, *The Process of Industrial Development and Alternative Development Strategies.* Essays in International Finance No. 141 (Princeton: Princeton University, 1981), p.17.

77. Gisselquist, p.184.

78. Nashashibi, p.15.

79. Ibid.

80. IBRD, *World Development Report,* p.55.

81. J.N. Robinson, p.74.

82. John Williamson, *The Lending Policies of the International Monetary Fund* (Washington: Institute for International Economics, 1982), p.24.

83. IBRD, *World Development Report,* p.89.

84. Bela Balassa, *Adjustment to External Shocks in Developing Economies.* World Bank Staff Working Paper, No. 472 (Washington: World Bank, 1981), p.29.

85. IBRD, *World Development Report*, p.17.

86. Nashashibi, p.14.

87. Cline, p.10.

88. Dod, p.649.

89. Nashashibi, pp.14–15.

90. Ibid., pp.16–17.

91. Williamson, p.27.

92. Nashashibi, p.17.

93. Ibid., p.15.

94. Jane Spivak Hughes, "The Countries of the Future Don't Look So Hot Today," *Euromoney*, January, 1983, p.108.

95. Seiber, *International Borrowing*, p.27.

96. IBRD, *World Development Report*, p.15.

97. Anderson, "Rescheduling," p.22.

98. Angelini, Eng and Lees, p.105.

99. OECD, p.26, 28.

100. Killick, p.20.

101. OECD, pp.12, 18–19.

102. Seiber, *International Borrowing*, p.98.

103. Charles Grant, "The Carnival Is over, but There's Always Next Year," *Euromoney*, April, 1982, p.3.

104. Seiber, *International Borrowing*, p.129.

105. Marilyn J. Seiber, "Alternative Proposals for Debt Relief," in *Developing Country Debt*, ed. Lawrence G. Franko and Marilyn J. Seiber (New York: Pergamon, 1979), p.189.

106. Seiber, *International Borrowing*, p.124.

Chapter 3

THE LENDERS

The Commercial Bank Focus

Because direct investment does not require repayment on a preset schedule, relevant external capital flows to LDCs issue from three basic sources: foreign governments, multilateral development banks and commercial markets. Apart from short-term, trade-related credits, official government-to-government loans have declined of late, and their beneficiaries are primarily low-income LDCs receiving Official Development Assistance (ODA) from the member nations of the Development Assistance Committee (DAC). Consequently, their role in the growth of major developing country debt-service burdens is comparatively minor, as is their capacity to relieve these burdens at current funding levels. Multilateral development banks, among which the World Bank Group is by far the most important, have adopted a two-pronged approach to development, financing Hi-Income LDCs with project loans on near-market terms, and Low-Income LDCs with ''needs-oriented'' assistance on concessional terms. Limitations on the volume and type of loans which the MDBs can extend to major developing nation debtors work to constrain their role as cause and remedy of the present debt crisis. The critical component of the debt pressures confronting primary LDC borrowers is the stock and service of floating-interest loans granted to them by commercial lenders, particularly through the medium of syndicated Euro-loans. Since this element tends to outweigh all others in terms of total debt and yearly debt service due, the bulk of this chapter will be devoted to an analysis of this form of LDC borrowing. While the priorities of the LDC loan recipients are matters of growth, productivity and improvements in living standards, the interests of the commercial banks are largely those of profit, risk, market share and continuing opportunities to do business. The banks, then, frame the current LDC debt problems in terms of a different set of issues than that which the developing nations address, and this, in turn, leads them to an entirely different position on the nature, origin and meaning of the present situation.

Official bilateral loans from industrialized nations to the Third World have not grown as rapidly as total developing nation borrowings, and the recipients of these flows are now heavily concentrated among the poorest countries of the world. In 1979, total outstanding debt owed by all LDCs to DAC members stood at $27.4 billion,[1] a substantial sum, but merely a small fraction of the total debt owed by all developing countries. In fact, the share of official bilateral flows granted on soft, concessional terms as a part of total LDC borrowing has dropped from 28.5 percent in 1971 to a mere 11 percent in 1980.[2] The dangerous side effects of such loans (i.e., the political, diplomatic and military strings attached to them) have caused LDCs with access to alternative sources of finance to avoid this form of assistance,[3] while the very ineffectiveness of these strings in manipulating the policies of the borrowers has led official lenders to view such loans with disfavor.[4] Bilateral official loans may play an important part as emergency measures accompanying multilateral reschedulings of major borrowers, but as original sources of LDC debt and debt service the role of such flows is minimal.

The World Bank was established in 1945 as one of the two Bretton Woods institutions, the other being the International Monetary Fund. Chartered as the International Bank for Reconstruction and Development (IBRD), the mission of the Bank is to assist nations in their reconstruction and development.[5] Given this broadly defined mandate, it is not surprising to find that the Bank has reinterpreted its role over time. The parent IBRD has set up two major soft-loan windows in the form of the International Finance Corporation (IFC) and the International Development Association (IDA), but the IBRD remains the largest and most powerful member of the group, and it is the activities of the IBRD that are most relevant to major developing country debtors. From 1946 to 1980, the IBRD alone extended $59.3 billion in loans,[6] mostly to middle-income developing countries. These loans have been offered on near-market terms, providing a discount from market levels to borrowers and enabling the Bank to run at a profit. The volume of such lending has grown over the years so that, exclusive of IFC and IDA financing, the World Bank's lending program has expanded from $2 billion a year in 1973 to a projected $11.2 billion for fiscal year 1983.[7]

Originally, the World Bank Group's lending was almost solely for project financing, mostly large-scale infrastructural construction. With Robert McNamara's assumption of the Bank's presidency in 1968, the emphasis shifted to meeting the needs of the vast majority of LDC residents who had been bypassed in the process of industrial modernization.[8] Project lending remained the Bank's mainstay, but a limited number of balance of payments and "general" disbursements were granted to meet urgent human needs.[9] A major departure from the Bank's lending purposes occurred in 1980, when, for the first time, the IBRD issued Structural Adjustment Loans (SALs).[10] These funds were slated for use by developing nations suffering from stagflation, high interest rates, growing protectionism, increased oil-import costs and the worsening "climate of concessional aid;"[11] the major LDC debtors being prime examples of countries affected by these phenomena. The disbursement of SALs is conditional upon the borrower's meeting certain prestated objectives, but since they carry long-term maturities, World Bank conditionality is loose in comparison with that of IMF upper-tranche loans. Upper-tranche loans are highly conditional balance of payments loans from IMF. They are part of a tranche system in which each member nation's borrowing quota is determined and divided into five tranches. The first and second tranches can be drawn upon without stringent conditions and are termed "lower tranche." When these are exhausted, borrowers draw on the third, fourth and fifth tranches, or "upper tranches," carrying more stringent conditions. Despite the obvious need for such funds, SAL financing remains relatively modest, amounting to an annual average flow of just over $1 billion in its first two years of existence.[12]

Along with the International Monetary Fund, the World Bank is frequently mentioned by LDC debt analysts as a potential prime mover in resolving the LDC debt problem. However, like the IMF, the Bank's capacity to fulfill a central part is severely limited. The first limitation on the Bank's role resides at the very heart of the institution. The IBRD acquires funds from both governments and bond markets and then relends these monies to its borrowers. As a funding mix, this arrangement allows the bank to obtain financing at a cost which is closer to open market than to concessional levels. What is important here is that the Bank is a *profit-making institution* that can only offer non-IFC/IDA loans for projects with a satisfactory rate of return.[13] Moreover, since the World Bank must also sponsor concessional loans through its soft windows, it "has maintained an equilibrium between very short-term, high-yielding projects and poverty-oriented, long-term experiments."[14] Therefore, the profit that the Bank makes on hard loans through the IBRD must contain a premium to offset its losses on concessional loans. In 1982, the cost of borrowings to the Bank (weighted by amount and maturity) rose to 10.93 percent on average, up from 9.3 percent the previous year.[15] On 1 July, 1982, World Bank President A.W. Clausen announced that henceforth "the lending rate for all new loans will no longer be fixed for the life of the loan," but will be "adjusted every six months [to reflect] the average cost of a pool of IBRD borrowings."[16] What has occurred, first, is that along with rising costs of funds for the Bank, uncertainty concerning future costs has induced the IBRD to institute its own floating-interest loans. Some have suggested that the IBRD tap commercial banks to expand its funding base, but, again, since these added costs would ultimately be reflected in added debt service for the final LDC borrower, such an arrangement would not offer much promise of actual debt relief in the long term.[17] In general, the IBRD can offer funds to LDCs at a discount from the market level, but because it is a profit-making institution, it cannot simply disregard market levels in setting its own interest rates.

Secondly, there is an emerging controversy over just which nations are eligible for IBRD loans. The World Bank periodically "graduates" nations by "slowly phasing out IBRD lending as a borrowing country reaches a level of development, management capacity and access to capital markets that permits it to carry on without IBRD financing.''[18] Prime candidates for graduation include precisely those Hi-Income LDCs who have tapped commercial markets and now find themselves at a loss to repay these loans. Critics of the graduation process rightfully point out that, in effect, it serves to punish the more efficient and faster-growing LDCs while rewarding inefficient, stagnating countries. Despite the storm it has brewed, graduation continues apace, with industrialized nation representatives to the Bank pressuring for an acceleration of the process.[19]

The IBRD's lending program is heavily influenced by the policy stances of its developed nation contributors, for it is they who control the bulk of the votes on Bank executive boards and it is they who have the final say in determining participation in World Bank efforts. The expansion of loan volumes and the range of lending purposes by the IBRD is severely constrained by the political aims of the developed nation ''majority'' members.[20] This is most apparent in the degree of control that the United States has tried to exercise on the Bank over the course of successive administrations. From 1974 to 1977, U.S. Treasury Secretary William Simon carried on a running battle with McNamara's Bank, part of the conflict revolving around the latter's attempt to trade World Bank voting power to OPEC nations in return for an increased flow of petrodollars to the Bank.[21] McNamara's ''needs'' emphasis also ran afoul of the Carter Administration's human rights crusade, with the American government holding up funds to authoritarian regimes, regardless of the consequences for the victimized masses of these lands.[22] McNamara resigned in June, 1981, amidst a second unsuccessful attempt to trade votes for oil money,[23] this time involving the participation of the Palestine Liberation Organization (PLO), and while current Bank head Tom Clausen (formerly President of the Bank of America) enjoys more cordial relations with the Reagan Administration, it is doubtful whether any American administration can resist trying to put its own stamp on the course of World Bank lending.[24]

It has also been suggested that the World Bank could effectively increase its lending leverage without a corresponding increase in its borrowings through the mechanism of co-financing.[25] A co-financing arrangement involves funding from both the IBRD and a commercial source (e.g., an international bank syndicate) to an LDC, usually as long-term project investments. Co-financing offers the commercial bank lenders added insurance against rescheduling or outright default by the borrower. Through ''cross-default'' clauses, the debtor's chronic failure to meet service payments would result in both the commercial lender and the World Bank calling him into default. It is generally felt that an LDC borrower would be extremely reluctant to alienate a major source of discount financing such as the World Bank, and since the IBRD guarantees the use of funds, supervises their disbursement, monitors project performance and provides technical assistance, its participation improves prospects for successful performance.[26] For many potential bank participants, however, there are significant drawbacks to co-financing with the IBRD. The World Bank has an un-blemished loan performance record, it is true, but, counter the bankers, no American bank has ever been forced to write off a loan to a sovereign bor-rower, even though reschedulings have become commonplace.[27] Profit margins available to the banks under IBRD co-financing are thin, with spreads of only $^1/_2$ percent being offered, in part because LDCs drive a hard bargain on the basis of the reduced risk that Bank participation affords to its commercial part-ner.[28] Finally, should major servicing difficulties arise in the repayment of a co-financed loan, there could be a conflict of interest between the Bank and the commerical lender which, in turn, would provide undue leverage to the bor-rower.[29] Co-financing deserves to be encouraged, but it does not offer sufficient advantages to the banks to become a principal vehicle for lending to the Third World.

With official flows reduced and the funding capacity of the World Bank in-herently constrained, creditworthy LDCs have turned increasingly toward the commercial Euromarkets for their financial needs. It was in the aftermath of the first oil shock that syndicated Eurolending to LDCs shifted into high gear. Banks had already begun serving LDC clients on a large scale during the 1971–1973 export commodities boom, but after the doubling and redoubling of energy costs in 1973–1974, their lending took on a whole new form. First, there was a dis-proportionate increase in the share of loan flows directed toward sovereign gov-ernment borrowers,[30] and second, in contrast to the predominance of project lending in prior loans to LDC governments, banks now extended credits for balance of payments and general purposes.[31] Bank claims on Non-Oil LDCs grew from $35 billion in 1974 to $150 billion in 1979,[32] reaching $254 billion in 1980, $305 billion in 1981, and $382 billion in 1982.[33] The banks had clearly decided that loans to official borrowers in selected LDC nations were prudent additions to their portfolios, but there were, in addition, a wide range of ulte-rior motives behind their boosting of flows to sovereign LDC borrowers, and this leads naturally to a discussion of the first issue that commercial lenders confront when evaluating LDC debt: Why lend commercial funds to developing nation governments?

Issue 1: Why Lend to LDC Governments?

From the commercial lender's perspective, the first LDC debt-related issue is basically the counterpart of the initial issue confronted by the borrower: Why lend to sovereign LDC entities? The risks of such lending will be treated shortly as part of an analysis of country risk evaluation. For now, the focus of inquiry is centered on the factors that have favored increased loan flows from the banks of the industrialized nations to developing country borrowers. Much of this dis-cussion will be approached from the standpoint of U.S. commercial banks, but, with minor variations, the same forces that encouraged American bankers to expand LDC lending also influenced their European and Japanese colleagues.

A logical starting point for surveying the reasons behind greater international activities on the part of Western banks is their experience and performance within domestic credit markets. Following World War II, there was a gradual slow-down in the pace of economic growth in the United States.[34] During the 1950s and 1960s, domestic demand for commercial loans generally slackened, while competition for deposits increased sharply. Entering a "performance era" in deposit-taking and encountering new types of competition in loan-making (e.g., credit unions), American banks searched for new sources of funds and new credit customers and saw a world of opportunities abroad, primarily in the Euromarkets. The question of whether lending to LDCs is more profitable than granting credit to alternative borrowers remains largely unanswered. However, LDC lending allowed the banks to charge higher margins and fees than those available domestically, and some American banks—Citibank in Brazil, for instance—received extremely attractive returns on their Third World loans. Outright default by LDC sovereign borrowers was, and still is, very rare, and so the perceived risks of sovereign lending to developing nations appeared slight in comparison to domestic business, where U.S. corporate bankruptcies continued throughout the 1970s.[35]

The American money-center banks had been operating abroad for some time before the spurt of LDC sovereign borrowing in the mid–1970s. In general, U.S. banks followed their major multinational corporate customers overseas in the late 1960s, providing on-the-spot services to these clients in support of direct investment and trade. In one sense, then, large U.S. banks were forced to internationalize in order to prevent other banks, both American and foreign, from infringing on their multinational customers,[36] as well as to provide convenient services for foreign customers in their own lands.[37] Seeking to maintain their relationships with U.S. and foreign corporate customers, major U.S. banks moved beyond their national borders.[38] In a very short time, these banks established networks of branches and subsidiaries in Europe, Japan and the Third World. To support the overhead costs entailed in maintaining these networks during periods of low corporate demand in international markets, the American banks sought to expand their lending activities.[39] Sovereign lending appeared to be precisely the sort of continuous business needed to keep branches and subsidiaries from the embarrassment of having to close shop, and, like dealings with corporate customers, such lending held forth the prospect of forging a relationship with government and government-guaranteed borrowers. If occasionally this meant offering a comparatively low-profit or high-risk loan to an LDC customer, this could be justified on the basis of expectations for future profits from "spin-off" business with the borrowers.[40] Thus, even in periods when a borrower's market prevailed, the banks continued to lend to LDCs, despite the unattractive margins and fees, in part because of their perception that opting out too often would diminish opportunities for future business. Since the mid–1970s, these same banks have come to the realization "that corporate lending can generate a wider range of business than governments can,"[41] and lending for relationship business has been switched back to the MNCs[42] and private local firms in LDC nations.[43] Nevertheless, the concept of a relationship with private domestic and foreign borrowers stimulated U.S. bankers to expand their activities abroad and to look for similar relationships with sovereign LDC borrowers to offset overhead costs generated by foreign branches and subsidiaries.

With regard to American banks in particular, one of the primary paradoxes of their increased international activities is found in the influence that U.S. banking regulations had upon them in the early 1970s. These regulations, designed to curb credit expansion, had the unintentional effect of promoting the bankers to respond in ways that furthered their offshore lending. For example, the Voluntary Foreign Credit Restraint Program of 1965–1974 "encouraged banks to keep their foreign deposits in foreign offices for onlending to foreign customers,"[44] thereby creating a physical and ledger-sheet separation between the domestic and international businesses of these institutions. In 1971, these credit restraints were rescinded for loans in support of American exports,[45] and in 1974 the Program was eliminated altogether.[46] But other regulatory measures, such as the imposition of interest rate ceilings under Regulation Q, compelled American banks to look abroad, not only for loan customers, but also for sources of deposits. Indeed, during the credit crunch of the late 1960s, American banks were forced to fund domestic loans from the Eurodollar market.[47]

The growth of American bank lending to LDC customers and the high degree of exposure evident in the LDC loan portfolios of many major U.S. banks is presently a source of concern for U.S. monetary and financial regulatory authorities, especially the Federal Reserve Board, the Comptroller of Currency (COC) and the Federal Deposit Insurance Corporation (FDIC). Their worries about U.S. banking activities in Third World markets involve not only possible imprudence in lending exposure, but also unrestrained credit creation and the inflationary effects which such borrowings may generate.[48] In 1978, the Fed, COC and FDIC formed an Interagency Country Exposure Review Committee,[49] requiring U.S.-headquartered banks to submit consolidated balance sheets reflecting both domestic and international business for the Committee's inspection. Similarly, the Japanese Ministry of Finance put a virtual stop to all syndicated lending by Japanese banks in 1979–1980,[50] while the Bundesbank informally pressured German bankers to curb their lending to LDC borrowers.[51] In spite of these efforts, the regulation of industrialized nation bank activity on international markets remains fragmentary and filled with loopholes. Even after the 1978 stipulations had been put in place, one bank analyst concluded that "the high degree of Federal control which characterizes the domestic operations of U.S. banks does not hold true for their international operations."[52] Limits have been established on relative sums that can be lent to individual sovereign borrowers, but their intent can be obviated by the banks through lending to several "sovereign" borrowers within a single country. Special Federal Reserve Board measures adopted in March, 1980, to stem the flow of American bank loans to heavily indebted LDCs were phased out within four months,[53] and the lack of regulatory powers over short-term lending has allowed Japanese and German banks to elude country ceiling limits by expanding short-term loans and then rolling them over.[54]

The two oil price rises of 1973 and 1979 had a strong negative impact on the balance of payments positions of Non-Oil LDCs. Along with export revenues from industrialized nations, these deficits represented current account surpluses for most OPEC oil producers. OPEC surpluses, in turn, created sharp liquidity surges in international financial markets as petrodollars flowed into major American, European and Japanese banks. Limited in their own domestic absorption capacities, OPEC nations found themselves in the enviable position of being unable to spend all their oil-export receipts.[55] Unwilling to simply hand back these revenues as aid to Non-Oil LDCs,[56] OPEC members lacked the requisite financial machinery, expertise and confidence to undertake direct investment or direct loans to the rest of the Third World.[57] Consequently, the oil-rich OPEC nations "recycled" their petrodollars through the intermediation of the international commercial banking system, depositing vast sums with the banks who, in their turn, lent a major portion of these monies to developing nations suffering from increased energy-import costs. It has been estimated that, in 1974 alone, $22.5 billion were channeled from OPEC coffers into the European banking system,[58] that from 1974 to 1976 some $49 billion in petrodollars found their way into the treasuries of banks in New York and London,[59] and that of the whopping $240 billion OPEC surplus of 1979, about 80 percent was invested outside OPEC lands, one-half of that figure being in the form of bank deposits.[60] In line with their risk avoidance posture, the OPEC depositors selected only the "bluest chip" institutions to handle their accounts,[61] the lion's share being funneled to the largest American and European "names." The bankers characterized this recycling function as a "public-spirited" service[62] permitting a smooth transfer of funds back to severely strained LDC economies. But taking deposits and making loans is the basic stuff of commercial banking, and it would have been extremely uncharacteristic of the banks to have refused OPEC monies. Having taken on these funds, the bankers sought borrowers, and, with the industrialized nations in recession, the Non-Oil LDCs stood out as prime candidates for "recycled" lending.

Throughout the 1970s and the 1980s, banks experienced dramatic rises and falls in the margins and fees attainable from LDC Eurolending. See-sawing from a borrower's market allowing only thin spreads under conditions of excess liquidity to a lender's market allowing higher spreads during periods of tight liquidity, Euromarket lending went through a rapid succession of stages in profitability. The commodities boom of 1970–1973 resulted in strong bank competition for loans to LDC nations, followed by a lender's market as credit demand increased in the wake of the first oil shock, and another return to borrower's terms during the period 1975–1979.[63] Indeed, the borrower's market of the late 1970s enabled LDC debtors to renegotiate and refinance debts incurred in the 1974–1975 period,[64] but the Iranian Revolution led to another lender's market based on increased perception of risk associated with LDC lending.[65] In 1980–1981, spreads on LDC loans plummeted again to an average of less than 1 percent above LIBOR, but, as the magnitude of the debt problems faced by major LDC borrowers became apparent after mid–1981, margins rose to heights of 2 $1/2$ percent above LIBOR. These fluctuations in the profitability and perceived risk of bank lending to developing countries had the effect of offering something for everybody. Banks with conservative lending styles increased their LDC lending activities when risks were perceived as minimal, while those with a more adventuresome orientation enlarged their LDC loan portfolios during periods of high profit margins. Thus, the rate of growth in the volume of bank lending to LDCs remained remarkably stable over the decade from 1972 to 1982, as banks with different approaches to basic profit/risk calculations increased or decreased their LDC financing.

Issue 2: To Whom to Lend

Motivated in part by these factors, American, European and Japanese bankers confronted the second issue of the LDC debt problem seen from their angle, one that centered around their lending strategy: Which LDC borrowers were to be entrusted with funds and how could the risk of lending to the developing nations be limited? First and foremost, lenders were confronted with the task of assessing country risk as a distinct class apart from general credit risk. There are wide variations in the conceptualization of country risk, and the term itself "is subject to a wide range of interpretations."[66] Consider, for example, the differences among three different glossings of the term "country risk:"

1. "The likelihood of the occurrence of default, moratorium, forced rescheduling or merely extensive delays in the repayment of principal and interest at a national, rather than an individual company, level."[67]

2. The risk that "a country will fail to generate enough foreign exchange to service its foreign currency loans according to the terms laid down in the original agreement."[68]

3. "The risk involved in lending to an entity (public or private sector) in a foreign country in a currency other than the local one."[69]

For the sake of conceptual clarity, "country risk" in this discussion consists of two interrelated elements. First, there is the risk that, for economic or financial reasons, an LDC borrower will fail to accumulate enough foreign exchange receipts to meet debt-service obligations on loans denominated in foreign currencies. This foreign exchange risk may be termed "sovereign risk" when the borrower is a government or government-guaranteed entity, and "transfer risk" when the borrower is a private entity (the latter may or may not be constrained on foreign exchange remittances by statutory regulation). Second, there is a "political risk" involved in country risk. This second element exists because even though a country may have sufficient foreign exchange receipts to service external debt, political or social dislocations may inhibit its "will" to do so.[70] Hence, taken together, sovereign/transfer risk and political risk comprise country risk.

There are two aspects of sovereign lending that require attention at this point. First, unlike domestic borrowers or non-guaranteed private debtors, sovereign nations cannot go bankrupt.[71] On the other hand, it is extremely difficult to compel a sovereign nation to repay an external debt through purely legal means. The doctrine of "sovereign immunity" provides three privileges to government borrowers:

1. In general, they cannot be sued without their consent;
2. courts of one country cannot sit in judgement on the acts or omissions of a second country committed within the second nation's frontiers; and
3. property of a government or its instrumentality is immune.[72]

There are, of course, extralegal sanctions which can be imposed on a negligent sovereign debtor, ranging from a drop in its international credit standing to political, economic and diplomatic pressures from the lender's national government; but the era of gunboat diplomacy has long since vanished, and, short of war, there is ultimately no means of forcing a sovereign government to make good on its external debts.

Given this situation, commercial bankers have devised systems of country risk analysis to evaluate the creditworthiness of potential LDC borrowers from different Third World nations. Citibank's Irving Friedman credits himself with having "invented" country risk analysis in the aftermath of the first oil shock of 1974–1975.[73] Whether Friedman is the "father" of country risk analysis is not of great importance, but it was in the mid–1970s that bankers first sought to assess country risk on a systematic basis. In addition to the standard economic and financial data, country risk analysis encompassed political and social factors having a potential influence on a country's ability or willingness to service external debt.[74] A variety of country risk formats evolved, including structured qualitative, fully qualitative and checklist methods for measuring the sovereign and political risks entailed in lending to a given foreign borrower.

The experience of the international bankers in applying country risk analysis to their international lending strategies is similar to that of Western development theorists in applying models of development to the Third World: mixed and erratic. Over time, the shortcomings of country risk analysis have become more prominent than its purported usefulness. There was, first, a rage for quantification, especially among American bankers, and lending officials devoted stores of energy to assigning numerical values to political and social factors. European bankers frequently chided their American colleagues for relying on the numbers, preferring their own impressionistic approach to foreign lending based on personal knowledge of the borrower.[75] Essentially qualitative phenomena were quantified and then wrenched into place as part of a general country risk model which was unrealistically expected to represent the relevant workings of scores of diverse national economies, political systems and social structures.[76] Even "purely economic" calculations, such as DSRs, contain pitfalls when treated abstractly, including the failure to treat short-term debt,[77] the assumption that all export receipts can be mustered to service external debt,[78] and statistical distortions arising from early, voluntary repayments which raise DSRs on paper, even though they are positive events.[79] Even if all economic and financial factors are correctly calculated and modeled, there must still be a realistic appraisal of a country's ability to manage its debt servicing capacity.[80]

Then, of course, there is the matter of the irrational or unpredictable. Not only have there been periodic, unforeseeable events, (e.g., the Iranian Revolution and the Argentinian invasion of the Falklands); the impact of such events on debt-service performance has varied greatly. The 1979 Iranian Revolution created major disruptions in debt repayment, but the 1980 assassination of South Korea's president had no discernible effect on that nation's debt-service performance.[81] The unpredictable can emanate from sources outside of the borrower's borders, i.e., as externalities like the precipitous rise in dollar interest rates in the period 1980–1982. Finally, nations, particularly those committed to rapid economic development, undergo change over time. "Most countries survive in the world economy only as a result of frequent and often large changes in policy on the part of national governments, central banks, etc.,"[82] so that while "baseline" assumptions made when granting credit may be correct, there is no guarantee that they will remain so throughout the life of the loan.

A number of partial remedies have been adopted to compensate for the drawbacks in the current state of the art in country risk analysis. Commercial lenders now pay greater attention to key, short-term economic variables related to a nation's current accounts,[83] as in the Statement of International Financial Transactions (SIFT) "cash flow" method of measuring national creditworthiness.[84] Some bankers have elected to follow the market's assessment in determining the riskiness of lending to a particular LDC borrower, as in *Euromoney*'s country risk ratings or the informal survey techniques of *Institutional Investor*. Still others have called for a central, "official" country risk assessment, possibly from the World Bank or the IMF, but such procedures bear potential political conflict and economic embarrassment, and neither the Bank nor the Fund is willing to provide this kind of service to the banks.[85]

What this effort to improve existing country risk analysis systems reflects is the increasing distrust of bankers for their own country risk evaluations.[86] Hence, line officials often countermand the country risk analysis of a bank's central staff;[87] banks are warned of impending political disruption but continue to expand their lending to such borrowers,"[88] and the "herd instinct" has frequently overridden independent analysis, especially in the case of regional banks following the lead of money-center institutions.[89] Lastly, as the history of spreads offered to a variety of LDC borrowers on the basis of differential risk demonstrates, there has never been a spread among margins sufficient to reflect the difference between "prime" low-risk borrowers and "non-prime" high-risk borrowers.

One final problem inherent in assessing a nation's credit lies in the systemic consequences of all bankers arriving at the same country risk conclusions. Suppose, for a moment, that all of the data fed into country risk models were completely accurate, that the models themselves were perfect and that the interpretation of the results was absolutely correct. Bankers would simply channel loans to the best risks while ignoring the poorer ones.[90] Ironically, this leads to an over-concentration of lending, and thus increased risk to lenders taken collectively.[91] "A fairly standard country-by-country approach has sometimes resulted in over-concentration on certain regions or certain sectors,"[92] or certain nations. Competition for loans to "certified" nations would, of course, be quite keen, increasing the borrower's leverage and resulting in lower margin and less attractive risk/profit relationships.[93] Finally, countries do not exist as hermetically sealed units, despite the impression given by the country-by-country approach. Focusing on certain nations to the exclusion of others leads to a situation in which creditworthy countries find markets in loan-deprived trading partners dry, thereby hindering export performance for the nation deemed creditworthy. In short, if all bankers have the same "good" idea, the aggregate application of this idea may be self-defeating in the end.

Country risk analysis is exclusively concerned with the performance of bank assets, but, of late, there has been a new emphasis on the other side of the ledger, i.e., on the capacity of the banks to fund loans while remaining solvent. Simply because a bank undertakes a loan does not assure that funds will be available to it on a given date, in a specified currency and at a commercially viable cost.[94] Banks are now paying close attention to the liabilities involved in international lending activities, to "funding risk" or "market risk."[95] As previously mentioned, one of the motives behind increased American activity abroad was to diversify and expand sources of funding[96] in the "performance era" of deposit-taking.[97] Over the course of the past decade, the concern with funding loans has led to a vast increase in interbank lending.[98] "As banks intermediate short-term volatile deposits into longer-term relatively illiquid loans to LDC nations,"[99] they have come to rely on the interbank market to assure them of matching maturities and currencies contained in original loan agreements. In light of the current uncertainties pervading bank lending to LDCs, it is not surprising to find a conflict of interest between investors favoring short-term commitments and borrowers seeking longer maturities on their loans.[100] Currently, perceptions of increased funding risk have begun to influence the volume of medium-and long-term loans extended to developing nation borrowers. As one analyst contends, in the present environment banks "are not going to increase their exposure in a market that relies on 3 and 6 month deposits to fund commitments of five, seven and even ten years."[101] Mismatching of funds, concentrations of exposures and doubts "about certain nationalities of banks"[102] have evoked concern in the international banking community over the possibility of an interbank deposit crisis. One American banker was recently quoted as saying that "the only event that could kill the loan market would be an interbank crisis."[103] The rush of petrodollars into the banking system in 1974–1975 sparked fears about the potential effects of a precipitous withdrawal of OPEC funds on bank funding commitments.[104] These misgivings proved ungrounded, but, as the experience of the Central Bank of Hungary in the first quarter of 1982 underscored,[105] "there's no bank in the world that can afford to repay deposits all at the same time."[106]

Country risk analysis and the growth of the interbank markets are two means which bankers use in controlling and minimizing international lending risk. In addition, there have been three major innovations in the operational techniques of the Euromarket which have been instituted to facilitate risk-taking by commercial banks: floating interest rates, syndication and cross-default arrangements.[107] Variable or floating interest rates originated on Euromarkets in the early 1970s.[108] While the recent rise and volatility of variable interest rates represents a serious externality for LDC borrowers, rates pegged to LIBOR or the U.S. prime rate protect lenders from unforeseen trends in the cost of funds. Many recent loan agreements now give creditors the additional option of using either LIBOR or the U.S. prime rate as the base for determining variable interest rates.[109] However, the levels and volatility of these rates remain sources of concern for both lenders and borrowers. "In 1981, the 3-month Eurodollar deposit rate moved up or down by 2 percent a month,"[110] and the difficulties which such wide movements place upon the borrower are ultimately shared by the lender as they affect the debt-service capacity of the debtor.

Syndication is another means of handling international lending risk. While syndications vary, their basic mechanism is universal. In syndications on the Euromarket there is a "lead bank or syndicate manager (or group of managers) which negotiates the terms of the loan with the borrower . . . and incorporates them into a loan agreement and sells participations to a number of other banks."[111] Syndications allow for greater loan sizes, as epitomized in the $1 billion-plus "jumbos" granted to some LDC borrowers. They offer substantial fees for lead managers, publicity for participants, profitable working relations among banks, and, most important, a spreading of loan risk among several creditors. There are, nonetheless, drawbacks to syndication, two of which are of prime significance. First, occasionally a lead bank, usually a large money-center "name," will accept a loan mandate from, for example, an LDC sovereign borrower, and may fail to exercise sufficient prudence in granting or negotiating the loan. This occurs when the lead bank or banks concentrate on the fees generated by syndication and the relationship business forthcoming from the borrower, retaining only a small share of the overall financial responsibility. Participants who buy into the syndication, frequently medium- or small-sized regional banks, rely on the judgement of the syndicate leaders, only to realize that the leaders are more interested in the ancillary benefits of the loan to themselves than in the quality of the assets purchased.[112] Second, if a syndicated loan does get into difficulties and some sort of restructuring is required, syndication becomes an awkward arrangement on the lender's side as numerous and varied creditors press their own interests during negotiations. Due to these problems, syndication in sovereign lending has been greatly reduced from mid–1982,[113] the preference now being for "club loans" involving only small groups of major banks,[114] which are easier to arrange,[115] or for straight one-to-one loans,[116] which are even more convenient, although they do not offer the fees involved in syndication.

Finally, syndicated loan agreements are "peppered" with cross-default clauses.[117] Such provisions offer an added assurance to the lenders insofar as a borrower may be willing to renege on a loan from a single creditor, but will be more reluctant to "stiff" a number of banks, including the "names" which typically head syndication tombstones. There are two problems involved with such cross-default arrangements. Because any creditor can trigger the cross-default mechanism, it is possible that a single, anxious lender could initiate a wave of default declarations. On the other hand, because of the severity of the sanctions involved in calling a default under such arrangements, individual lenders may be extremely reluctant to initiate a default declaration. In general, "the tighter and harder the provisions of the agreement, the more difficult it may be for the lender to decide to invoke them."[118] Country risk analysis, expanded interbank activities, floating interest rates, syndication and cross-default clauses are all methods of limiting international lending risks. However, taken singly or collectively, they do not provide a foolproof method for evaluating or controlling such risk, and each involves its own unique shortcomings.

Issue 3: Who Is to Blame

Statements from official lender governments of the industrialized nations contain a strong assumption about who is responsible for the current LDC debt problem. From their perspective, Western officials find the borrowers to be at fault. More specifically, it is the pursuit of expansionary policies and the maintenance of high levels of consumption by the LDCs that has resulted in a failure to adjust to external shocks and mounting balance of payments deficits. More will be said of the position of Western governments on the developing nation debt crisis in this chapter, particular attention being devoted to the U.S. government's stance. As for the banks, they are in an extremely delicate position when confronted with the question of culpability. In general, reflecting their commercial-legal backgrounds, the bankers have refrained from assigning blame for the LDC debt crisis, avoiding broad policy platforms and concentrating on narrow negotiating issues. The bankers could place the onus of responsibility on the borrowers, but because of the need to retain their good faith, such a posture would be damaging to their interests. Alternatively, the banks could charge the industrialized and OPEC nations with contriving the external shocks that have afflicted debtor economies. Again, the banks' interests lie with keeping lines of communication open to OPEC depositors and, more important, to their own governments, which may be called upon to help commercial lenders collect their Third World loans. Finally, the banks themselves share some of the blame for the present circumstances. No one forced them to extend credit to these countries, and all of the loans issued from the banks to the LDCs were made under expectations of profit. At this juncture, it is necessary to examine the LDC debt crisis within a geo-political context, for both official and commercial lending to the Third World has been influenced by powerful political forces. In light of such forces, the matter of responsibility for the current quandary from the lenders' standpoint becomes even more complicated.

Western government creditors of the developing nations have compelling interests in these lands beyond the sums extended to them as bilateral official loans. They are involved in the crisis for a range of strategic and political reasons, a significant one being the desire to keep debtor nations within the ambit of Western capitalism during these turbulent times. Moreover, it is the banks of the industrialized powers who have extended loans to debt-laden LDCs, and their failure represents a loss to developed nation governments.[119] Should a debt impasse develop as the result of a moratorium, default or intractable rescheduling difficulties, this could result in a spasm of punitive trade restrictions.[120] For a nation like the United States, with 36 percent of its exports sold on LDC markets[121] and an estimated 800,000 American jobs dependent upon these exports,[122] the trade consequences of the LDC debt problem are serious indeed. In addition, U.S. direct investment within major LDC debtor countries is substantial, and a debt-related economic conflict could threaten these corporate holdings.[123] To a degree, the "loosening" of American monetary policy by the Federal Reserve Board since mid-1981 was motivated by a need to relieve LDC borrowers from part of the effects of high dollar interest rates, although much of this relief was offset by the interest rate pressures of continued deficit spending by the Federal Government.[124]

While official bilateral creditors do not have a strong financial stake in heavily indebted LDCs compared to the banks, they retain major interests in how the present crisis will evolve, and, understandably, they have attempted to influence the actions of their national commercial banks in handling these difficulties. Since Western governments have control over foreign economic relations as part of their sovereign rights, there can be little doubt that they play a profound part in shaping the environment in which their banks operate. If, for instance, the United States sought to improve its relations with a particular LDC by expanding official resource flows to it, this, in turn, would multiply the lending opportunities available to U.S. banks in this nation. Seiber's observation that "there is a tendency for U.S. banks to lend where the United States wishes to protect its interest"[125] is something of an understatement, for it is the "special relationship" countries (Mexico, Brazil, South Korea, etc.) who have been afforded a disproportionate amount of commercial loans from American banks.

Traditionally, bankers have been reluctant to acknowledge the influence which their governments exert on their lending programs.[126] However, since the most recent round of reschedulings in 1982, Western government pressures on their international banks have become much more overt. This trend toward coordinating bank lending policy by U.S., European and Japanese governments is likely to increase in the immediate future as LDC reschedulings become more commonplace and momentous. Banks have been affected in their LDC lending policies for some time now, a prime example of which is the influence of the West German government in expanding German bank lending to Poland as part of the Federal Republic's Ostpolitik rapprochement with the East.[127] German bankers were urged by their government to continue lending to Poland long after prudence began to dictate otherwise; in the tactful words of one German banker; "There were a lot of forces for continuing our exposure to Poland."[128] Governments have sometimes reversed the signals they send to their banks regarding LDC lending, cautioning prudence at first and then prodding them to continue lending in support of faltering LDC regimes.[129] After the Carter Administration's freeze on all dollar-denominated Iranian assets in American banks in 1979,[130] U.S. bankers began to speak of a "Washington Risk" associated with international lending.[131] Hence, the banks may be partially culpable for imprudent, overly competitive lending to major LDC debtors, but their actions were taken with the tacit consent of their governments and, on occasion, with encouragement to do so from these governments.

Issue 4: What Is to Be Done

A fourth issue that commercial lenders to major LDC debtors must face is analogous to the adjustment process choices that these debtor nations confront, and can be reduced to the broad question: What is to be done? The matter of rescheduling LDC debts will be treated in Chapter 4, so that the present inquiry extends to the independent policies that banks have adopted in response to their LDC debt exposure. Two broad trends are discernible in the current answer of the commercial lenders to this question: retrenchment and specialization.

In the late 1970s, the concern of developing nation debt analysts was centered on the rapidly expanding volume of commercial lending to select developing nations and its influence on their debt-service burdens. In the early 1980s, the focus has shifted to worries about the effects of "over-rapid correction" in stemming commercial loan flows to these nations.[132] A fairly common scenario is at the root of these fears. Months before a nation enters into a deep debt-related problem (usually signaled by a request for IMF assistance), the banks provide a new wave of short-term, balance of payments financing, typically on hard terms. When the crisis eventually surfaces, these same banks may refuse to roll over short-term credits or provide fresh funds, despite the fact that the debtor government may have instituted an austerity program under Fund supervision.[133] This squeeze on short-term credit becomes the basis of a liquidity crisis, as LDC governments and financial institutions find themselves unable to meet foreign currency obligations of the day.[134] As Deutsche's Bank's Wilfred Guth comments, "Today we face a problem opposite to that of indiscriminate lending—the danger of over-hasty withdrawal of banks from international business."[135] The International Monetary Fund has echoed these concerns (see Chapter 4), finding its lending and adjustment programs thwarted by bankers who wait for an infusion of IMF funds to a troubled LDC and subsequently "try to collect short-term loans, make no new loans, and cut their losses."[136] This concern has become all the more intense due to a slowdown in the number of new entrants into LDC loan participations. In the past, as some banks exercised prudence in their LDC lending, others took up the mantle, accepting greater risks for higher spreads and fees.[137] "In each year over the last decade, an average of 72 new managers entered the publicized syndicated loan market,"[138] the latest wave coming from the Japanese, who have enlarged their share of LDC lending at the expense of the Americans. In 1982, however, there was a noticeable reduction in the number of new bank participants in syndicated Euroloans,[139] and the process of new entrants replacing cautious veterans may be nearing an end.

Retrenchment is most acute among U.S. regional banks. As participants in syndicated Euroloans to the Third World, the "regional banks have often tended to follow the lead of the large money center banks,"[140] both contractually and in the sense of relying upon the latter's country risk assessments. The amount of debt held by the regionals in some major LDC debtor nations is significant as a percentage of total commercial debt. Forty-four percent of Mexico's debt to U.S. banks, 39 percent of Brazil's and 36 percent of Argentina's belong to American regionals.[141] While their collective interests are large, on an individual basis the exposure of the regionals relative to their assets and capital is significantly less than that of their money-center counterparts. This disparity contains a potential conflict between money-center banks, who are "locked into" LDC debt by higher degrees of exposure, and the regionals, who can opt out of the problem fairly easily. The potential for conflict is even greater given regional complaints about being misled or treated condescendingly by the big banks, an experience which makes them less prone to help out their former leaders.[142] Even a downturn in the growth of short-term credits from the regionals to major LDC borrowers could destabilize efforts to remedy their problems (and, hence, those of the money-center banks), while regionals threaten an abatement of such flows.[143] The large banks, aware of the crucial role of the regionals, have used moral suasion in urging the regionals to at least maintain current levels of LDC lending.[144] This campaign has been largely unsuccessful, in part because even if the regionals elected to maintain current funding levels, in the present environment they would still find it "difficult to raise funds on the intermarket on competitive terms."[145] The money-center banks may have permanently bought into the LDC debt dilemma, but the regionals can extricate themselves from it, and their capacity to continue buying in is seriously limited at present.

The second type of adjustment response that commercial lenders to LDC nations have made falls under the broad rubric of specialization. Specialization as a commercial lender adjustment policy has taken three principal forms: a concentration on profit as opposed to volume of lending; a shift to short-term, trade-related financing; and specialization in services and markets. Prior to mid–1981, volume of lending and market share enjoyed high priority as objectives of bank lending policy.[146] As large volumes and market shares of LDC debt stock are now viewed as liabilities, the desire for safe gearing ratios has caused international bankers "to abandon asset growth for its own sake."[147] Simultaneously, the banks have reduced medium- and long-term loans in favor of shorter maturities, providing stop-gap financing to LDCs with little relation to their overall development plans.[148] Generally, the banks have moved away from comprehensive country risk analysis and toward short-term, balance of payments, cash flow computations reflecting prudential concerns.[149] Trade financing, offering relationship business with developed country exporters, is now the preferred mode of lending to LDCs,[150] and there has been a shift away from fungible, "general" loans toward "export credits tied to specific supplies and financing tied to specific projects."[151] Finally, commercial lenders have adopted specialized service niches and segmentation of credit markets.[152] The banks now pay greater attention to fee-earning services over pure lending, with some institutions concentrating on narrow segments of the LDC loan market, e.g., the energy sector.[153]

The Current Position

Ironically, the current move toward specialization may contribute to a principal debt-related problem confronted by major commercial lenders to LDCs: the concentration of exposure by a small number of banks in a handful of nations. Partially as the consequence of standardized country risk analysis, commercial bank loans to the Third World are concentrated in a few nations deemed creditworthy and having a strong demand for loans. A recent OECD report centered on four such nations, Brazil, Mexico, Argentina and South Korea, finding that between 1978 and 1982 bank exposure in these four countries rose from $40 billion to $140 billion,[154] so that at the beginning of 1983 these four LDCs accounted for "85 percent of the net floating interest debt and almost all of the total net private bank exposure."[155] As a share of total bank lending, LDC loans were one-third of total international portfolios, a sum equal to only 6 percent of domestic lending by all banks.[156] Sharpening the focus, however, we find that the number of banks having substantial LDC claims is limited principally to the largest American, European and Japanese institutions. This mutual concentration by country *and* by bank has led Henry Wallich to remark that "the number of the U.S. banks with exposure in a single developing country in excess of 30 percent of capital jumped to 80 by end-year 1980, from only 36 in mid–1979."[157] It is in the Latin American countries that this country exposure is most intense. By the end of 1980, Brazil, Mexico and Argentina alone "had loans outstanding from the nine largest American banks amounting to 100 percent of those banks' capital and reserves.''[158] Further concentrations of bank exposure have come about from an emphasis on sovereign lending in the mid–1970s[159] and the trend toward short-term credits in the early 1980s.[160] Federal regulations have been imposed on the country exposure ceilings of American banks, but, given the loopholes previously mentioned, these are more in the nature of guidelines than firm rules. Banks set their own country exposure ceilings, but quite frequently simply raise the ceilings when an attractive lending opportunity arises.[161] How large the loan loss provisions of these banks are against non-performing LDC assets is a matter of conjecture, but despite recent increases,[162] it is unlikely that these stores amount to more than 5 percent of net exposure.

While the present LDC debt crisis is unique in many ways, from the perspective of the commercial lenders it pivots on a classic dilemma. In the past, the bankers were content to roll over principal on LDC debts seemingly *ad infinitum*.[163] Their preoccupation was with timely payments on debt service, and not with the ultimate recovery of the capital which they had lent.[164] Now, as cash flow bottlenecks emerge in LDC servicing of external debts, commercial lenders have begun to worry about the eventual fate of their original investment capital. Marilyn Seiber succinctly describes the predicament that major LDC creditors currently encounter: ''The banks' dilemma is that without long-term prospects for the improvement of the world's economy, prudence dictates increasing reluctance to loan. But without additional loans to finance already heavily borrowed countries, banks face defaulting customers and no more hard cash flowing in.''[165] If banks curtail LDC lending for prudential reasons, they will place immediate pressure on LDC debt-service capacity, and without the benefit of refinancing, many developing country borrowers may be forced into reschedulings, moratoria and defaults, events which all parties wish to avoid. A related question is whether any new loans should be made on liberal terms in recognition of the difficulties facing the borrower, or on stringent terms to compensate lenders for increased risks.[166] With major money-center banks locked in by virtue of medium- and long-term loans to LDC debtors, and by the current urgings of their governments and the IMF to continue flows, the problems of the LDCs can no longer be held at arm's length by the banks. In essence, the problems of the borrowers have become those of the lenders, and a semipermanent bond has been created between them as a consequence of the gravity of the problem.

Major commercial lenders, sensitive to their positions as intermediaries, have kept comparatively silent on large issues pertinent to LDC debt, retaining flexibility of movement while allowing their governments to formulate official policies. In the main, the industrialized nations have followed a hard line in their stance toward LDC debt that is only now beginning to show signs of softening. The basic premise of this policy is that there is no general developing nation debt problem.[167] Rather, the LDC debt problem is a country-by-country, case-by-case matter, with ultimate responsibility for the problem and its resolution resting with the borrowers.[168] Western government creditors insist on a clear distinction between balance of payments assistance, on the one hand, and debt relief and development financing, on the other. Debt problems are essentially balance of payments difficulties in the view of the industrialized countries, and relief must proceed on an *ad hoc* basis, at the lenders' discretion and without an automaticity in relief.[169] Because debt problems are "local," creditor governments see no need for a New International Economic Order, or for the expansion of the World Bank and IMF, contending that the present system can adequately meet such problems.[170] Lastly, in what sounds like a variation of the trickle-down theory, American officials, among others, argue that the best thing for debt-burdened LDCs would be a recovery in the industrialized nations, with benefits being passed on in the form of lower interest rates, greater LDC export demand, and, possibly, increased concessional flows.[171] What is eminently apparent, then, is that the position of the lenders, or at least the official expression of that position, is in diametric opposition to that of the borrowers. The task of reconciling these positions and the interests they reflect falls largely to the negotiators, and it is their function that now demands consideration.

Notes

1. Seiber, *International Borrowing*, p.53.
2. Ibid., p.61.
3. Angelini, Eng and Lees, p.x.
4. Kuczynski, p.1023.
5. Hurni, p.7.
6. Seiber, *International Borrowing*, p.19.
7. Samuel Alberto Yohai, "How the World Bank Might Recycle Assets," *Euromoney*, January, 1983, p.47.
8. William Clark, "Robert McNamara at the World Bank," *Foreign Affairs*, Fall, 1981, p.168.
9. Hurni, p.44.
10. Seiber, *International Borrowing*, p.100.
11. IBRD, *Annual Report: 1982*, p.39.
12. Charles Grant, "Don't Call the IMF: It's Running out of Quotas," *Euromoney*, August, 1982, p.52.
13. Hurni, p.42.
14. Ibid., p.104.
15. IBRD, *Annual Report: 1982*, p.15.
16. A.W. Clausen, "The World Bank: Helping One Another," *Vital Speeches*, 1 October, 1982, p.754.
17. Yohai, p.47.
18. IBRD, *Annual Report: 1982*, p.35.
19. Kuczynski, p.1026.
20. Goodman and Worth, p.81.

21. Clark, p.179.

22. Ibid., p.180.

23. Ibid., p.178.

24. Sampson, p.211.

25. Rogers S. Leeds, "Why We Need More Co-Financing," *The Banker*, August, 1980, p.21.

26. Sherry Buchanan, "Bedding down with the World Bank," *Euromoney*, April, 1982, p.111.

27. Ibid., p.112.

28. "A Nightmare of Debt: A Survey of International Banking," *The Economist*, 20 March, 1982, p.17.

29. Buchanan, p.115.

30. Sampson, p.141.

31. Angelini, Eng and Lees, p.18.

32. Seiber, *International Borrowing*, p.79.

33. OECD, p.43.

34. Angelini, Eng and Lees, pp.16–17.

35. Jack Egan, "Banks on the Brink: Flirting with Global Collapse," *New York*, 25 October, 1982, p.28.

36. Christopher M. Korth, "The Management of International Lending Risks by Regional Banks," *The Journal of Commercial Bank Lending*, October, 1981, p.30.

37. Gisselquist, p.162.

38. Peter Field, "The Shunning of the Sovereign Borrower," *Euromoney*, May, 1982, p.37.

39. Grant, "Stuffees Have Left," p.35.

40. Field, "Sovereign Borrower," p.38.

41. "Nightmare," p.77.

42. Steven I. Davis, "International Bank Expansion: Time for a Reassessment," *The Banker*, May, 1981, p.63.

43. Wilfred Guth, "International Banking: The Next Phase," *The Banker*, October, 1981, p.33.

44. Gisselquist, p.162.

45. Ibid., p.172.

46. Angelini, Eng and Lees, p.6.

47. Mueller, p.11.

48. Charles M. Williams, "International Lending in the Decade Ahead," in *Offshore Lending by U.S. Commercial Banks*, ed. F. John Mathis (Washington: Banker's Association for Foreign Trade, 1981), p.271.

49. Korth, "International Lending Risks," p.34.

50. Seiber, *International Borrowing*, p.89.

51. Goodman and Worth, p.79.

52. Korth, "Developing a Country-Risk Analysis System," *The Journal of Commercial Bank Lending*, December, 1979, p.54.

53. "Phaseout of Credit Restraint Measures," *Federal Reserve Bulletin*, July, 1980, p.559.

54. "Nightmare," p.94.

55. Sampson, p.122.

56. Seiber, *International Borrowing*, p.102.

57. Guth, p.31.

58. Marilyn J. Seiber, "Debt Escalation: Developing Countries in the Eurocurrency Market, in *Developing Country Debt,* ed. Lawrence G. Franko and Marilyn J. Seiber (New York: Pergamon, 1979), p.49.

59. Angelini, Eng and Lees, p.29.

60. Seiber, *International Borrowing* p.95.

61. Seiber, "Debt Escalation," p.49.

62. Ibid., p.59.

63. Ibid., pp.45–50.

64. Seiber, *International Borrowing,* p.82.

65. Ibid., p.83.

66. William H. Riley, "How Regional Banks Approach Country Exposure and Country Risk," *Journal of Commercial Bank Lending,* March, 1980, p.34.

67. Korth, Developing A Country-Risk Analysis System," p.55.

68. J.N. Robinson, p.71.

69. Seiber, *International Borrowing*, p.111.

70. Angelini, Eng and Lees, p.121.

71. Sampson, p.141.

72. Angelini, Eng and Lees, p.77.

73. Peter Field, "Meet the New Breed of Banker: The Political Risk Expert," *Euromoney,* July, 1980, p.9.

74. Korth, "Developing a Country-Risk Analysis System," p.60.

75. Sampson, p.257.

76. Tim Anderson, "More Models Than Vogue Magazine," *Euromoney,* November, 1982, p.45.

77. Calverley, p.29.

78. Nowzad and Williams, p.40.

79. Ibid., p.47.

80. Group of Thirty, p.8.

81. "Nightmare," p.94.

82. Korth, "Developing a Country-Risk Analysis System, p.73.

83. Anderson, "More Models," p.43.

84. Emmanuel Gonzalez, "Call a Country a Company and It Looks Better," *Euromoney,* February, 1983, p.52.

85. Herbert G. Grubel, *A Proposal for the Establishment of an International Deposit Insurance Company.* Essays in International Finance, No. 133 (Princeton: Princeton University Press, 1979), p.6.

86. Gonzalez, p.48.

87. Field, "Meet the New Breed," p.21.

88. Ibid., p.12.

89. Anderson, "Rescheduling," p.15.

90. Field, "Sovereign Borrower," p.30.

91. Korth, Developing a Country-Risk Analysis System," p.56.

92. Field, "Meet the New Breed," p.19.

93. Field, "Sovereign Borrower," p.33.

94. Robert B. Palmer, "The Funding Risk in International Lending," in *Offshore Lending by U.S. Commercial Banks*, ed. F. John Mathis (Washington: Banker's Association for Foreign Trade, 1981), p.250.

95. Tim Anderson and Peter Field, "The Tremors That Threaten the Banking System," *Euromoney,* October, 1982, p.17.

96. Field, "Sovereign Borrower," p.41.

97. Palmer, p.249.

98. Gisselquist, p.160.

99. Angelini, Eng and Lees, p.82.

100. Palmer, p.253.

101. Tim Anderson and Quek Peck Lim, "Syndicated Lending—Out for the Count," *Euromoney,* February, 1983, p.37.

102. Anderson and Field, p.19.

103. Grant, "Stuffees Have Left," p.35.

104. Angelini, Eng and Lees, p.25.

105. Padraic Fallon and David Shirref, "The Betrayal of Eastern Europe," *Euromoney,* September, 1982, p.19.

106. Ibid., p.20.

107. Seiber, "Debt Escalation," p.44.

108. Gisselquist, p.160.

109. Goodman and Worth, p.81; Dod, p.654.

110. Geoffrey Bell, "Debt Rescheduling—Can the Banking System Cope?" *The Banker,* February, 1982, p.17.

111. Robert N. Bee, "Syndication," in *Offshore Lending by U.S. Commercial Banks,* ed. F. John Mathis (Washington: Banker's Association for Foreign Trade, 1981), p.178.

112. Dini, p.58.

113. Anderson and Lim, p.36.

114. Seiber, *International Borrowing*, p.86.

115. Grant, "Stuffees Have Left," p.37.

116. Ibid.

117. Riley, p.37.

118. James R. Greene, "Financing Foreign Governments and Official Entities," in *Offshore Lending by U.S. Commercial Banks,* ed. F. John Mathis (Washington: Banker's Association for Foreign Trade, 1981), p.244.

119. Seiber, "Alternative Proposals," p.188.

120. Gisselquist, p.241.

121. Seiber, *International Borrowing*, p.12.

122. Leeds, "External Financing of Development," p.21.

123. Gisselquist, p.224.

124. Egan, pp.28–30.

125. Seiber, *International Borrowing*, pp.16–17.

126. "Nightmare," p.48.

127. Ibid.

128. Anderson, "More Models," p.43.

129. Lord Roll, "End the Chaos and Build a New System," *Euromoney,* September, 1982, p.121.

130. Leeds, "External Financing of Development," p.28.

131. Seiber, *International Borrowing*, p.114

132. Dini, p.63.

133. Ibid., p.58.

134. Anderson "Rescheduling," p.22.

135. Grant, "Stuffees Have Left," p.135.
136. Gisselquist, p.165.
137. "Nightmare," p.78.
138. Bell, p.17.
139. Quek Peck Lim, "The Big Shift," *Euromoney,* November, 1982, p.16.
140. Riley, p.35.
141. Erik Ipsen, "After Mexico, the Regionals Retreat," *Euromoney,* January, 1983, p.60.
142. Grant, "Stuffees Have Left," p.36.
143. Ipsen, p.58.
144. "A Boom in Broking Out Loans," *Euromoney,* November, 1982, p.40.
145. Grant, "Stuffees Have Left," p.36.
146. Lim, "Big Shift," p.21.
147. Grant, "Stuffees Have Left," p.35.
148. "Nightmare," p.38.
149. Calverley, p.26.
150. Ipsen, p.63.
151. IBRD, *World Development Report,* p.14.
152. S.I. Davis, p.63.
153. Lim, "Big Shift," p.18.
154. OECD, p.4.
155. Ibid., p.8.
156. Ibid., p.4.
157. Richard F. Janssen, "Bankers Shed Their LDC Loan Worries," *Business Week,* 22 June, 1981, p.35.
158. "Nightmare," p.38.
159. OECD, p.45.
160. Roman I. Senkin, "Using Country Risk Assessments in Decision Making," *Journal of Commercial Bank Lending,* August, 1980, p.35.
161. Goodman and Worth, p.80.
162. Lim, "Big Shift," p.28.
163. Sampson, p.314.
164. "Nightmare," p.83.
165. Seiber, "Alternative Proposals," p.188.
166. Quek Peck Lim, "The Borrower's Trump Card Is His Weakness," *Euromoney,* October, 1982, p.35.
167. Seiber, *International Borrowing,* p.47.
168. Seiber, "Alternative Proposals," p.189.
169. Seiber, *International Borrowing,* p.125.
170. Ibid.
171. Kuczynski, p.1027.

Chapter 4

THE NEGOTIATORS

Overview

External debt-service problems manifest themselves in balance of payments deficits and foreign exchange shortages.[1] When this occurs, the difficulty may be of such magnitude as to require a restructuring of all or part of a country's stock of debt. There is a tendency on the part of both debtors and creditors to avoid renegotiation of original loan terms. Borrowers are aware that deviations from payment schedules damage their credit standings, and lenders view reschedulings as at least a temporary impediment to their cash flows. Consequently, a nation may be already heavily in arrears before it elects to undergo the rescheduling of its debts. If allowed to continue without a successful rescheduling/refinancing accord being reached, debt-service problems can lead to three undesirable events: a unilateral moratorium on payments by the debtor; an outright repudiation of debt by the debtor; or a declaration of default by the creditor. The consequences of such drastic actions are extremely grave for both parties, and, over the years, instances of them have been rare. Short of moratoria, repudiations and defaults, there are basically two courses of action which borrower and lender can take in concert:

1. Refinancing through the extension of new loans from the original lender, a portion of which is used to service existing debt.
2. Rescheduling through a lengthening of maturities and grace periods contained in the initial agreement.

These two restructuring modes are not mutually exclusive and are often used in conjunction with one another. This is usually the case in large, multilateral debt restructurings which include official and commercial loans to government and government-guaranteed borrowers, and which may also include provisions regarding non-guaranteed private debt.

To the casual observer, the multilateral rescheduling of sovereign debt may seem like a three ring circus, but, for conceptual purposes, the overall process resembles the workings of three moving concentric circles arranged in "bull's eye" fashion. To be sure, there is no set, uniform procedure for the rescheduling process as a whole, but the broad outlines of its typical structure and sequence are fairly distinct. Large-scale restructuring of sovereign debt begins with a debtor government setting the innermost circle into motion by approaching a multilateral institution, most frequently the IMF, to arrange a standby line of credit. Subsequently, the Fund and the debtor country negotiate an emergency loan, the disbursement of these funds being contingent upon the borrower's compliance with agreed upon conditions in adjusting its fiscal and monetary policies. With this phase completed, the second circle is approached by the debtor with the assistance of the IMF, IBRD or OECD. The middle ring is occupied by official creditor governments meeting under the informal aegis of the Paris Club. Putting this circle into motion usually requires the pre-existence of an IMF conditional loan agreement. Official creditors reach an overall accord in Agreed Minutes with the debtor which serves as the basis for bilateral reschedulings of a portion of the principal, interest and/or arrears owed to official lenders, possibly including an adjustment of interest charges in favor of the borrower. These agreements, along with any refinancing which may be offered, are also made contingent upon continued conformity to the conditions of the IMF loan. Paris Club reschedulings may include an "initiative clause" under which the debtor promises to enter rescheduling negotiations with commercial lenders, e.g., the banks, according to the principle of "comparable treatment" of all creditors. Reaching the outermost perimeter of the rescheduling process, the debtor confronts *ad hoc* committees of major bank representatives. These creditors negotiate a rescheduling/refinancing of a part of the commercial debt owed on principal, interest and arrears, sometimes with a change in interest charges favoring the lender. A common accord is reached spelling out the basis for fair treatment of commercial lenders, and this agreement may also be made dependent upon the borrower's meeting Fund loan conditions.

There are a number of aspects of this three-circle structure that must be noted. First, the circles become looser and more informal as the debtor moves from the IMF, through the Paris Club and into commercial rescheduling. Second, the movement of the second and third circles almost always requires that the first ring already be in motion, but this relationship is not strictly serial, so that all three circles may be in motion at once. Third, the harmonious working of the process as a whole is by no means assured. The different rings may move in opposite directions or otherwise run afoul of each other. Finally, the critical element lies in the gravitational linkages among the three circles, centering on the Fund's efforts to meet the debtor's needs and set a path for official and commercial creditors to follow. Since it is the IMF that lies at the "eye of the hurricane" in the rescheduling process, any discussion of the issues confronting negotiators and their positions on those issues must start with a survey of the IMF's role in the present LDC debt dilemma.

The International Monetary Fund

The International Monetary Fund was created as the "twin" institution of the IBRD under the Bretton Woods Agreement (1944–1945) for the broad purpose of maintaining "stability in international relationships."[2] The switch from fixed to floating exchange rates created a new set of responsibilities for the Fund which have dramatically altered its mission. Carl Neu explains this change as follows: "Until the early 1970s, the Fund's primary function was the management of a system of fixed exchange rates. Today, in a regime of floating rates, its major function is to encourage its member nations to adopt policies that will facilitate the international flow of trade and capital and to avoid actions that would restrict these flows."[3] The Fund's lending program is the chief instrument that it employs to meet these objectives. These loans enable countries facing balance of payments problems to meet their short-term obligations without having to resort to "beggar-thy-neighbor" policies, and when the loans are conditional this also introduces a spur to discipline in the borrower's fiscal and monetary policies.[4] It is this purpose—essentially, the mechanical maintenance of a capitalist, free-market global economy, not debt relief or development assistance—that forms the rationale for and central mission of, the Fund.

The IMF began accumulating capital for its lending programs in 1947 with a collection of gold and currencies from its member nations.[5] Virtually all major industrialized and developing countries belong to the Fund, but most Council for Mutual Economic Assistance (COMECON) nations, notably the Soviet Union, are not members. The IMF's members make annual contributions of funds in their own currencies according to a quota system based broadly on ability to pay. The size of a member's quota determines its voting power on Fund executive boards and also provides a limit for quota borrowings by the contributor. In addition to quota funding, the IMF has negotiated general agreements to borrow with the central banks of its major members; has established special facilities from time to time (e.g., the Witteveen facility financed by contributions beyond quotas);[6] and has enjoyed a vast increase in the nominal value of its gold holdings during the 1970s.[7] On 17 January, 1983, Group of Ten nations from the industrialized world voted to establish a $20 billion emergency fund to assist the IMF in its lending programs for deeply indebted countries.[8]

Despite standard and extraordinary funding from its member nations, the IMF's capital is not presently sufficient to meet the balance of payments needs of major LDC debtors by itself. In 1980, the Fund's Managing Director, Jacques de Larosière, proposed that the Fund borrow on commercial markets and relend these monies to its debt-troubled members. In one sense, this proposal was "equivalent to an indeterminably large increase in IMF resources," for, "simply to state that the IMF could or may borrow represents an expansion of its financial power."[9] As in the case of the IBRD, there are several obstacles to the Fund's tapping of commercial credit markets, two of which are especially significant. First, commercial lenders to the IMF would expect the Fund to pay interest charges at market or near-market rates. Because the IMF relies on offering a discount on its loans as an incentive for the borrower's acceptance of the conditionality attached to them, the benefits of using commercial funding sources are highly constrained.[10] Equally important, majority voting power on IMF executive boards is controlled by the industrialized nations, who generally oppose the Fund's borrowing on commercial markets. To date, the "major industrial nations" have refused "to allow the Fund to establish itself, even on a modest scale, as a borrower in the private market."[11]

During the 1970s, the Fund created a number of new windows for its member nations, e.g., the "oil facilities" of 1974 and 1979, and the Supplementary Financing Facility, offering conditional loans to assist nations adjusting to major external shocks.[12] The Fund also issues Special Drawing Rights (SDRs) which amount to a system of forced credit from balance of payments surplus nations to deficit countries. It is, however, from quota subscriptions that the Fund obtains the bulk of the funding needed to finance its balance of payments adjustment loans. Members contribute a yearly quota of their currencies to a central pool and are allowed to borrow a set percentage of that contribution in any given year. Arranged in a system of credit tranches (each tranche being roughly equivalent to one-fifth of quota), the degree of conditionality entailed in borrowings under this program moves from no conditions for the first 20–25 percent of quota, to moderate conditionality in the next two tranches, to tight conditionality for the two upper tranches. It is the quota funds that the IMF provides at concessionary rates of interest, averaging 6.6 percent at the beginning of 1983.[13] As an outcome of the Fund's involvement in Turkish reschedulings, the IMF has loosened the ceilings on its quota lending, now allowing members to borrow up to 600 percent of quota over three years compared with the previous limit of 125 percent of quota in one year.[14]

Given the centrality of the IMF in the global financial system, it is somewhat unexpected to find that "net disbursements from the IMF tend not to be an important source of financing."[15] From 1974 to 1979, IMF lending averaged $4.1 billion a year,[16] with about $1.4 billion going to Non-Oil LDCs, an amount equal to about 5 percent of their yearly current account deficits.[17] As of 1982, the Fund and the World Bank together extended financing to Non-Oil LDCs equivalent to one-tenth of their current account deficits.[18]

Why has the Fund's lending program been so modest in proportion to the balance of payments deficits of Non-Oil LDC members? The answers come from both the supply and the demand side of the ledger. First, while IMF resources are substantial, relative to global capital movements they are small and getting smaller. In 1960, the "sum of all the quotas contributed by its member countries was equivalent to 12 percent of world imports," but "by 1980, this had diminished in real terms: to 4 percent of world imports."[19] Many of the currencies coming to the IMF from the Third World are virtually unusable, and approval for a sale of the Fund's gold reserves is procedurally difficult, requiring an 85 percent majority vote. On the other side of the coin, heavily indebted nations have avoided borrowing from high-conditionality facilities, including the upper tranches of the quota program and the special facilities, because of their objections to the Fund's conditional adjustment programs. Under the present dire circumstances, major LDC borrowers have been compelled to borrow from the Fund's conditional facilities, but one major reason why Fund lending has been so small in the past is that borrowers seek such funding only after all other sources have been exhausted.

Since 1980, there has been a significant change in the lending philosophy of the IMF. As a balance of payments institution, the Fund's focus has always been on loans to meet temporary balance of payments deficits.[20] According to its standard classification system, there are three types of balance of payments deficits to which Fund programs can be addressed: those which are self-reversing; those due to excessive demand; and those due to overvaluation of the borrower's currency.[21] All three types of deficits recognized by the Fund prior to 1980 were transitional in nature and correctable through mechanical adjustments, e.g., curbs on credit and devaluation. Thus, Fund programs were short-term in duration, as were the Fund's expectations for balance of payments improvements following conditional adjustment loans. The IMF has avoided longer-term lending in the past, insisting that it is chartered as a balance of payments institution, not a development agency.[22]

In 1980, de Larosière announced the Fund's intention to provide financing for medium- and long-term purposes.[23] The change was prompted by a concern with the externalities that had created structural distortions in national economies, leading to deficits which arise "from circumstances *beyond a country's own control*."[24] Termed "structural deficits," such problems are the products of "exogenous change that appears to be permanent, [such as the rise in energy import costs] and which can only be eliminated by depressing output below full capacity or by structural change."[25] Despite neoclassical assumptions that structural distortions naturally disappear through the operation of market mechanisms, in practice, eliminating such distortions requires new investments for import-substitution and export-promotion. Acknowledgement of structural deficits and the need for structural adjustment financing was implicit in the creation of the Fund's special facilities, but formal recognition of a Fund role in treating semi-permanent problems of deficit nations came about only after the second oil shock.

The entrance of the IMF into structural adjustment lending coincided with the IBRD's initiation of its SAL loans, which, like the Fund's quota loans, are conditional.[26] In fact, the Fund and the Bank have begun to converge in their efforts to assist debt-laden LDCs.[27] John Williamson summarizes the blurring of the division of labor between the IMF and the IBRD: "The former distinctions between the roles of the Fund and the Bank, macro versus micro, demand versus supply, adjustment versus development, financial versus real, program versus project loans, short-term versus long-term—have been severely eroded."[28] It is too early to evaluate the scope and impact of combined Fund/Bank structural adjustment lending programs, but the very fact that the Fund has moved in this direction indicates an awareness of the intimate interconnections among balance of payments positions, external debt and national economic development.

Of all the major multilateral institutions concerned with global economic problems, including the World Bank, the Bank for International Settlements (BIS) and various agencies of the United Nations, the IMF is by far the most influential.[29] Therefore, when LDC debt analysts search for a centralized means of alleviating the debt problems of major Third World borrowers, they frequently call for an expansion of IMF powers and resources. Arthur Burns, W. Michael Blumenthal, David Rockefeller, Morgan Guaranty and New Zealand's Prime Minister Robert D. Muldoon have all identified the IMF as the sole institution capable of orchestrating overall debt assistance to the developing nations.[30] At the same time, under the stewardship of Managing Director de Larosière, the IMF has expressed a willingness to grow beyond its original mission in response to the present LDC debt quandary.[31] All of this naturally evokes the question: If the IMF is already the most influential of all international financial bodies, why is an expansion of its powers and resources necessary?

The IMF's muscle rests upon its ability to impose and monitor the borrower's performance in meeting conditions attached to its loans. It is the Fund's conditional lending programs, then, that provide it with greater leverage vis-à-vis its borrowing members than that possessed by the IBRD, BIS or UN. While conditional lending is a potent instrument for affecting the policies of nations with severe deficit problems, "the Fund has no comparable leverage in dealing with surplus countries that do not need to use the Fund's resources or with deficit countries, like the United States, that avoid seeking to use conditional tranches."[32] While the Fund can directly influence the monetary and fiscal policies of LDC borrowers, it cannot do so in the case of developed countries and OPEC nations who remain free to manage their domestic and international economic policies, often at the expense of the LDCs. Moreover, while the Fund's membership is widespread, it is not universal, and the non-membership of COMECON nations precludes Fund activities in these Eastern countries[33] More important, "the ability of the IMF . . . to influence debtor nations is limited by the willingness of alternative lenders to disregard IMF leadership."[34] LDC borrowers will not accept the "stick" of conditionality attached to the "carrot" of its loans if others (e.g., commercial banks) offer loans without conditions, even when the latter are granted on harder terms than those available from the Fund. Finally, like the World Bank, the IMF is "as weak or as strong as its controlling members care to make it,"[35] and majority voting power rests with the industrialized countries who, until quite recently, opposed an expansion in the IMF's role.

Conditionality of lending is the principal means through which the Fund exercises such influence as it has upon member nations. It was in the early 1950s that the IMF began to fit conditions to its loans,[36] largely at the urging of the

Eisenhower Administration for a "get tough" policy with deficit Latin American nations.[37] Starting with the 1954 Peruvian letter of intent, the Fund institutionalized conditional lending, a function which has drawn the IMF into the approval and design of adjustment programs for meeting conditions required for continued loan disbursements. By 1959, conditionality had become embedded in the IMF's credit tranche system, which established gradations of conditionality with liberal treatment of lower tranche drawings "and more rigorous expectations for corrective action in subsequent tranches."[38] The tranche arrangement, it should be noted, favors developed nations who may have occasional recourse to lower-tranche borrowings but rarely require upper-tranche loans. IMF loan conditions comprise an adjustment package which forms the basis of a viable adjustment program formulated and adhered to by the borrower as a means of correcting its balance of payment problem, with external debt service as an element of the deficit.[39] While the borrowing country designs its own adjustment program, typically the Fund does not approve of its stated objectives and seeks to improve the program through more stringent and thoroughgoing conditions. This negotiating procedure brings the IMF into the process of fashioning the economic policies for the debtor nation, including decisions that have powerful effects on domestic conditions. At the same time, the Fund insists that adjustment take place without recourse to heightened trade and exchange controls, and this interest also disposes the IMF to go beyond policy approval and into policy-making.[40]

As to IMF conditions themselves, they take three basic forms:

1. *Preconditions*: Actions taken by the borrower before an adjustment program is approved by the IMF.

2. *Performance criteria*: Stated objectives for the borrower's adjustment which must be met for the Fund to continue loan disbursements in the absence of a new agreement on conditions.

3. *Policy understandings*: Actions which the debtor agrees to take, but which do not carry specific sanctions for non-performance.[41]

It is through the performance criteria that the IMF is able to monitor and supervise conditional loan adjustment programs, for it is the ongoing conformity of the debtor to these conditions that determines the continuing flow of funds. Qualitative performance criteria are broadly defined objectives, usually centered on the borrower's avoidance of trade and exchange restrictions. Quantitative performance criteria are explicit objectives couched as ceilings on government deficit spending, current account deficits, credit expansion, external borrowings, inflation rates, etc., or as minima for GNP growth rates, increased productivity, export growth, build-ups of reserves and repayment on external borrowings.[42]

Apart from the epidemic of reschedulings in 1982, major LDC borrowers have assiduously avoided the "conditionality wringer."[43] Developing nation leaders have charged that IMF conditions inhibit flexibility in meeting developmental aims, impede growth, undermine stability and represent an incursion on sovereign powers. Prior to 1974, 58 percent of net credit purchases from the IMF included drawings from upper, high-conditionality tranches, but in the following two years "only 19 percent of such purchases extended into upper tranches."[44] This low degree of utilization for highly stringent loans is partially a reflection of increased lending from alternative sources during the period, i.e., the banks. It also suggests that IMF conditional loans are seen by borrowers as entailing more demands than incentives, as forming more of a barrier than a bridge between themselves and the Fund.[45]

Since the IMF rarely accepts the original adjustment program proposed by the borrowers and has an active role in the design of the programs that receive its own approval, it necessarily influences the borrower's mix of policies.[46] The direction of this influence, of course, is a product of the IMF's recognizable and orthodox approach to balance of payments adjustments. The Fund places heavy emphasis on monetary policy,[47] financial discipline and open market principles. The Fund's inevitable call for realistic devaluations in the borrower's currency is the hallmark of its neoclassical, capitalist credo.[48] From a purely economic standpoint, the chief objection to the Fund's approach is that it is highly recessionary in nature, leading to a contraction in economic growth and a stagnation or reversal in national development. From a political point of view, it is the arrogation of sovereign powers to the IMF that is of gravest concern. In statements designed for the consumption of local polities, LDC officials frequently characterize the IMF as a dictatorial arm of the industrialized world. Even when these objections are absent from a working relationship between the Fund and the borrowing country, there may still remain a conflict on the pace that adjustment should take. The Fund expects fairly rapid results in its adjustment programs, primarily because its loans range from one to three years in maturity. In conjunction with its recessionary approach to adjustment, the Fund's insistence on rapid improvement frequently results in Draconian austerity measures which ignore political and social conditions.[49] IMF-sponsored "shock treatment" is sometimes described as killing the patient in the course of effecting a cure, and it is the widespread social disruption that often erupts in reaction to the Fund's remedies that constitutes the most damning criticism of its adjustment programs. In several cases, "IMF riots" have flared up as LDC governments have attempted to meet Fund performance criteria through cuts in social spending, reductions in real wages and sharp rises in unemployment.[50] Ironically, whether the IMF's orthodox approach to adjustment is an effective means for bettering a nation's balance of payments position is debatable. Studies of the effectiveness of Fund-sponsored programs "disclose little systematic effect"[51] between actual performance and what would have occurred without such measures.

In the IMF's opinion, not only do conditional loans provide funding and introduce discipline into the borrower's policies; they also assist the debtor in regaining a favorable credit standing on commercial credit markets. A salient contention of the IMF's stand on conditionality is that "if the Fund does not insist on conditions that promise a reasonable prospect of adjustment, its 'seal of approval' will be devalued, benefiting no one."[52] According to this line of thinking, the IMF's, monitoring and supervision of adjustment programs for upper-tranche borrowers represent a verification of that nation's commitment to recovery in its balance of payments position and debt-service capacity. The Fund "has . . . come increasingly to be accepted by private lenders as a dependable certifier of international creditworthiness."[53] In fact, the IMF contends that nations with access to capital markets (e.g., Hi-Income LDCs) have just such a certification in view when they undertake conditional loans from the Fund.[54] Turkey is the most frequently cited example of a successful "shock treatment" providing a stamp of improved performance and a renewal of commercial lending.[55] Developed country leaders challenge this assertion, contending that the Fund's seal of approval does not guarantee that private lenders will resume flows to the borrower, and noting that it took more than four years between the institution of the first adjustment program in Turkey and the resumption of commercial lending to Turkey. Going to the Fund for assistance actually downgrades a country's commercial credit, these same officials argue, since it is a signal to the banks that conditions are dire in that nation. Moreover, when a borrower fails to meet IMF conditions, the outcome is yet another black mark against the debtor and a further debasement of the Fund's seal of approval.[56]

Ostensibly, the IMF is politically and ideologically neutral, its mission being the broadly stated maintenance of international financial stability. The Fund's critics dispute this claim, replying that the IMF's doctrinaire monetarism is inherently biased in favor of "free-market" forces and against socialist governments. From this angle, the Fund is seen as a prop for the continued economic domination of the industrialized nations, especially the United States, operating under the guise of strict neutrality. On the surface, "exclusive use of English for many years surely helped to give the casual observer the notion that the IMF was a U.S. or Anglo-U.S. institution,"[57] but the strongest evidence in support of these charges can be seen in the evolution of conditional lending. During the Bretton Woods conference of 1944–1945, a division of opinion was expressed between the Americans, who desired conditional IMF lending according to a preset repayment schedule, and the British, who favored automatic lending which would continue until substantial progress had been made in the borrower's balance of payments.[58] The Fund's Articles of Agreement are silent on the matter of conditionality, but by the early 1950s conditional lending was already well established in response to United States insistence.[59] More recently, the Fund's critics observe that from late 1979 to mid–1981, when global economic conditions were generally on the upswing, the Fund offered loans with less stringent conditions than those extended in the following year, when world economic conditions took a turn for the worse.[60] This pattern of pro-cyclical lending can be seen as a manifestation of the Reagan Administration's efforts to fight domestic inflation by curbing international credit creation at precisely the time when anti-cyclical, low-conditionality lending was required.[61] In late 1982, the United States reversed its position and "decided to support a strengthening of the resources of the IMF,"[62] presumably supporting increased accessibility by debtor nations to IMF funds. This about-face by the United States can be interpreted not as an altruistic interest in the Third World, but merely as a re-evaluation of America's economic and political stake in the fate of major LDC borrowers. From the viewpoint of its detractors, the Fund does what the industrialized nations want done, this control being virtually assured by the voting power of the United States and its like-minded allies within the IMF.

The Paris Club

The next stage in the overall rescheduling process for major sovereign debtors is the renegotiation of official, bilateral debt through the multilateral forum of the Paris Club. First convened in 1956 in response to Argentina's request for official debt relief,[63] the Paris Club consists of representatives from the principal OECD creditor nations and is customarily chaired by the French Minister of Finance. The Club meets on the application of the debtor, and, almost invariably, the completion or near-completion of an IMF conditional loan agreement is pre-requisite to such requests.[64] Since 1956 more than twenty countries have undergone Paris Club reschedulings, many returning several times to the Club over the period. Until quite recently, the amounts rescheduled by the Club exceeded $1 billion in only one instance (Indonesia, 1970), but since 1978 these sums have grown enormously to three, four and five billion dollars.[65]

The use of a multilateral framework for the rescheduling of bilateral debt provides several advantages over independent, government-to-government reschedulings. The multilateral format is much more expedient for both creditors and debtors since "it would be impractical, time-consuming and inefficient for a debtor country to enter into separate reschedulings with each of its numerous creditors."[66] The framework allows the establishment of uniform principles, procedures and policies for the official rescheduling of debt, affording equal treatment to all lender governments.[67] As a centralized body, the Paris Club facilitates retrospective linkages of official reschedulings and IMF adjustment programs, and forward linkages to commercial reschedulings contained in initiative clauses calling for comparable treatment of official and commercial debts.[68]

The general procedures of the Paris Club have become fairly standardized over the years, and debtor applicants know what to expect. The Club works on the guiding principle that debt relief must be "provided in the context of a stabilization program designed to improve the balance of payments position"[69] of the debtor country. The Club's stabilization program is the adjustment package accompanying a previously agreed upon, highly conditional loan from the IMF.[70] LDC officials are well aware of this connection between the Fund and the Club and of the three basic forms which it can take:

1. Direct commitment to implement a Fund-sponsored stabilization program previously negotiated.
2. Direct commitment that any future rescheduling of official debt will require conformity to IMF conditions now in place or to be negotiated in the future.
3. Implicit commitment to a set of specific measures contained in a stabilization program currently in force.[71]

Of these three modes of connection between the Club and the Fund, the first is by far the most common, and so debtors realize that in order to reschedule official debt, they must first go to the Fund and its conditionality "wringer."

When an IMF package is in place and emergency loans are being disbursed by the Fund, the debtor usually asks the IMF to "sound out" official creditors on their willingness to restructure a part of the debtor's official borrowings.[72] If there is a favorable response to this overture, a three-stage process is set in motion. The first phase is a comprehensive review of the data relevant to a country's current debt-service capacity, this accounting being assisted by IMF, IBRD, BIS and OECD presentations. With the facts determined, a first round of negotiations between the debtor and the assembled Club members begins, generally leading to an "umbrella agreement" which serves as a guideline for bilateral negotiations and helps assure parity in the treatment of creditors. This is followed by a second series of negotiations between the debtor and individual creditor governments within the guidelines provided by the umbrella accord.[73] Bilateral arrangements have usually conformed to the Agreed Minutes of the first negotiating phase, but matters such as interest rates are ultimately left to the bilateral bargainers.[74] Provision may also be made for a reconvening of the parties under a "goodwill clause," but the Club's capacity to monitor and supervise debtor performance after negotiations is largely based on the conditionality mechanism of the IMF.

The first significant point to note concerning the typical terms offered in Paris Club reschedulings is that only a portion of the borrower's total official debt is eligible for rescheduling. Generally, a Paris Club rescheduling "involves the debt service payments due over a specified period of time—most often between one and four years—on a specified class of external public debt."[75] The Paris Club stretches out maturities and grace periods for officially guaranteed export credits and straight government loans, mostly short-term borrowings.[76] Rarely are interest payments or accumulated arrears rescheduled by the Club, and normally "the amount rescheduled is limited to about 80 percent of the principal payments due over a three-year period."[77] While there are some departures from the rule, the Paris Club will not reschedule payments owing on previously rescheduled debt.[78] An IMF-sponsored paper by Bahram Nowzad and Richard Williams surveying several Paris Club reschedulings reports that "grace periods offered on rescheduled debt ranged from $2^{1}/_{2}$ to $5^{1}/_{2}$ years, bringing total maturities to a range of $7^{1}/_{2}$ to 10 years."[79] Favorable rates of interest to the borrower are usually suggested in the Agreed Minutes, which often remind creditor governments of the export gains they have received from their short-term trade credits, but in theory each individual creditor is free to wrangle such terms from the borrower as he can.[80] In most cases, the new rate of interest is quite close to the original charge, but there have been cases where governments have insisted on near-market or market levels of interest. Chandra Hardy has observed that, since 1971, "there have been no concessional debt reorganizations" through the Paris Club, only extensions of grace periods and maturities, and estimates that, since 1974, these reschedulings have resulted in "no loss to the creditors."[81] Terms may include an initiative clause stating the debtor nation's intention to reschedule a portion of its commercial debt and/or a statement on the accumulation of arrears on this debt.[82]

Three aspects of the Paris Club system demand special attention: the *ad hoc* character of the proceedings; their short-term focus; and the complete absence of any regard for the debtor's development plans. Despite some broad principles and procedural rules, the Paris Club has remained an informal, *ad hoc* body.[83] Paris Club representatives assert that since debt situations vary so greatly, they must be approached in a flexible, case-by-case manner.[84] The lack of detailed standards is also a product of the creditors' desires "to avoid setting undesirable precedents"[85] that may give the borrower the unwarranted impression that debt relief is in any way automatic and preset. In large part, the informal character of the Paris Club is the intended consequence of the creditor nation's desire to avoid the institutionalization of debt.[86]

Part and parcel with this *ad hoc* orientation, the Paris Club operates on the premise that the debtor's difficulties are basically short-term problems which can be quickly adjusted. The short-term focus of the Paris Club's rescheduling provides lenders with an additional means of controlling debtor policies, because the debtor nation will need the further cooperation of the Club if he encounters future debt-servicing obstacles.[87] The Paris Club's "short-leash" approach is mirrored in its meeting only to prevent imminent default,[88] as Hardy puts it, the convening of the Club "takes place not to avoid a liquidity crisis, but in response to one."[89] For heavily or chronically indebted LDCs the general pattern is a series of Paris Club reschedulings year after year, each meeting coming only when the situation has already reached crisis proportions.

Finally, Paris Club members have repeatedly stated that "debt rescheduling should not be used as a vehicle for development aid."[90] Hence, official reschedulings through the Club proceed without any reference to the debtor's development plans. "Rescheduling is not part of the procedure to deal with a country's basic economic problems,"[91] and if the rescheduling offers inadequate relief or works against the borrower's purposes, this is neither the fault nor the concern of the creditors, according to the official wisdom.

Commercial Reschedulings

Paris Club initiative clauses form a tie between the reschedulings of official and commercial sovereign debt. Frequently the renegotiation of bank loans follows immediately after a debtor government has completed a Paris Club accord. Sometimes the bankers undertake restructuring of commercial debts without a prior Paris Club agreement, but, like the creditor governments, they usually demand that an IMF-sponsored adjustment program be in place before entering into discussions with the sovereign debtor.[92] While commercial lenders advertise loan agreements in the "tombstones" which appear in financial journals, they do not publicize their rescheduling activities. Bank reschedulings are not clandestine, but there is an aura of secrecy and confidentiality about them, making analysis of their workings all the more difficult. If the Paris Club restructurings occur in an informal framework, bank reschedulings display no standardized framework at all. There is no universal format for the restructuring of sovereign debt owed to the banks on their sovereign Euroloans, each case requiring a new process and pre-negotiations among creditors to establish principles and procedures for the case at hand.[93] Often these pre-negotiations run into information gaps as new data on aggregate debt owed come to light and additional creditors come forward to press their claims.[94]

Cross-default clauses written into syndicated Euroloan contracts comprise a compelling reason for banks to work in unison, beyond the exigencies of a multilateral forum. Cross-default clauses allow individual creditors to unilaterally initiate a process in which all commercial creditors may call a sovereign debtor into default in the event of one lender issuing a default declaration against the borrower.[95] Thus, not only does a multilateral approach permit the creditors to present a united front to the debtor,[96] it also assists the creditors in keeping each other in line, preventing rash action by any one bank. Again, as with the Paris Club, bank negotiating cartels provide an assurance of comparable treatment of creditors, repressing any partiality the borrower may have for large[97] or accommodating banks.[98]

The procedures for commercial reschedulings vary greatly, but among major debtors who have borrowed from hundreds of banks through syndicated loans, reschedulings typically take the form of parallel but independent negotiations between the debtor and several groups of banks represented by self-appointed steering committees.[99] The bankers have been eminently successful in avoiding unilateral declarations of default, the last instance of such a sanction occurring in the case of Cuba (1962).[100] Nevertheless, there is "a tendency for individual banks or groups of banks to pull in different directions."[101] While this frequently happens between banks of different nationalities, the most widespread and disconcerting conflict arises from the disparities between money-center syndicate leaders and the regional bank participants. As members of the rank and file, the regionals find themselves with little influence and few options within the rescheduling process as a whole, with steering committees being manned exclusively by the personnel of the big banks.[102] This asymmetrical leverage predisposes the regionals to play the role of spoilers, refusing to endorse terms which they have had little part in setting.[103]

As the Nowzad and Williams study finds, most commercial reschedulings "took place in the context of, and were influenced by parallel discussions with other creditors and institutions, particularly the Paris Club and the Fund.''[104] Initiative clauses in Paris Club Agreed Minutes connect official and commercial reschedulings, and while bankers have permitted reschedulings without the debtor's acceptance of an IMF adjustment program,[105] such cases are unusual.

The absence of even an informal structure such as that of the Paris Club for commercial reschedulings contributes to two interrelated and exasperating features of bank reschedulings: delay in their commencement and lengthiness of negotiations. Bank reschedulings on just a portion of one year's commercial debt service take from six months to four years to complete.[106] There is a tendency to wait until the final hour before negotiations are begun. In one case, formal discussions on commercial debts did not commence until four years after the appearance of arrears on those obligations, and in another, there was a time lag of five years between the emergence of arrears and the signing of a restructuring agreement.[107]

The amount of commercial debt eligible for rescheduling in any given negotiating round is even more limited than in official restructurings. The banks refuse to reschedule more than one year's debt service at a time, and usually limit maturity-stretching to payments on principal alone, demanding timely repayment of interest and accumulated arrears.[108] Prior to the late 1970s, the bankers preferred the face-saving mode of simply refinancing old debts, extending new monies to the debtor and fattening their loan portfolios. In the 1980s, the bankers have grown more anxious about funds already disbursed, and they now favor rescheduling over refinancing.[109]

Commercial creditors have been far from generous in the terms attached to rescheduled sovereign loans. Their emphasis in demanding hard terms has clearly been on compensation for increased risk rather than on lightening the borrower's debt-service burden.[110] According to the Nowzad and Williams study, "Most of the restructuring agreements provided grace periods of about three years and total maturities of 5 to 7 years, except that overdue interest, *if* included, was rescheduled with no grace period and a repayment period of 2 to 5 years. The agreements generally provided for interest at spreads ranging from $1\,{}^3/_4$ to 2 percentage points over LIBOR.''[111] Whereas official reschedulings usually offer concessional terms close to those contained in original loan contracts, commercial reschedulings are always offered at a margin above market. *The Economist* has observed that ''some of the interest rates charged by the banks for more recent reschedulings are so much higher than the original rates it seems inevitable that the banks have got a good deal out of most reschedulings.''[112] Paris Club initiative provisions may call for comparable treatment of official and commercial debts, but the banks tend to drive a harder bargain with faltering debtors than do government creditors. The banks have infrequently attempted to impose their own adjustment programs on rescheduling nations, but, as the case of Peru in 1976 illustrates, these efforts have been disastrous, primarily due to the borrowers' objections about bank interference in sovereign affairs.[113] Having neither the leverage nor the expertise of the Fund, the banks rely upon the IMF for monitoring and supervising debtor adjustment programs.

The same basic criticisms that have been lodged against Paris Club reschedulings can be applied with greater force to commercial restructurings: commercial restructurings are chaotic in form, myopic in focus and operate against the debtor's development aims. Commercial reschedulings are entirely *ad hoc* in form.[114] Of the "rules" that have emerged in the course of commercial reschedulings (e.g., the principle that interest and arrears are not eligible for treatment), virtually all have been violated in one instance or another, confounding negotiations and undercutting the lender's bargaining position. The one precept on which the bankers have remained firm is the limitation of eligible debt to one year's debt service.[115] The banks base their approach to rescheduling "on the need to achieve a return to normalcy in the shortest time possible,"[116] thereby limiting crimps in cash flow and renewing investor confidence. A rapid return to smooth repayment schedules may promote a sort of stability for the bankers in the short term, but as an *idée fixe* it poses grave hazards for both debtors and creditors, because "the larger the proportion of debt subject to annual review and recommitment, the greater the danger that any change adversely affecting a country's debt situation will trigger a loss of confidence and hence a crisis."[117] Given delays in the initiation of commercial reschedulings and the length of negotiations when they are finally begun, the "one year at a time" principle is completely asynchronous with the borrower's debt-service needs. Commercial reschedulings afford no guarantee of resumed lending to the debtor, and rarely is any sort of refinancing given as part of these restructurings.[118] Indeed, one motive behind the debtor's agreement to hard terms is its perception that such settlements must be attractive to the bankers to encourage a resumption of lending.[119] If this tactic works, sovereign borrowers may receive new loans to finance development, but in the context of the uphill debt profiles they now face, most of these new monies must be earmarked to pay existing debt service. The year 1982 was the first in which there was a net outflow of funds from some major LDC debtors to commercial creditors, and without more substantial debt relief, this pattern will continue for several years.[120] In a very real and calculable sense, commercial loans have become more of a burden on national economic development than a stimulus to it, for funds raised from other sources, primarily LDC domestic flows, must now be diverted to meet external obligations. Moreover, there is the neglected matter of the human resource costs caused by the short-term scope of commercial reschedulings. If, as is currently the case, able LDC economic and financial experts are perpetually preoccupied with the renegotiation of debt contracted in the past, how can they devote their energies to development planning for the future? The underlying orientation of the banks, then, runs counter to both the capital and human resource needs essential to the debtor nation's economic development.

Linkages

The rescheduling of sovereign debt breaks down into three distinct rounds held together by formal and informal linkages. These connections give the overall process a unity in the broadest sense, but the entire form remains fragmentary and makeshift.[121] In a recent poll of international bankers, 50 percent of the respondents felt that existing arrangements for official and commercial reschedulings were adequate to handle upcoming workouts, 40 percent were uncertain and 10 percent believed the system to be inadequate.[122] Having already examined the salient shortcomings of each of the three rescheduling rounds taken individually, it is now time to consider the interconnections among the rounds, the most important being the linkages and potential ties between the tightest rescheduling ring—IMF conditional lending—and the loosest element—commercial bank reschedulings.

The International Monetary Fund has repeatedly expressed its concern over the independence of bank policies prior to and during the negotiation of Fund-sponsored adjustment programs. According to the IMF, these policies are uncoordinated with Fund efforts and often counterproductive to their purposes. Quite frequently the banks increase short-term lending to a heavily indebted nation at precisely the time when its debt-service burden demands emergency financing from the Fund. Once adjustment negotiations have begun, the bankers reduce or stop new lending to the borrower and merely seek to collect on loans already extended. Due to the severe and chronic nature of LDC debt burden, the banks can "extricate themselves from such a situation without loss only if loans from some new sources"[123] are made available to the debtor. A major new source of funding that permits the banks to reduce exposures and unlock themselves from debt-troubled developing nations is, of course, the IMF and its conditional loans. By waiting for an IMF agreement to be negotiated prior to commercial rescheduling, the bankers anticipate that the debtor, mindful of its international credit standing, will use Fund monies to repay existing commercial (and official) obligations. Thus, the pre-existence of a Fund loan disbursement before commercial rescheduling provides the banks with a mechanism for influencing the debtor's policy in the direction of orthodox discipline and with an escape route from high levels of exposure. Thus, one further motive behind delays in bank restructurings is that they allow the creditors to wait and see what the IMF will do and how they can best turn the Fund's actions to their own advantage.

This potential for abuse has elicited charges of bank "bailouts" from diverse quarters, including the IMF itself. As one Fund official has remarked, "We're in the business of saving countries. . . . saving banks isn't our business."[124] In spite of the IMF's criticism of the banks on this score, some left-wing critics see the "capitalist" Fund in tacit league with the international banks, claiming that the Fund "is primarily concerned with bailing out banks from loans that run into trouble, rather than helping member countries."[125] Indeed, even the *Wall Street Journal* has objected to *de facto* bank bailouts that have come to light, cynically dubbing a bill for increased Fund quotas the "Banker's Relief Act of 1978."[126] At bottom, the control mechanism of the rescheduling process as a whole is lopsided because, while the Fund exercises control over the debtor through conditionality, it has no equivalent power over the lenders, and the lenders reap the advantage of constraining borrowers by proxy while remaining free to control commercial reschedulings and flows on new loans to the debtor.

The banks strenuously object to any measures that would empower the Fund with formal influence over their actions similar to that which the Fund possesses over its member nations. The bankers are understandably cool to any formal links with the IMF, maintaining that they cannot allow the Fund to dictate their lending strategies.[127] "If we made a binding commitment to the Fund," one banker asserts, "we'd be in a very weak position vis-à-vis the borrowers."[128] Anthony Sampson has offered telling insight into a fundamental dilemma confronting the bankers in contemplating standardized linkages with the Fund. If the bankers were to swap part of their independence in sovereign lending for a guarantee of assistance from the Fund to their debtors, what risk would the commercial lenders be taking?[129] Were the Fund to act as an automatic lender of last resort or administer an insurance pool for commercial loans, risk would be drastically reduced, but so would the rationale for profit. Thus, greater institutionalization of international commercial debt through formal ties between the Fund and the banks would dilute the basic profit-risk formula upon which the latter operate.

The bank bailout syndrome inherent in the current overall structure of sovereign rescheduling also bothers official creditor governments.[130] The central banks of these governments have often intervened to save domestic corporations on the verge of bankruptcy, but they have generally taken the position that their purpose "is to protect the confidence and stability of the system, not to make good the losses of badly-run banks."[131] Again, banks can wait until Paris Club reschedulings have been signed and then absorb much of the relief provided to debtors, using the borrower's breathing space as an opening for reducing exposures.

In the latter part of 1982, the IMF and official creditors took a landmark step toward reducing the capacity of commercial lenders to exploit IMF and Paris Club reschedulings. In June, 1982, de Larosière cautioned bankers for their imprudence in continuing large loan flows to heavily indebted developing countries. By September, 1982, the managing director had changed his tune, exhorting the bankers to be flexible in their use of exposure ceilings and to maintain current levels of new lending.[132] In the course of negotiations with Mexico and Brazil, de Larosière saw that the banks could effectively pull the rug out from planned adjustment through a drastic pullback from new lending to these nations. The managing director decided to squelch such a move by exhibiting a new brand of Fund activism. The IMF undertook the orchestration of commercial bank lending for the first time.[133] As one financial analyst bemoans, "In short, the Fund and central banks have invented a new type of loan—assessed on existing loan exposure and fixed by the examples of Brazil and Mexico at about 7 percent of a bank's outstanding exposure—that penalizes the banks and allows borrowers to tap another source of Funds."[134] Unable to tolerate complete independence of policy by the banks, de Larosière designed his own linkage between the Fund and commercial lenders, making approval of Fund loan disbursements and adjustment programs contingent upon the banks' commitment to extend fresh monies to the debtor nations.

As this historic event reveals, in the 1970s, the IMF had become "much more a lender of last resort," providing funds to sovereign debtors who found other windows closed to them.[135] The idea of the Fund's becoming a lender of last resort requires some qualification. If such a role merely implies that the Fund selectively and conditionally provides financing when others will not, then the Fund already performs such a function. If, on the other hand, a lender of last resort is expected to automatically provide funds when other credit sources have dried up, then the Fund has neither the will nor the power to act as such.[136] It is here that the notion of "moral hazard" becomes relevant, for if the Fund automatically and unconditionally offered financing to debt-troubled borrowers or administered an insurance pool against sovereign loan losses, this might encourage profligacy on the part of the borrower and imprudence on the part of the lender. As an underwriting axiom puts it, "the availability of insurance against a certain hazard tends to induce behavior that leads to an increased incidence of that hazard."[137] For the Fund to play a role as lender of last resort would remove a measure of accountability from both creditor and debtor, and along with the financial limitations on Fund resources, this hazard deters the IMF from acting as an ultimate insurer of international loans.[138]

More modest liaisons between the Fund and the bank have been proposed as a means of harmonizing lending and rescheduling policies. Part of the Fund's importance within the restructuring process is its command over the facts involved and its capacity to interpret them. Therefore, one suggestion for establishing links between the Fund and the banks calls for the IMF to share selected pieces of information about borrowing governments with the banks.[139] Such collaboration, however, might violate confidentiality between the Fund and its member nations and the willingness of countries to supply the IMF with data in the first place.[140] Information-sharing on this "personal" basis would naturally favor the largest and most important creditors to the competitve disadvantage of small- and medium-sized banks.[141] Finally, if the IMF were to disclose alarming information to the banks, this might stir them into taking just the course the Fund wishes to avoid: a radical cut-off of credit to the debtor nation.[142] While there is a need to increase interaction among the IMF, official creditors, the banks *and* the debtors to counterbalance current asymmetries, the dimensions of the rescheduling framework have not taken cohesive form, and the channels needed for a coordinated structure await future action.

Positions on Debt Rescheduling

Each of the four principal parties involved in the debt rescheduling process has evolved a distinct general position on the issues surrounding external debt relief. The IMF has endorsed the concept of structural deficit lending, but it continues to see itself as a neutral, balance of payments institution. Debt-service problems are primarily the responsibility of the debtor, who must initiate any request for IMF assistance and must comply with Fund conditions to receive emergency loans. The abuses of the rescheduling process by commercial lenders have caused the Fund to adopt a hard-line stand vis-à-vis the banks, counteracting the potential for bailouts.

The commercial banks view rescheduling as an extreme event and avoid renegotiations of contracted LDC debt until a liquidity crisis is under way.[143] They call for a case-by-case approach to restructuring, with only broadly stated principles remaining in any way fixed. The banks acknowledge that their lending tends to increase sharply as borrower difficulties arise, but this is seen simply as a matter of filling a need created by increased demand.[144] The banks have avoided setting their own conditions on debtor policy, preferring to rely on those of the Fund, but they do not favor any formal linkages with the IMF which might constrict their maneuverability.

Official creditors do not acknowledge the existence of a generalized LDC debt problem.[145] Current problems are viewed as balance of payments difficulties, and therefore transient and subject to rapid adjustment by the debtor.[146] The Paris Club mechanism, with its informal, short-term, non-development approach, is perfectly capable of handling such developing nation debt problems as now exist.[147] As to the bankers, creditor governments reject an automatic rescue of commercial lenders by their central banks.[148]

LDC debtors see debt relief as being one and the same with balance of payments assistance and development financing.[149] From the viewpoint of major Third World debtors, the current rescheduling mechanism is woefully fragmentary and makeshift, and much greater formalization is required in both official and commercial reorganizations. This codification ought to include some degree of automaticity, as, for instance, anticipatory rescheduling triggered by a nation's reaching a set debt-service ratio.[150] Developing nation leaders argue that increased power should be placed in the hands of the IMF and the IBRD for influencing the course of official and commercial rescheduling, and that both Paris Club and bank reorganization must take a long-term view of the debtor's problems and prospects.[151] At the same time, LDC officials downplay the importance of the Fund's seal of approval, observing that going to the Fund does not necessarily ensure the amount or terms of new funds which may or may not be made available from official and commercial lenders. Seeing no need for additional certification of creditworthiness, the LDCs favor a relaxation of Fund conditionality and want greater say in the form and pace that adjustment programs take.[152]

Notes

1. Seiber, *International Borrowing*, p.63.
2. Hagen, p.303.
3. Carl R. Neu, "The International Monetary Fund and LDC Debt," in *Developing Country Debt*, ed. Lawrence G. Franko and Marilyn J. Seiber (New York: Pergamon, 1979), p.237.
4. Ibid.
5. Gisselquist, p.208.
6. Seiber, *International Borrowing*, p.103.
7. Gisselquist, p.208.
8. Paul Lewis, "$20 Billion Aid Accord for IMF," *The New York Times*, 17 January, 1983, p.D–1.
9. Gisselquist, p.20.
10. H.O. Ruding, "Lenders Ought to Consult the IMF," *Euromoney*, February, 1980, p.36.
11. International Monetary Fund, *Summary Proceedings: Annual Meeting, 1982* (Washington: International Monetary Fund, 1982), p.36.
12. Gisselquist, p.201.
13. Charles Grant, "Don't Call the IMF," p.51.
14. Seiber, *International Borrowing*, p.103.
15. Dod, p.651.
16. Seiber, *International Borrowing*, p.103.
17. Neu, p.239.
18. Ruding, p.52.
19. Ibid., p.51.
20. Seiber, *International Borrowing*, p.106.
21. Williamson, p.16.
22. Ibid., p.14.
23. Sampson, p.304.
24. Williamson, p.15.
25. Ibid., p.57.
26. Ibid., p.22.
27. Sampson, p.305.
28. Williamson, p.22.
29. Gisselquist, p.224.
30. Seiber, "Alternative Proposals," p.204; "LDC Debt: Vital U.S. Role," p.79; Donal Curtin, "Muldoon: Why There Will Be a Crash," *Euromoney*, February, 1983, p.70.
31. Seiber, *International Borrowing*, p.103.
32. Frank A. Southard, *The Evolution of the International Monetary Fund*. Essays in International Finance, No. 135 (Princeton: Princeton University, 1979), p.21.
33. Fallon and Shirref, p.28.

34. Gisselquist, p.54.
35. Sampson, p.296.
36. Gisselquist, p.207.
37. Sampson, p.101.
38. Southard, pp.18–19.
39. Seiber, *International Borrowing,* p.66.
40. Neu, p.239.
41. Williamson, p.37.
42. Ibid., p.36.
43. Gisselquist, p.207.
44. Sidney Dell and Roger Lawrence, *The Balance of Payments Adjustment Process in Developing Countries* (New York: Pergamon, 1980), pp.113–114.
45. Ibid., pp.115–116.
46. Williamson, p.25.
47. Neu, p.241.
48. Art Pine, ''IMF Becomes a Leader in Rescuing Debtor Lands, but Its Austerity Measures Are Called Too Rigid,'' *The Wall Street Journal,* 11 January, 1983.
49. Hardy, p.37.
50. Sampson, p.298.
51. Williamson, p.53.
52. Ibid., p.5.
53. Neu, p.240.
54. Williamson, p.19.
55. Grant, ''Don't Call the IMF,'' p.52.
56. Williamson, p.19.
57. Gisselquist, p.218.
58. Southard, p.16.
59. Ibid., pp.17–18.
60. Williamson, p.51.
61. Ibid., pp.57–58.
62. Peter Field, David Shirref and William Ollard, ''The IMF and the Central Banks Flex Their Muscles,'' *Euromoney,* January, 1983, p.36.
63. Gisselquist, p.188.
64. Group of Thirty, p.13.
65. OECD, pp.44–45.
66. Nowzad and Williams, p.17.
67. Ibid., p.21.
68. Ibid.
69. Ibid., p.22.
70. ''Nightmare,'' p.27.
71. Nowzad and Williams, p.24.
72. Angelini, Eng and Lees, p.144.
73. Seiber, *International Borrowing,* p.66.
74. Nowzad and Williams, pp.22–23.
75. Gisselquist, p.188.
76. ''Nightmare,'' p.27.
77. Hardy, pp.34–35.
78. Nowzad and Williams, p.23.
79. Ibid.

80. William Ollard and Anne Sington, "The Unique Club of Michel Camdessus," *Euromoney,* August, 1982, p.54.

81. Hardy, p.34.

82. Nowzad and Williams, pp.22–24.

83. Ibid., p.22.

84. Ibid.

85. Christopher Davis, "A New Approach to Rescheduling," *The Banker,* January, 1980, p.109.

86. Grubel, p.8.

87. Seiber, *International Borrowing,* p.66.

88. C. Davis, p.107.

89. Hardy, p.34.

90. Nowzad and Williams, p.22.

91. Ollard and Sington, p.54.

92. OECD, p.24.

93. Group of Thirty, p.14.

94. Ibid., p.15.

95. "Nightmare," p.35.

96. Gisselquist, p.213.

97. Robert A. Bennett, "Brazil's Bank Loan Bid Stirs Concern," *The New York Times,* 18 November, 1982, p.D–1.

98. "Nightmare," p.55.

99. Nowzad and Williams, p.34.

100. "Nightmare," p.36.

101. Group of Thirty, p.16.

102. Williams, p.264.

103. "Nightmare," p.35.

104. Nowzad and Williams, p.30.

105. Hardy, p.37.

106. Group of Thirty, p.15.

107. Nowzad and Williams, pp.34–35.

108. "Nightmare," p.28.

109. Nowzad and Williams, p.35.

110. Hardy, p.37.

111. Nowzad and Williams, p.36.

112. "Nightmare," p.36.

113. Seiber, *International Borrowing,* p.17.

114. Group of Thirty, pp.13–14.

115. "Nightmare," p.22.

116. C. Davis, p.105.

117. Ibid.

118. Nowzad and Williams, p.39.

119. Ibid.

120. Ibid., p.140.

121. Group of Thirty, p.13.

122. Bell, p.19.

123. Neu, p.243.

124. Seiber, *International Borrowing,* p.137.

125. Williamson, p.56.

126. Gisselquist, p.216.
127. Seiber, "Alternative Proposals," p.205.
128. Field, Shirref and Ollard, p.44.
129. Sampson, p.300.
130. Angelini, Eng and Lees, p.45.
131. Dini, p.61.
132. Field, Shirref and Ollard, p.37.
133. Ibid., p.36.
134. Ibid.
135. Williamson, p.12.
136. Neu, pp.236–246.
137. Grubel, p.15.
138. Neu, p.243.
139. Ruding, p.36.
140. Sampson, p.299.
141. Seiber, "Alternative Proposals," p.206.
142. "Nightmare," p.41.
143. Seiber, *International Borrowing*, p.65.
144. Nowzad and Williams, p.33.
145. Seiber, "Alternative Proposals," p.190.
146. Seiber, *International Borrowing*, p.63.
147. Ibid., pp.126–127.
148. Grubel, p.7.
149. Hardy, p.37.
150. Seiber "Alternative Proposals," p.199.
151. Ibid.
152. Hardy, p.38.

Chapter 5

CASE 1: TURKEY

Chronology

Turkey was the first major LDC borrower to undergo large-scale, multilateral restructurings of official and commercial debts in the 1970s. As the "sick man of Europe," the country survived the 1950s only with the help of massive aid and concessionary loans from its anti-communist NATO/OECD allies.[1] Economic performance during the period 1962 to 1976 improved on some counts, with average annual increases of 6.9 percent in GNP, 9.8 percent in industrial output and 10.7 percent in fixed investment.[2] While the nation's internal economy displayed impressive growth, its external sector remained weak. Turkey's balance of trade was unfavorable throughout the period, with exports stagnating, imports curbed only by protectionism, and foreign exchange receipts coming largely as wage remittances from Turkish workers abroad. In 1973, workers' remittances "almost matched the foreign exchange earnings of exports of goods"[3] from Turkey, but problems appeared on this front as recession hit the Common Market countries of Western Europe and Europe Economic Community (EEC) governments imposed employment and remittance restrictions on Turkish guest workers. Remittances to Turkey dropped from $1.4 billion in 1973 to less than $1 billion in 1976 and 1977.[4] Industrialized nations, West Germany in particular, achieved lower inflation and unemployment rates by restricting Turkish workers, but this contributed to rising unemployment in Turkey and a domestic inflation rate of 37 percent in 1977. Like other LDCs, Turkey reeled under the combined effects of oil price hikes, rising dollar interest rates and deteriorating volumes and terms of trade.[5] Simultaneously, the government changed hands repeatedly, as the Republican People's Party (RPP) and the Justice Party (JP) took turns in leading fragile coalitions. Neither faction would tackle the urgent need for balance of payments adjustment, as successive administrations took the collective decision "not to reduce the pace of Turkey's economic growth at all."[6] Despite the powerful externalities that riddled the economy in the mid–1970s,[7] the Turks continued the industrial modernization

Table 2
Selected Economic Performance Indicators for Turkey, 1976–1978

	1976	1977	1978
Consumer Prices (annual rate of growth)	+17.4%	+26.1%	+61.9%
Balance of Payments Current Account ($ million)	−1,964	−3,419	−1,332
Exports ($ million)	1,960	1,754	2,287
Imports ($ million)	4,565	5,158	4,093
External Debt (Gross, $ million)	3,582	4,287	6,227

Source: Adapted from Benjamin J. Cohen, *Banks and the Balance of Payments: Private Lending in the International Adjustment Process* (Montclair, New Jersey: Allan Held, Osmun, 1981), p. 220.

program which they had embarked upon at the beginning of the decade, pursuing economic growth at the expense of other objectives, e.g., equity of distribution.[8]

As shown in Table 2, from 1976 to 1978, economic conditions in Turkey eroded greatly. Real growth in GNP fell from 7.7 percent in 1976 to 4 percent in 1977, and 3 percent in 1978, and stagnated completely in 1979 with zero growth and an actual decline in industrial production, as unemployment grew to a reported 20 percent for 1979–1980.[9] Lacking requisite foreign exchange to pay for essential imports needed as inputs for domestic production, Turkish plants operated at 50 percent capacity in 1979/1980, many being forced to close entirely "for lack of foreign exchange to import needed oil or materials."[10] Financial and statutory constraints on imports fueled inflation, consumer prices rising at a 60 percent yearly pace in 1979, 70 to 80 percent nationwide in 1980, and reaching 140 percent in Ankara and Istanbul for the first three months of 1980.

The worsening of Turkey's domestic economy was accompanied by a soaring increase in its annual debt-service obligations. The nation's debt profile eroded rapidly as the Turks supplemented concessionary long-term loans from official sources with short-term commercial financing, much of the latter coming through the Convertible Lira Deposits (CTLD), of which more will be said later. Table 3 reveals the growth of Turkish external debt from 1975 to 1980, and the rise of commercial loans as a share of total debt and as a component of debt service.

The pattern that bank lending to Turkey took in the mid 1970s has been severely criticized by international debt analysts. From 1974 to 1979, the banks lent huge sums to the Turkish government, predominantly on short term, in a manner which "was hardly of a nature consistent with development" [11] and which "was clearly unrelated to the country's capacity to service it." [12] It is further charged that the bankers felt secure in their Turkish assets because the nation's strategic importance to NATO led them to believe that OECD nations would readily intervene in the event of a full-blown debt crisis. The bankers have a decidedly different interpretation of their Turkish credit policy in the mid–1970s. They maintain that commercial lenders "carried" the Turks as official credits shrank, [13] and, they observe, the OECD nations did not come to Turkey's rescue until Tito's death, the Iranian Revolution and the Soviet invasion of Afghanistan sharpened the West's interest in Turkey. Finally, in a study of Turkey's creditworthiness as of 1975, the country was compared, on the one hand, with eighteen similar countries, only one of which went to rescheduling, and, on the other hand, with ten similar countries, eight of which underwent rescheduling, so that the chances for Turkey's having to reschedule could be alternatively set at 5 percent or 80 percent depending on the model used to assess country risk. [14]

While the expansion of bank lending to Turkey in the mid–1970s can be partially justified, the virtual cut-off of all commercial credit to the nation in the late 1970s is considerably more difficult to rationalize. By February, 1977, Turkey's central bank ceased to pay out foreign exchange, and in March Wells Fargo led the last syndicated loan to Turkey of the decade, a six-month facility. As Turkey's leaders contemplated the prospect of going to the International Monetary Fund, the economy relied on "debt rollovers, credit-line drawings and unpaid suppliers credits," [15] with commercial lenders being unwilling to provide any fresh monies. When the first rounds of IMF/OECD rescheduling were set in motion, the banks adopted a wait and see posture, delaying commercial debt negotiations and resumption of lending until Fund and official

Table 3
Turkish External Debt and Debt Service, 1975–1980
(in $ million)

Year	Total Debt	Private Debt	Total Debt Service	Private Debt Service
1975	3,614	60	358.6	11.8
1976	4,390	476	487.8	44.3
1977	5,389	729	450.6	68.7
1978	7,315	955	592.7	97.7
1979	11,581	3,449	914.0	145.7
1980	14,534	4,234	1,135.7	363.5

Source: OECD, p. 113.

creditors completed a restructuring of Turkey's public debt. The attitude of the Turkish government did not favor the rapid completion of such an accord. Justice Party Prime Minister Suleyman Demirel was unable to impose an austerity program on the economy in 1977, primarily because of a coalition with the Islamic National Salvation Party, a faction adamantly opposed to reductions in growth, consumption and social welfare spending. The RPP assumed power in 1978, and Prime Minister Bulent Ecevit was firmly against IMF-type adjustment, blaming the United States, the Common Market and the commercial banks for his country's external debt difficulties.[16]

Returning briefly to the mid–1970s, it is apparent that commercial lenders did exploit Turkey's need for external capital, but it is also apparent that the Turks provided them with the apparatus to do so in the form of the Convertible Lira Deposit Scheme (CTLD). Turkey is unusual among major LDC borrowers in that it never tapped the medium- and long-term Euroloan markets. "Instead, it fell into debt by encouraging short-term bank loans, by drawing on short-term bank credit lines and by stretching payment on trade credits."[17] It was not, then, the amount of external debt owed per se in the late 1970s that made Turkey's debt-service burden unbearable; rather, it was the use of short-term loans at commercial rates that distorted the country's external debt repayment schedule. In April, 1978, Turkey's short-term debt amounted to a total of $6,657 million, of which $4,033 million was owed to banks and $2,086 million was owed as trade arrears, primarily to OECD governments.[18] It was in this context that the "notorious"[19] and "appalling gamble"[20] of the CTLDs takes on full meaning. At its core, the CTLD scheme initiated by Demirel in 1975 was quite simple (and simple-minded). "Foreign banks were offered a government guarantee on the value of funds deposited for one or two years in Turkey,"[21] the Turkish banks selling the foreign exchange to the Central Bank, using the lira for lending to domestic customers, and the Central Bank, in turn, selling the foreign exchange to Turkish importers. The plan had the one advantage of encouraging remittances from Turks abroad. Far outweighing this benefit was the fact that effective interest rates on deposits in Turkish banks exceeded LIBOR and average margins greatly, so that the Turks "paid" far more for these funds than they would have on direct loans from the same banks.[22] The mechanism produced an inflow of foreign exchange in 1975, 1976, and early 1977, but it then resulted in a heavier outflow of foreign exchange as these deposits became due. The banks were eager to place monies in a system in which Swiss francs, for example, could be lent at Turkish interest rates and then converted back into francs at a government-guaranteed rate of exchange.[23] The impact of the CTLDs upon Turkey's external debt structure was wholly negative.

In 1975, most of the country's foreign debt was of a long-term nature (above ten years), and carried an average interest rate of only 3.5 percent. Following the introduction of the Convertible-Lira Deposit Scheme, by the end of 1977, some two-thirds ($8.5 billion) of the estimated total debt ($12.5 billion) was short-term, and debt-service had risen above $2 billion a year.[24]

The Turks may have suffered a battering at the hands of the banks, but they themselves abetted the assault by handing commercial lenders the CTLD club.

The Turkish economy was beset by the three main externalities affecting LDCs in the 1970s: rising energy prices, high dollar interest rates and a downswing in volumes and terms of trade. Unlike other Middle Eastern states, the Turks were extremely vulnerable to OPEC price hikes,[25] domestic production accounting for only 15 percent of the nation's crude oil needs.[26] Heavily reliant on truck transport[27] and still in the process of constructing large-scale energy projects (e.g., the Ataturk dam on the Euphrates), the Turks watched in horror as the first oil shock created a $600 million current account deficit for 1974 and a $2 billion deficit in 1975.[28] The oil-import bill for Turkey in 1973 was $200 million, an amount equal to 17 percent of national export receipts. By 1980, the cost of imported oil reached $3.1 billion, the equivalent of 110 percent of Turkish export earnings.[29] According to one source, the second oil shock resulted in an oil-import bill of $1.7 billion in 1979, $3.6 billion in 1980, and $3.9 billion in 1981, with a time lag before its full effect could be fully measured.[30] Simultaneously, the United States Federal Reserve anti-inflation monetary policy, in conjunction with unflagging deficit spending by the American government, caused dollar interest rates to rise steeply and the Turks' floating-interest debt to balloon correspondingly.[31] Exports, never one of Turkey's strong suits, suffered from the inflation of production costs and from recession/protectionism in the markets of the West, while the price of imported goods from the industrialized countries became much more expensive.[32]

As the situation worsened, some form of balance of payments adjustment became inevitable. In late 1978/early 1979, Ecevit undertook sporadic austerity measures, including the IMF-ordered devaluation of the lira, but failed to follow through in a disciplined and comprehensive manner.[33] Demirel assumed control of a coalition government in October, 1979, and one of his first moves was the appointment of Turgut Ozal as Deputy Prime Minister. Ozal became the architect of an anti-inflationary, export-promotion austerity package, bringing technocratic zeal to IMF-type "orthodox" stabilization.[34] Under Ozal's direction, the Turkish government replaced economic growth with curbing inflation as its chief priority and sought to establish price equilibria between domestic and external markets. Ozal's strategy called for an end to subsidies for State Economic Enterprises (SEEs), an accompanying deregulation of prices charged for SEE goods and services, an opening of the economy to foreign investment, and devaluation of the lira totaling 48 percent (more than was requested by the IMF).[35] On 24 January, 1980, the government proclaimed its Economic Stabilization Program and the beginning of the "capitalist revolution" in Turkey. Under the January decrees, the lira was officially depreciated by one-third, and banks were allowed to retain 80 percent of their foreign exchange receipts. Import taxes were reduced, especially on inputs needed for the production of tradeables; export subsidies were granted; and oil exploration in Turkey was opened to foreign firms. In April, 1980, the government announced a further devaluation of the lira and abolished interest rate ceilings on bank deposits, followed in September by a statute making strikes illegal. State Economic Enterprises were weaned from subsidies and forced to price their products according to costs and market conditions.[36] Bank interest rates on deposits were "freed at a stroke," causing rates to leap fourfold to 40 percent and 50 percent annually. To ensure that a "gentleman's agreement" among Turkish bankers would not defeat the liberalization of deposit rates, the Turkish government invited foreign banks to set up business in Turkey, thereby introducing new competitive forces into the financial sector.[37]

The effects of the January stabilization program and the accompanying measures were immediate and widespread.[38] Inflation, which had run at close to 100 percent for 1980, fell to between 35 percent and 40 percent by end-year 1981.[39] After three years of negative rates in real GNP growth, the Turkish economy expanded at a 4.4 percent clip in 1981. In the course of a single year, 1980/1981, government budget deficits dropped from 5 percent of GNP to 1 percent.[40] As debt relief became available through IMF and official reschedulings, the country's debt-service ratio reached the manageable level of 17 percent by August, 1981, and at the end of 1981, short-term bank debt had been cut to a total of $800 million.[41]

Since mid–1981, Turkey's debt profile has improved strongly. It is now projected that all current commercial debts outstanding will be repaid by 1986.[42] As of February, 1982, only $4 billion of the nation's total $18 billion external debt carried commercial rates of interest, the bulk of the stock bearing concessionary rates on loans from official, bilateral sources and the IBRD. International commercial lenders are well aware of this turnabout in Turkey's debt structure and debt-service capacity. In March, 1982, the state-owned airline THY received the "first publicized medium-term loan by a Turkish borrower [in] five years.[43] Despite Ozal's resignation in the summer of 1982, the banks have maintained their renewed confidence in Turkey, granting a $200 million, three-year export finance credit in December, 1982, at the comparatively favorable rate of 1 $1/4$ percent over LIBOR.[44] Whether the Fund's seal of approval helped to restore Turkey's access to commercial credit is a matter of conjecture. As will be seen below, however, it was only through four years of arduous negotiations that Turkey received the debt relief that contributed so heavily to the success of its adjustment.

Rescheduling of Turkey's official and commercial sovereign debt in the late 1970s and early 1980s "was far more difficult than anyone realized" it would be.[45] In contrast to the relative ease with which official loans to Turkey were restructured in 1959 and 1965, the 1977–1982 rounds of external debt renegotiations were extremely complex, with major setbacks arising throughout the process as a whole.[46] As 1977 came to a close, the Turkish government met with IMF officials to arrange a conditional emergency loan to assist it in meeting balance of payment deficits. With Ecevit and the RPP maintaining a shaky hold on the Turkish government, the opening discussions between the Turks and the Fund "started off with governmental reluctance to make policy changes on the scale the Fund considered necessary."[47] By January, 1978, Ecevit had already rolled over short-term bank credits and encountered a stone wall from the bankers on any new funds or standby loans.[48] The Turks then approached the OECD nations for a rescheduling of long-term official loans, but the industrialized countries refused to consider debt relief without an IMF adjustment program in position.[49] After initial resistance, the Ecevit Administration came to terms with the IMF in March, 1978. The Fund granted Turkey a $370 million standby credit,[50] and the Turkish government committed itself to cuts in public spending, severe credit restraints, initiation of commercial debt negotiations and a 23 percent devaluation of the lira.[51] Two months later, under the auspices of the OECD, creditor nations agreed to defer payments on $1.5 billion in export credits and concessionary loans. Four-fifths of the payments on principal due for one year's debt service was rescheduled, but no refinancing was provided.[52] In December, 1978, the IMF's monitors in Turkey reported that the Turks were not complying with the conditions attached to its standby credit, and suspended further disbursements in the absence of more stringent austerity measures, including another official currency devaluation.[53] While the amount of IMF funds withheld was not a critical element in Turkey's overall restructuring, the Fund's judgement that Turkey's adjustment program was not sufficient had a crucial impact on OECD creditors, who refused to furnish the Turks with new loans if a second IMF adjustment package was not approved.[54]

In May, 1979, key NATO members pledged $962 million in financial assistance to Turkey as soon as a new IMF accord had been reached.[55] This sum was raised to $1.5 billion at the end of the month, again contingent upon an IMF agreement. On 19 July, 1979, the Turks and the Fund signed a new conditional loan for $250 million. Final approval was then given by OECD official creditors to reorganize 85 percent of principal and interest payments due over the period 1 July, 1979–30 June, 1980, net debt relief amounting to approximately $850 million.[56] Encouraged by the IMF and OECD agreements, some 254 international banks restructured $2.6 billion in commercial credits and awarded $400 million in new loans during the summer of 1979. The entire $3 billion package carried a seven-year maturity with interest charges set at 1 $3/4$ percent over LIBOR.

At the outset of 1980, the Turks were still unable to meet their external debt obligations, and the Turkish government instituted its national austerity package. This concerted adjustment effort on the part of the Turks led to approval of a $1.6 billion quota loan from the IMF, an amount equal to 600 percent of Turkey's yearly quota, with disbursements scheduled over a three-year time span.[57] The loan set a historic precedent, being the largest in IMF history at the time and representing the first instance in which the Fund granted a loan having a maturity in excess of one year.[58] In July, 1980, the OECD again rescheduled $2.3 billion in debt falling due between July, 1980, and July, 1983, another departure from the "one year at a time" principle.

During 1981, the Turkish government sought a rescheduling of bank loans previously restructured in 1979, specifically requesting a drop in spreads from 1 $^3/_4$ percent to 1 $^1/_4$ percent above LIBOR. The Turks felt that their adjustment program warranted a gesture of confidence on the part of the banks and a signal that fresh loans would be restored to Turkey shortly.[59] The bankers, however, balked at the notion of rescheduling loans already reorganized and would not extend fresh credits to the Turks. From September, 1981, to mid–1982, the Turks gathered concessional loans from various sources, negotiating a $460 million aid package from West Germany, $250 million from Libya and IBRD structural adjustment loans of $300 million in 1981 and $304.5 million in 1982. In the fall of 1982, a massive $5.1 billion rescheduling was agreed on between the OECD Aid to Turkey consortium, the IMF and the banks, but, once again, the banks would only stretch out maturities and grace periods, remaining unwilling to refinance.[60]

In John Williamson's estimation, "Turkey is a good example of successful Fund supported shock treatment."[61] From an economic/financial standpoint, the January, 1980, austerity program formulated by Ozal in response to IMF pressures was eminently successful. If political and social conditions are taken into account, the 1980 package was Draconian in the extreme, contributing to widespread disorder, unemployment, reduction in real wages and, most telling, the ouster of civilian government. Thus, according to another analysis, the IMF's approach was too ambitious in its design and pace and was executed without regard to the fragility of political and social relations within Turkey.[62]

While the Fund can be charged with undue interventionism in setting Turkish fiscal and monetary policy, the commercial banks, on the other hand, can be accused of draining official debt relief into their own treasuries by refusing to grant new credits and merely rescheduling existing debt. In December, 1980, as the Turks contemplated going to the banks for a renegotiation, a vitriolic dispute arose between the banks and the IMF.[63] The Fund viewed the bankers' fickleness as entirely self-interested and counterproductive to the improvement of Turkish debt-service capacity. In the mid–1970s, the IMF observed, "huge loans [were] showered on Turkey without intelligent conditions by the international banks.[64] "Having made their quick profits, [the banks] were glad to leave it to Western governments and the IMF to cope"[65] with Turkey's debt woes. The Fund insisted that its purpose was not to bail out the banks, but, given the bankers' hasty cut-off of all commercial credit to the Turkish government, it was apparent that they had simply absorbed official monies as payments on previously contracted loans. OECD governments voiced similar objections, asserting that much of the debt relief that they had provided was nullified by the collective retrenchment policies of the banks.[66] The resumption of commercial lending to Turkey in late 1982 was far too little and far too late to compensate for debt relief indirectly devoured by the banks.

Commentary

Examining Turkey's overall development strategy in light of the adjustments it was forced to make in 1980, the salient characteristic of the Turkish approach to national economic development was its strong protectionist, import-substitution orientation. Since the Turkish Revolution of 1923, the country's industry had atrophied under the protection of a defensive "infant industry" trade wall. Imports were strictly limited through trade barriers, while exports were inhibited by special taxation and a chronically overvalued lira.[67] Surveying Turkish trade policy in the 1960s and 1970s, a research team comments that "protection has been largely automatic because authorities have generally prohibited imports of any goods once domestic production began."[68] The same study dismisses any "infant industry" rationale for Turkish protectionism since "protected Turkish industries did not experience rapid increases in output per unit of input,"[69] as would be the case if protectionism had successfully fostered industry. Along with bureaucratic barriers to exports, protectionism of domestic production led to high rates of consumer inflation and the establishment of monopolies and oligopolies within protected industries, creating entrenched demand for continuation of "favorable" trade policies.[70]

All of this changed overnight, as Ozal assumed control over Turkish economic and financial policies, alarming the Turks with his rallying cry of "Export or die."[71] In the first year of the new export-promotion program, Turkish export receipts rose $700 million, from $2.2 billion to $2.9 billion, a growth rate which impressed even staid IMF officials.[72] With the textile industry providing a platform for its export drive, and the potential of the neglected agrarian sector to serve as "the bread basket of the Middle East," the outward orientation initiated by Ozal continues as a welcome, if overdue, remedy for curing the "sick man's" previous dismal balance of trade performance.[73] At the same time, under the 1980 package, the principle that "everybody is entitled to import whatever is required for export production" has been faithfully implemented, with protectionism and import-substitution measures reduced, inflation of consumer goods dampened, barriers against foreign inputs for export production lowered and a decline in oligopolist control.

The Turks have also taken a new course with regard to workers in Europe (800,000 in Germany alone),[74] who continue to provide foreign exchange flows back to Turkey in excess of $1 billion a year.[75] In the mid–1970s, the Turks were hit hard by their fellow EEC members, who did not welcome Turkish workers during a period of widespread domestic recession and unemployment.[76] The Turks have moved to diversify their remittance sources by sending teams of building contractors into neighboring Middle Eastern countries, e.g., Saudi Arabia, Libya, Egypt and Iraq.[77] Should the current downtrend in OPEC oil prices continue, the Turks will gladly forego foreign exchange receipts from these nations and accept oil and gas in lieu of currency.[78]

The unwieldy size of the public sector was a second feature of the Turkish economy that constrained its economic performance and debt-service capacity. Government deficits ran as high as 5 percent of GNP in the late 1970s, partially as a result of Turkish defense spending related to its ongoing dispute with Greece.[79] More important, the public sector was a major investor in all types of economic activities, especially industrial modernization. Since January, 1980, the government has de-emphasized its role in financing industry and manufacture, concentrating on projects related to energy, transport, agriculture and health.[80] According to one Turkish official, the new focal point of industrial policy "is not to add new capacity, but to make best use of existing resources."[81] Capacity utilization, then, is currently the overarching criterion guiding the development of Turkish industry.

The primary example of prior public sector overkill in nurturing Turkish industry can be seen in the State Economic Enterprises (SEEs). SEEs were established by the Gursel government in 1960 as a means of promoting infant industry and giving a second-stage boost to industries already begun by the private sector.[82] The enterprises were financed and supervised by the government and the central bank, and were allowed to price goods below manufacturing costs, generating a continuing stream of deficits in public budgets. Production planning occurred "at the top" without the benefit of market signals from below.[83] SEEs could be found in every nook and cranny of the economy,[84] taking the form of slaughterhouses, meat production facilities, feed industries, and tobacco, soft drink, cement, sugar, fertilizer, iron and steel enterprises, among others. Over the years, successive Turkish governments "deliberately scattered their investments . . . to provide employment rather than produce efficiently."[85] In 1979, for example, wages took up nine-tenths of all monies earned from the sale of SEE products.[86] The inefficiencies of the SEEs are most apparent in the relative performance of public sector basic metal industries compared with those in the private sector. In 1979, while the SEEs accounted for 65 percent of employment in this industry and only 40 percent of production, the private sector accounted for 35 percent of employment and 60 percent of production.[87] The private sector, moreover, came to resemble its public counterpart, as a handful of industrial holding companies expanded into virtually every area of productive activity.[88] Under the 1980 package, SEEs must live by the dictates of the marketplace, and industrial sprawl is being reversed as non-competitive businesses drop by the wayside.

Turkey's "capitalist revolution" brought reform in two other areas relevant to its debt-service capacity: taxation and foreign investment. Tax evasion has always been widespread in modern Turkey,[89] and in 1980 it was estimated that 85 percent of all professional workers reported incomes below taxable levels.[90] These abuses led to reductions in public revenues and inhibited productive activity by placing heavier burdens on salaried workers.[91] The Turkish government has tightened its taxation procedures, introducing a value added tax based on the West German system and closely scrutinizing tax statements from professionals.[92] As to direct foreign investment in Turkey, prior to 1980 it was virtually non-existent. Between 1954 and 1980, a mere $228 million in foreign investments came into the country.[93] On paper, Basic Law 6224 regulating foreign investment was quite liberal, but its interpretation by bureaucratic officials was not. Ozal tried to induce a more favorable climate for multinational activity in Turkey during the late 1960s, but by 1974 a general xenophobia had once again emerged. Under the January, 1980, plan, a Foreign Investment Department was established, and in two years (1980–1981) more foreign investment was placed in the country than had been invested in the previous twenty-five years.[94] By closing tax loopholes and opening the economy to foreign investment, the Turks have enhanced the capacity of the public sector to pay external debts and have improved the private sector's ability to garner foreign exchange earnings.

To this point, the analysis of Turkey's most recent debt crisis has treated political and social factors as simply a side-light on economic performance. In point of fact, both domestic and international political forces had strong influences on Turkey's assumption of foreign debt and its efforts to service it. The potential for domestic conflict in Turkey is inherently great. Regional rivalries cut across longstanding ethnic and religious hostilities among the nation's Sunni majority and its large Shiite and Kurdish minorities.[95] Strong political factions can be found on the Marxist left and the neo-Fascist right. Their warrings have repeatedly fractured the Turkish polity, prompting the centrist military to intervene with caretaker governments three times since the formation of the state. There are perhaps a dozen minor parties in Turkey, but basically, like the United States, Turkey runs on a two-party system. The Republican People's Party, led by Bulent Ecevit in the 1970s, is roughly equivalent to the Democratic Party in the U.S., based on a center-left coalition of workers, civil servants and urban voters. The Justice Party, headed by Suleyman Demirel during the period, is similar to the Republican Party in the United States, representing business, landowning and traditional interests.[96] Together, the RPP and JP captured an average of 80 percent of the popular vote over the 1970s, but unlike the friendly rivalry between America's Republicans and Democrats, the two major Turkish parties have perennially projected "an uncompromising, hostile and aggressive attitude toward each other."[97] With the Turkish polity and parliament split down the middle, neither the RPP nor the JP was able to reduce growth rates or current consumption without fear of undermining their popular support, and both solved the problem by borrowing abroad. As debt service on these loans became more burdensome, neither Ecevit nor Demirel "ever enjoyed sufficient parliamentary support to put through unpopular stabilization measures,"[98] so that adjustment was delayed until the last minute and took drastic form when it occurred. Despite their differing ideological backgrounds, both Ecevit and Demirel blamed the Western nations, their banks and "their" IMF for Turkey's ills when they were not busy sniping at each other. During the 1970s, government power passed back and forth between the RPP and the JP, each party enlisting strange bedfellows to hold together slim parliamentary majorities, e.g., the alliance between the JP and the leftist-oriented Islamic Salvation Party. Political violence between the Marxist Left and the Right's "gray wolves" was a daily occurrence in Turkey, taking 2,500 lives in 1978–1979 and 2,000 in the first seven months of 1980 alone.[99] With the JP and the RPP stalemated in the dead center of the political spectrum, extremists pulled apart the social fabric. Under conditions of widespread disorder and political crisis, diligent management of national economic development was a luxury that the nation's political leadership could not afford.[100]

On 12 September, 1980, the Turkish military, unable to tolerate domestic violence, assumed absolute control of the government, abolishing the constitution, imprisoning opposition legislators and declaring martial law in all of the country's sixty-seven provinces.[101] The coup was led by General Kenan Evren, a staunch defender of Kemalist centerism. Political conflict had taken on new dimensions after Demirel's imposition of the 1980 austerity package. The same adjustment that Western governments, bankers and Fund officials roundly applauded carried high social costs in terms of rising unemployment, reduction in real wages and cuts in social spending, all coming virtually overnight. Social tensions became even more intense as the economy was deflated, especially within the "gecekondos" (urban slums). When the military completed its takeover, Evren's first task was to continue with the austerity program (Ozal remaining as its director) while repressing terrorism.[102] It was only through the use of martial law that this task was accomplished. Evren cracked down hard on both left- and right-wing extremists, using force to produce order where law alone would not. On 7 November, 1982, Turkish voters overwhelmingly approved a new national constitution, installing Evren as President for a seven-year term. Adjustment was executed only by force of arms, and while democracy was eventually restored, it proved fragile in meeting the political and economic challenges that besieged the nation.

Turkey's strategic importance to NATO was another factor that influenced the country's accumulation of debt and its reorganization. In the mid–1970s, bankers in the West were encouraged by their governments to extend credit to Turkey, the Germans in particular following Bonn's lead in strengthening ties to Ankara.[103] The West's interest in maintaining stability in Turkey enhanced the Turks' bargaining position in the rescheduling of both official and commercial external debts.[104] When Ecevit suggested in 1978 that the behavior of OECD nations in handling Turkish debt might be linked to Turkey's continuing membership in NATO, both the OECD and the IMF bent their rules, allowing the rescheduling of more than one year's debt and a multi-year Fund loan for the first time. Turkey's links with the West had been weakened by American and European partiality toward Greece in the Cyprus conflict, the U.S. arms embargo of 1975–1978 causing the greatest damage.[105] OECD and IMF debt relief for Turkey was backed by compelling realpolitik motives, while Turkey's perception of unreliable OECD partners has caused it to seek improved ties with the Middle East and the Soviet Union.[106]

Notes

1. Sampson, p.261.
2. Morris Singer, "Turkey in Crisis," *Current History,* January, 1981, p.29.
3. Robert N. McCauley, "A Compendium of IMF Troubles: Turkey, Portugal, Peru, Egypt," in *Developing Country Debt,* ed. Lawrence G. Franko and Marilyn J. Seiber (New York: Pergamon, 1979), p.142.
4. Ibid.
5. Singer, p.30.
6. Ibid.
7. Hagen, p.360.
8. Singer, p.29.
9. Ibid., p.31.
10. Hagen, p.360.
11. Benjamin J. Cohen, *Banks and the Balance of Payments: Private Lending in the International Adjustment Process* (Montclair, New Jersey: Allan Held, Osmun, 1981), p.219.
12. "Nightmare," p.41.
13. "Global Ripples from Turkey's Financial Crisis," *Businessweek,* 15 December, 1980, p.91.
14. "Two Statistical Approaches," *The Banker,* January, 1981, p.79.
15. McCauley, p.145.
16. Ibid., pp.145–148.
17. Ibid., pp.142–143.
18. Ibid., p.146.
19. "Turkey: Back Again," *The Banker,* February, 1981, p.77.
20. Fallon and Shirref, p.22.
21. B. Cohen, pp.217–218.
22. McCauley, p.145.
23. Field, Shirref and Ollard, p.38.
24. B. Cohen, p.218.
25. "Turkey: Back Again," p.77.
26. Singer, p.77.
27. "A Programme to Make Capitalism Work," *Euromoney,* February, 1982, p.8.
28. B. Cohen, p.217.
29. "Energy?: The Answer Is the Dam on the Euphrates," *Euromoney,* February, 1982, p. 13.
30. "Programme," p.9.
31. "Turkish Tea and Sympathy in the Royal Garden," *The Economist,* 17 January, 1981, p.79.
32. "Turkey: Back Again," p.77.
33. Singer, p.28.
34. Ibid., p.29.

35. "Akturk: The Planner Who Longs to Plan Less," *Euromoney*, February, 1982, p.16.

36. "The State Enterprises Can't Simply Be Handed Over," *Euromoney*, February, 1982, p.25.

37. "Pushing the Banks into Export Financing," *Euromoney*, February, 1982, p.30.

38. IBRD, *Annual Report: 1982*, p.86.

39. James Brown,"Turkey's Policy in Flux," *Current History*, January, 1982, p.27.

40. IBRD *Annual Report: 1982*, p.8.

41. Calverley, p.31.

42. "Preparing for the Day When Turkey Can Borrow Again," *Euromoney*, February, 1982, p.15.

43. "Another Year Older and Deeper in Debt," *The Economist*, 6 March, 1982, p.88.

44. "Turkish Banker's Delight," *Euromoney*, December, 1982, p.12.

45. Curtin, "Muldoon," p.70.

46. Gisselquist, p.188.

47. Williamson, pp.54–55.

48. Sampson, p.262.

49. Singer, p.31.

50. McCauley, p.148.

51. B. Cohen, pp.218–219.

52. McCauley, p.148.

53. B. Cohen, p.219.

54. McCauley, p.149.

55. B. Cohen, p.218.

56. Seiber, *International Borrowing*, p.72.

57. Gisselquist, p.23.

58. Seiber, *International Borrowing*, p.24.

59. "Turkish Tea," p.79.

60. Field, Shirref and Ollard, p.37.

61. Williamson, p.35.

62. B. Cohen, p.219.

63. "Global Ripples," pp.74–75.

64. Seiber, *International Borrowing*, pp.91.

65. Sampson, p.262.

66. "Turkey: Back Again," p.77.

67. "How to Sell Garlic, Tractors and Fish," *Euromoney*, February, 1982, p.26.

68. Anne O. Krueger and Baran Tuncer, "An Empirical Test of the Infant Industry Argument," *American Economic Review*, December, 1982, p.1146.

69. Ibid., p.1149.

70. Singer, p.40.

71. "How to Sell," p.26.

72. "Akturk," p.16.

73. "How to Sell," p.28.

74. "Akturk, p.18.

75. Brown, p.13.

76. C.H. Dodd, *Democracy and Development in Turkey* (London: Euthen, 1979), p.15.

77. "How to Sell," p.27.

78. Ibid.

79. Brown, p.26.

80. "Akturk," p.16.

81. Ibid., p.18.

82. "The Road to Capitalism," *Euromoney,* February, 1982, p.4.

83. "Akturk," p.18.

84. "State Enterprises," p.24.

85. Ibid.

86. Ibid., pp.24–25.

87. Ibid, p.24.

88. "Road to Capitalism," p.4.

89. "It Was a Black Economy: Now at Least It Will Be Gray," *Euromoney,* February, 1982, p.22.

90. "Akturk," p.18.

91. Ibid.

92. "Black Economy," p.22.

93. "At Last the Foreign Investor Is Welcome," *Euromoney,* February, 1982 (Spec. Suppl.), p.31.

94. Ibid., pp.31–32.

95. Singer, p.27.

96. O.N. Baburoglu, "Toward a Theory of Stalemated Social Systems: The Turkish Case," in *Dependence and Inequality: A Systems Approach to the Problems of Mexico and Other Developing Countries,* ed. R. Felix Geyer and Johannes van der Zouwen (Oxford: Pergamon, 1982), p.99.

97. Ibid., p.90.

98. B. Cohen, p.219.

99. Singer, p.28.

100. Baburoglu, p.101.

101. Singer, p.29.

102. Brown, p.26.

103. Sampson, p.261.

104. Seiber, *International Borrowing,* p.45.

105. Brown, p.38.

106. Brown, pp.27–37.

Chapter 6

CASE 2: MEXICO

Chronology

When Gustavo Diaz Ordaz selected Luis Echeverria as his successor to the Mexican Presidency, he certainly did not expect that his former protégé would immediately set about reversing the development course followed throughout his administration.[1] From 1964 to 1970, the Ordaz government based its development planning on the "engine of growth" model, stressing rapid modernization of industry through government subsidies to the private sector.[2] Taking office in 1970, Echeverria transformed the previous partnership between government and business into a relationship of competition and mutual enmity.[3] Echeverria's anti-capitalist rhetoric could be dismissed as a cost-free means of broadening his popular base,[4] but it was the President's policy of greater government ownership and control over industry that divided Echeverria from the business community. Echeverria envisioned an enlarged role for the public sector in financing and managing Mexico's industrial plant, with profits from the modern sector being siphoned off by government to support increased social welfare spending. From 1970 to 1975, the government's share of total investment in Mexico grew from one-third to one-half,[5] accompanied by large-scale increases in education, health, housing and rural development outlays.[6]

Echeverria's development strategy and reform programs brought some temporary relief to Mexico's workers and peasants, but from a purely economic standpoint they were ruinous. The public sector deficit expanded from 1 percent of GDP in 1970 to 5 percent in 1975,[7] while the nation's current account deficit multiplied fourfold, from less than $1 billion in 1972 to nearly $4 billion in 1975.[8] The government was unwilling to raise taxes and met public deficits through the artifice of simply printing more money. Consequently, inflation, which had been held to less than 5 percent a year in the early 1970s, spiraled to 11 percent in 1973 and a startling 60 percent in the last six months of 1976.[9] Inflationary forces and the impact of the first oil shock generated an enormous capital flight out of Mexico as investors sought shelter from the domestic storm. Despite his nationalist stripe, Echeverria turned increasingly toward foreign borrowing to finance his lopsided development program. The nation's public external debt climbed from $4.8 billion in 1974[10] to $13.5 billion in 1975 and $20 billion in 1976.[11]

As the summer of 1976 approached, rumors of an imminent massive devaluation created further anxiety in the private sector and propelled capital across the border. In August, 1976, the central banks announced that the traditional privilege of converting pesos into dollars at a fixed exchange rate would be rescinded, the peso was set free, and a devaluation of 42 percent was the outcome. To meet this liquidity crisis, Echeverria received $600 million in assistance from the United States Treasury and a $1.2 billion emergency loan from the IMF.[12] The Fund credit was granted under liberal conditionality, the government pledging to reduce public deficits, cut inflation and limit foreign borrowings.[13] Needless to say, during his last months in office Echeverria did nothing to tarnish his reformer's image, and little concerted adjustment was actually executed.

In December, 1976, Jose Lopez-Portillo assumed the Mexican Presidency, and once again there was a sharp turnabout in public policy. The new President tried to restore harmonious relations between the public and private sectors, downplaying his predecessor's portrayal of Mexico as the natural leader of a militant Third World.[14] Lopez-Portillo had an ace in the hole which the nationalist Echeverria Administration had refused to play, Mexico's vast petroleum resources. Starting in 1976–1977, Mexico's government-owned oil industry increased its production flow enormously.[15] The new government abandoned strict conservation of the country's natural resources and began to use Petroleos Mexicanos (PEMEX), a state-owned oil and gas producer and the chief organization in Mexico's nationalized oil and gas industry, as a new engine of growth for Mexican development. By 1979, "oil was virtually the only factor keeping [the nation's] balance of payments from going completely out of control.[16]

The performance of Mexico's economy in the first half of the Lopez-Portillo regime was mixed. On the one hand, under conditions of crisis management in 1976–1977, Mexico suffered from substantial inflation, continued high rates of unemployment and a GDP growth rate barely equal to that of population growth.[17] On the other hand, from 1976 onward, there was a steep reduction in current account deficits, imports leveling off and exports rising by one third over 1976–1977.[18] In 1978 and 1979, GDP growth accelerated to 7 percent and 8 percent respectively, rates well in excess of population growth.[19]

There was one broad point of continuity between the Echeverria and Lopez-Portillo administrations: fiscal and monetary expansionism. The country's money supply grew by 15 percent in 1976, 29 percent in 1977 and 17 percent in 1978, with consumer inflation running at 29.1 percent, 26.0 percent and 31.0 percent over these years.[20] As the government's commitment to monetary and fiscal austerity evaporated, Lopez-Portillo increased foreign borrowing, so that "foreign credit came to be regarded as a substitute for, rather than as a complement to adjustment." [21]

Inflationary forces and the accumulation of external debt did not deter the Mexican government from continuing its pursuit of rapid economic development. If anything, the pace of development was intensified and its scope widened. In March, 1979, Lopez-Portillo announced a Global Plan for Development for "industrial, agricultural, educational and rural development, under which the government proposed to utilize newly available resources to relieve unemployment and malnutrition and to accelerate the industrial development process." [22] The plan called for the use of Mexican petrodollars to fight a war on two fronts. Oil earnings would be channeled to support industrial development, as under Ordaz, and to support improvements in living conditions, as under Echeverria. Both of these broad objectives could be reduced to a single aim, the creation of employment. [23] The target of the Global Plan was the generation of 4 million new jobs to accommodate Mexico's burgeoning workforce. [24] According to the priorities set under the Global Plan, if full speed ahead meant high levels of inflation, then inflation would simply have to be tolerated until stable growth could be achieved. [25]

The results of the first two years of the Plan were predictably mixed. Growth in GNP averaged an impressive 8 percent a year, [26] with agricultural productivity improving by 6 percent annually. [27] However, despite rapid growth of oil-export earnings, Mexico's balance of trade remained negative. In 1980, the value of manufactured imports ran to $12.6 billion, while manufactured exports reached a level of $3.4 billion, this gap contributing greatly to the year's $6.6 billion current account deficit. [28] Inflation was even greater than expected, averaging 30 percent in 1979, 1980 and 1981. [29] The Mexican workforce, then, experienced a crisis of rising expectations; jobs were more available, paychecks rose in nominal terms, but real wages fell as consumer goods became more expensive. [30] At the same time, under expectations of an even more intense tapping of PEMEX resources, foreign capital streamed into Mexico. The growth of Mexican sovereign debt and annual debt-service requirements is traced in Table 4. Both total sovereign debt and yearly debt service jumped in 1981, reaching $54.4 billion and $13.4 billion respectively. [31] Mexico may have been counting on its petroleum reserves to finance development in the long term, but in the short run it was external capital that was keeping the economy liquid.

The national economy continued on a downhill course throughout 1981, with the confidence of both international and domestic investors moving in the same direction. [32] High dollar interest rates bloated annual debt-service payments, domestic inflation inhibited capital formation, and, unlike most Hi-Income LDCs, Mexico found its balance of trade eroding as a result of declining world oil prices. [33] The government responded with a series of isolated and uncoordinated measures (e.g., import restrictions and budget cuts), but their aggregate effect was minimal. [34] The country's economic leadership publicly acknowledged the

Table 4
Mexican External Debt and Debt Service,
1975–1980

(in $ million)

Year	Total Debt	Debt Service
1975	16,562	2,484
1976	21,568	3,630
1977	26,729	5,210
1978	32,529	7,100
1979	37,607	11,439
1980	43,475	9,257

Source: Adapted from OECD, p. 91.

need for greater adjustment, but a coherent stabilization program was not implemented, largely due to the political unpopularity of reducing growth and consumption.

In April, 1982, the Mexicans encountered a serious setback in an unexpected quarter. The Monterrey-based Grupo Industrial Alfa (ALFA), a highly diversified conglomerate with major holdings in steel, metal and chemical production, "suspended payments on $2.3 billion of debt owed to more than one hundred Mexican and foreign banks."[35] ALFA's collapse was all the more shocking because up until this announcement the firm was a longstanding growth leader on the Mexican stock exchange. As a privately owned corporation, ALFA had been atypically favored by the Echeverria Administration, expanding laterally in the 1970s by moving into diverse industrial activities. ALFA's planners had predicated their company's financial strategy on international interest rates in the range of 10 percent to 12 percent, and were stunned as they continued above 17 percent in 1981.[36] When a self-appointed steering committee of Mexican and American bankers met to consider ALFA's balance sheets, they found its major profit centers on solid ground, with only the more recently acquired, marginal enterprises being beyond redemption.[37] Despite the potential for a resurrection of ALFA, considerable damage had already been done in terms of Mexican credit. Even though the corporation's external debt was not guaranteed by the government, the entire economy suffered from its collapse, Standard & Poor's downgrading the credit rating of the state-controlled NAFINSA (a conglomerate with industrial, agricultural and credit holdings) in the wake of ALFA's bankruptcy.

In April, 1982, the Lopez-Portillo Administration abandoned its piecemeal approach to adjustment in favor of a spartan seventeen-point austerity program.[38] Formulated by Jesus Silva Herzog, the plan resembled the deflationary adjustment programs prescribed by the IMF. The April measures included a commitment to an 8 percent reduction in government spending, a decrease in public deficits from 12.5 percent of GDP to 9.5 percent, and limitations on foreign borrowing.[39] The recessionary nature of the program is evident in its call for a complete halt to government-funded construction (resulting in a loss of 500,000 jobs) and for reserve restrictions on domestic banks leading to interest rates of 55 percent on internal lending.[40]

The stabilization program proved unequal to the task for which it was designed, inflation reaching 60 percent by August, 1982, and the government's deficit actually increasing to 15 percent of GDP.[41] Following a 30 percent devaluation of the peso in February, 1982, and a series of mini-devaluations thereafter, capital fled Mexico under assumptions of an imminent, massive devaluation. These fears intensified on 13 August as the government imposed foreign exchange restrictions and froze all U.S. dollar bank accounts.[42] Simultaneously, Mexico's sovereign debt grew sharply, reaching a total of $80 billion at end-year 1982, with $31 billion due on loans of less than one year, and $25.2 billion owed to American banks.[43] Table 5 reflects the rise of commercial debt as a percentage of total debt and GNP over the years 1978 to 1982.

The nation's sovereign borrowers had come to rely upon commercial financing carrying floating interest rates, and as the banks became reluctant to grant maturities of more than twelve months, the Mexicans accepted short-term credits, creating a distortion of the national debt profile and a bunching of external debt obligations.

The final blow to investor confidence in Mexico's capacity to service its foreign debt as contracted came on 1 September, 1982, when Lopez-Portillo nationalized the nation's private banks and established a complete system of foreign exchange controls.[44] The twin measures caught Mexican bankers and businessmen by surprise since they had always been opposed by Lopez-Portillo's ruling party, the Institutional Revolutionary Party (PRI)[45] This new interventionism was the brainchild of the "nationalist/Marxist radical" Carlos Tello Macias, and its anti-free-market thrust alienated the country's business elite and many government officials, including Silva Herzog, who submitted his resig-

Table 5
Estimated Total Net Floating-Interest Debt for
Mexico, 1978–1982, as a Percentage of (1) Total
Net Debt, and (2) GNP

Year	Total ($ billion)	(1)	(2)
1978	19.9	60	22
1980	32.2	70	20
1982	59.3	78	23

Source: OECD, p. 33.

nation in protest only to have it refused by the President.[46] These moves were based on the President's perception that the largely unregulated Mexican banking system had acted as a conduit for capital flight. He accused the banks of playing a central part in a $39 billion capital outflow from Mexico over three years, with an estimated $16.4 billion winding up as private deposits in Texas banks.[47] While the bankers had not masterminded this outrush, they were instrumental to it; but, ironically, the government itself had contributed to the movement by freezing dollar accounts on 13 August and defreezing them immediately thereafter, prompting investors to make their move abroad before the gates were shut for good.[48]

Lopez-Portillo had previously extended partial treatment to his country's private bankers, allowing them to make financial gains through low-risk intermediations. The banks had enjoyed low interest rates on savings deposits (running at 4.5 percent at the time of nationalization) and high returns on domestic loans. As part of the September decrees, interest rates on savings deposits leaped to 20 percent, rates on loans for productive activities declined and those on borrowings for low-cost housing were reduced by 23 percent.[49] Mexico's economic leaders had repeatedly denied the possibility of exchange controls, Silva Herzog calling such measures unworkable in November, 1981[50] and Lopez-Portillo reiterating this position in April, 1982.[51] The September proclamation mandated a two-tier exchange system for converting pesos into dollars. Exporters, importers of essential goods and companies with large dollar-denominated debts were allowed a preferential rate of fifty pesos to the dollar, a rate of seventy pesos to the dollar being set for all other transactions.[52] Even with special treatment targeted for essential foreign inputs, Mexican plants closed quickly for lack of foreign exchange needed to purchase foreign imports.[53]

Well before formal debt restructuring discussions were begun, Mexico was receiving various forms of emergency assistance from foreign governments and multinational institutions. Mexican authorities worked in close cooperation with American officials throughout the summer of 1982, and the U.S. Federal Reserve's willingness to indirectly lower dollar interest rates at the expense of giving momentum to inflationary forces was, in part, a response to the burdens of heavily indebted LDCs. The Fed's Chairman, Paul Volcker, began to exert influence on American bankers to continue providing Mexico with new credit, reversing the Fed's prior call for prudential handling of country exposure ceilings.[54] The Bank for International Settlements readied $1.85 billion in emergency credits to Mexico, with one-third of the loan being made available prior to the completion of an IMF conditional drawing.

When the IMF convened its annual meeting of member nations in Toronto in September, 1982, its director, Jacques de Larosière, was well aware that Mexican officials were delaying negotiations with the Fund until the last minute. Like Brazil, Mexico had always distinguished itself from other, less creditworthy LDCs by expressing a stand against generalized debt relief.[55] The managing director had to prod Lopez-Portillo and his heir apparent, Miguel de la Madrid Hurtado, into swallowing their objections and contracting an upper-tranche Fund loan with stringent conditionality. On 10 November, 1982, the IMF and the outgoing Lopez-Portillo Administration came to tentative terms. Under the agreement,[56] Mexico undertook a strong dose of IMF deflationary stabilization. In terms of fiscal policy, government budget deficits, running at 16.5 percent of total economic output, were to be reduced to 8.5 percent by 1983 and 3.5 percent in 1985, meaning cuts in social spending, reductions in subsidies to the private sector, a freeze on public sector hiring, tax hikes, tightened credit and increased prices on products from government-owned enterprises. Monetary order would be restored through a reunification of the exchange rate and a major devaluation of the peso.[57] These measures ultimately took form as part of de la Madrid's Program of Economic Reordering, a ten-point austerity package announced shortly after de la Madrid's assumption of the Presidency and followed on 20 December, 1982, by an inevitable 53 percent official devaluation of the peso. In return, the IMF extended a $3.92 billion loan to the Mexican government, thereby fulfilling BIS requirements for disbursement of the remainder of its emergency credit.

Having brought the Mexicans to the bargaining table, de Larosière was now faced with the equally difficult task of bringing the nation's commercial creditors into line. Armed with a broad Mexican "letter of intent" to pursue stabilization, the managing director conferred with money-center bankers at a meeting of the Federal Reserve Bank of New York on 16 November, 1982.[58] The Fund's leadership decided to adopt a new hard line vis-à-vis the bankers to avoid a *de facto* bailout of the banks. The gist of this more militant attitude can be readily understood by looking at the outlines of the deal that de Larosière laid before the bankers. He informed bank representatives that the IMF was discussing an adjustment loan with Mexico, but that no proposal would be submitted to the Fund's board for approval without a firm commitment from commercial lenders to grant new loans to Mexico. Specifically, de Larosière called for a total $6.5 billion reorganization of Mexico's official commercial debt, of which $5 billion was to be refinancing through fresh credits. The Fund set a deadline of 15 December for bank action, underscoring its firm intent and the gravity of Mexico's predicament.[59] Confronting the prospect of rescheduling Mexico's bank debts without pivotal IMF money, expertise and monitoring power, the banks quickly went along with the Fund's demands,[60] completing a "jumbo" loan with Mexico on 3 March, 1983, with Citibank leading 530 others in a $5 billion, six-year loan, albeit at a high margin above LIBOR. More will be said of bank lending policy toward Mexico in the period immediately preceding this rescheduling, but for now it must be stressed that the banks were virtually compelled to play a part in the Fund's plans, their alternative being to go it alone as they had tried to do in Peru six years earlier, i.e., with little chance of success.

Commentary

Mexico differs from most Hi-Income, Non-OPEC LDCs (and all of the other case countries investigated in this book) insofar as it has become a net exporter of oil and gas. According to Mexican officials, the country is the fourth largest producer of oil in the world and the fifth largest producer of natural gas.[61] From 1977 to August, 1982, the Mexican government claimed a twelvefold increase in proven reserves of oil and gas, with PEMEX reporting a tripling of actual production.[62] In September, 1981, Lopez-Portillo announced that Mexico was pumping out an average of 2.5 million barrels of gas daily, one-half of which was exported. He assured the Mexican public that the country's oil resources would not dry up from more intensive exploitation, pointing to proven reserves of 70 billion barrels, probable holdings of 30 billion barrels and potential reserves of 300 billion barrels.[63]

The importance of petroleum to Mexico's economy since 1976 is evident when oil revenues from 1976 ($420 million) are compared with those of 1981 ($13 billion).[64] During the years 1980 to 1982, "more than 50 percent of the earnings" from oil and gas "went to the state via taxes on PEMEX."[65] Because oil is a nationalized industry, "petroleum has transferred resources directly to the public sector as tax revenues,"[66] allowing the government to funnel these monies into development projects, subsidies to private industry and public welfare programs.

A number of analysts have optimistically described Mexico's energy holdings as a panacea for both its external debt and its development capital needs. According to this line of forecasting, the combination of enormous energy holdings, world demand and the country's proximity to U.S. markets makes solution of Mexico's current and future problems virtually assured.[67] An economist calculates that if Mexico "only earmarks 25 billion barrels of oil for export until the end of the century it can pay easily" its accumulated external debts.[68] Another scholar concludes that "a strategy of economic growth for the Mexican economy based on carefully planned policy on oil prices and crude oil exports is possible as shown by simulation results."[69]

Unfortunately, there are serious limitations involved in the country's relying upon oil exports to repay debt and finance further development. First, while Mexican oil production and transport costs are comparatively low, it has taken massive infusions of capital to build production facilities. In 1980, for example, eighty-two banks extended a $2.5 billion syndicated short-term credit to PEMEX, followed the next year by a $1.5 billion loan.[70] In 1977, PEMEX owed a total of $3 billion to its international creditors. By mid–1982 this figure had risen to $20 billion. Repayment of this debt, of course, represents a burden on the economy as a whole, and expanding production will require capital investments of a similar order. Second, if Mexico decides to pump more oil for export, this will contribute to a reduction in price per barrel on world markets.[71] In June, 1981, PEMEX tried to prop up its price on petroleum by $2 per barrel above a weakening market, resulting in $7 billion in oil revenue losses from cancelled contracts as its customers simply went elsewhere. The current oil glut and reduction in demand and price does not bode well for Mexico.[72] An IBRD official surmised in January, 1983, that "if oil falls below $25 a barrel, Mexico would have no choice but to declare a moratorium on its debt."[73]

Then there are the political pressures against the expansion of oil production for export. In 1977, 90 percent of the nation's oil exports were sent to U.S. markets. By 1980, only 60 percent of the nation's oil outflow went to America, Mexican authorities fearing overdependence on U.S. energy markets.[74] Some interests in Mexico oppose any increase in oil exports no matter what their destination, asserting that all production will soon be needed for domestic consumption as the nation's industrial capacity reaches maturity.[75] Other opponents of the government's strategy argue that concentration on capital-intensive oil production "siphons resources away from economic activities that employ far more."[76]

A final set of problems involved in Mexico's reliance upon oil and gas to provide capital for its needs comprises what has come to be called the "oil syndrome." The syndrome involves the acceleration of inflation as foreign exchange receipts from oil exports flow into the country, "accompanied by growing external dependence and internal economic disorder."[77] "Petrolization," as it is alternatively known, typically results in the growth of capital and luxury imports, foreign indebtedness, public deficits, inflation, and skewed income distribution,[78] the gush of oil money distracting rather than reinforcing national economic development efforts. Bottlenecks arise as increased production must be accommodated and growing volumes of imports distributed, with human resource and infrastructural shortages being most severe.[79] Indeed, Mexico's ports and railroads are already showing signs of strain with increased oil transport and import inflow.[80] Many doubt that oil exchange earnings can be absorbed quickly enough into domestic investment "before they generate an uncontrollable domestic inflation," and, according to Robert Looney, oil's inflationary potential jeopardizes the country's import-substitution policy (and employment related to import-substitution) and carries the further danger of leading to volatile disturbances in the peso's exchange rate.[81] Mexico's vulnerability to the oil syndrome has prompted analogies between its current situation and that of Iran and Venezuela in the late 1970s, and while there are objections to such parallels,[82] oil revenues are both a potential boon and a danger, depending on how Mexico manages them as part of a balanced development strategy.

The size and role of the public sector are other features of the Mexican economy directly connected to its accumulation of external debt and its ability to meet foreign loan obligations. Since the late 1960s, the Mexican government has gained control over key economic sectors—including oil, electricity, communications, transport, basic industries and a portion of the financial sector—through the convenient vehicle of nationalization.[83] In Richard Weinert's interpretation, this process has been largely pre-emptive, guided by the perceived need to inhibit MNC penetration of the Mexican economy.[84] Aside from direct state ownership of critical industries, the government has taken an activist stance in regulating both the country's internal and external economies. While there has been a shift toward export-promotion since the mid–1960s, increased exports, mainly of oil and gas, have been paired with continued import-substitution and the protection of domestic producers from foreign competition.[85] Generous subsidies were provided by the Mexican government to private industry and agriculture, as well as to state-run enterprises. Subway fares of one peso were charged for services costing the state seven to forty pesos to finance, while the domestic price of gasoline was artificially kept to fifty-five cents a gallon before April, 1982.[86] All of this contributed to intolerable public deficits and levels of inflation, as inadequate tax revenues were supplemented by external borrowings and undisciplined expansions of the money supply.[87] When the details of the IMF's 1982 accord with Mexico were revealed to commercial creditors, they were not impressed by the target figures, reasoning that a government which "overspends announced budgets by as much as 30 percent a year" will not change its profligate ways even at the risk of non-compliance with Fund conditions and the accompanying sanctions.[88] With Tello playing a central role on de la Madrid's economic team, increased state intervention and deficit spending became even more likely. As to the new President himself, de la Madrid's initial statements as President included a strong commitment to state development planning as a "revolutionary task," and a warning that control of inflation must be kept subordinate to the achievement of growth in the government's hierarchy of priorities.[89]

As in most Latin American developing countries, direct investment has had, and continues to have, considerable influence on the shape of Mexico's economy and public economic policy. American direct investment alone in Mexico now totals in excess of $7 billion,[90] with $1.4 billion of U.S. direct investment flowing into Mexico during 1981.[91] Weinert explains the inordinate leverage of MNCs in Mexico thus: "Foreign firms account for 35 per cent of total industrial production and represent 45 per cent of the share of capital of the 290 largest firms. The influence of foreign capital is magnified because it is mostly found in sectors dominated by a few firms."[92] He goes on to describe how this focused MNC investment can thwart the government's purposes: "A Mexican subsidiary may not respond to local market conditions, but may orient production patterns to the global needs of its multinational parent."[93] If this occurs, state economic objectives can be frustrated as foreign firms fail to respond to the signals of state policies. The Mexican government has carved out strategic sectors in which MNCs cannot operate (e.g., oil, transport, communication), and in 1973, the nationalist Echeverria Administration enacted a Law to Promote Mexican Investment and Regulate Foreign Investment, under which "all new companies [must] have at least 51 percent Mexican capital irrespective of activity."[94] Recently this proviso has hamstrung co-financing between Mexican investors and MNCs as the latter "can't find a Mexican company able to ante up its share of the initial capital"[95] given the country's dry domestic credit markets.

The structure of the nation's industrial sector also displays shortcomings pertinent to its economic performance and capacity to repay foreign borrowings. The government has been an indispensable ally to private industry in its competition with MNCs, but, charge left-wing critics, it has also supported the industrialists in their disputes with Mexican workers.[96] Combined with protectionist trade barriers to foster import-substitution, Mexico's development strategy has favored capital-intensive industrial modernization and has "biased the structure of production away from more labor-intensive products."[97] Oil revenues have been used by the government to finance industries having minimal labor input requirements, of which oil itself is a prime example.[98] This bias was written into the 1979 National Industrial Development Plan, which continued to downplay labor-intensive, "inefficient" industry.[99]

There are at least five other problems that have emerged in Mexico's approach to industrial development. First, reliance on domestic markets has resulted in plants which are too small to realize the economies of scale necessary to compete on world markets. Second, there has been a heavy spatial concentration on industrial activity in the regions of Monterrey, Guadalajara and the Valley of Mexico.[100] Efforts to spread industry more evenly across the nation have been impeded by the small size of population centers in outlying areas, making assimilation of large industrial centers into existing towns costly and disruptive.[101] Third, production has been concentrated on finished, durable consumer goods without a corresponding development of processing facilities for intermediate products, and with raw materials utilized as export commodities.[102] Fourth, in the 1960s and 1970s, "industrial production output was concentrated in a few enterprises, including foreign-owned companies. Small and medium sized manufacturing firms operated under unduly high costs and were neglected by government policy. They had insufficient access to bank credit and used little modern technology."[103] Under this arrangement government-controlled industries and private oligopolies thrived, while small- and medium-sized firms folded, leading to a reduction in competition and greater disparities in wealth and income distribution. Lastly, as *dependencia* critics contend, the capital-intensive industrial development mode has made the country "too dependent on other countries for capital goods, especially new technology and financial assistance.[104]

If the government has tended to treat the modern industrial sector as a pampered or spoiled infant, it has handled the agrarian sector as it would a poor stepchild or worse. Mexico suffers from intractable land tenure and farm production difficulties,[105] with successive governments adopting a passive, trickledown approach to agricultural development.[106]

Agriculture is surely the weak link in any chain of integrated development policies in Mexico. The National Industrial Plan itself points out that a doubling of public sector investment between 1977 and 1982 will barely arrest the decline in agricultural output, and if that output grows no faster than the 3 percent minimum rate projected in the Plan, food imports will require 20 percent of petroleum export revenues in 1982 and 54 percent in 1990.[107]

With the country's population growth rate remaining high, if somewhat reduced from a decade ago, Mexico's food requirements are enormous. When droughts hit the nation's farmers, as in 1980 food must be imported to make up for a widening in the "food deficit," so that in 1980 imports of food grain were two and one-half times as large as those of the previous year.[108] Advances in agricultural production, e.g., the Green Revolution, have been chiefly in the form of irrigation and infrastructure construction, benefitting the latifundia and middle classes, while measures like seed improvement, which would benefit small landholders as well as large, have been overlooked.[109] All in all, the pace of Mexico's national economic development has been impressive, but it has also been seriously unbalanced and, as such, unable to function as the basis for self-sustained growth. Mexico has borrowed heavily to finance rapid industrial modernization, and now the drawbacks of this developmental model constrain the country's capacity and political will to repay its foreign loans.

Petroleum exports are the axle of Mexico's economic development plans, and they have also served as a powerful magnet attracting foreign capital into the country. Commercial lenders have viewed Mexican oil reserves as a welcome variation on the Hi-Income LDC pattern of enormous energy import costs. Even before Lopez-Portillo unleashed the nation's petroleum power in 1976, foreign creditors saw "exceptional economic potential" in Mexico.[110] Mexico has rich mineral resources, including silver, copper, sulfur and zinc deposits, a young and willing workforce, and a large domestic market.[111] The Mexican economy has experienced an "average real growth over the last thirty years of about 6 percent a year compounded, while the U.S. economy was growing at 3.2 percent annually."[112] In fact, as a Wharton forecast summarized in 1981, Mexico's growth has been too rapid, the economy being like a "grossly overloaded truck going uphill."[113] Nevertheless, along with its natural and human resources, the pace of Mexico's economic growth imbued international bankers with strong confidence in the nation's future.

In the course of less than two years, late 1979 to mid-1981, commercial lenders did a complete about-face in their attitude toward sovereign borrowing by Mexico. In late 1979, the government-owned conglomerate NAFINSA received a syndicated Euroloan at a margin of a mere one-quarter percent over LIBOR, while other government-guaranteed borrowers enjoyed similar soft terms on their bank loans.[114] As late as 1981, keen-edged bankers were exhorting Mexican borrowers not to be overly cautious in their assumption of foreign credit, and they permitted public and private debtors to refinance loans made in the mid-1970s at reduced spreads.[115] As the summer of 1981 approached, however, rising dollar interest rates and plunging global oil prices raised Mexico's debt-service charges by $2.5 billion,[116] and investor confidence in the Mexican economy began to wane. Margins on sovereign loans rose and syndications became more difficult. As the months passed, PEMEX was able to negotiate a $2 billion jumbo on the Euroloan market at seven-eighths percent over LIBOR or the U.S. prime rate (lender's option), and National Financiera received a $1.2 billion Eurocredit at five-eighths percent above LIBOR. The decline of Mexico's credit rating became apparent as the Mexican Republic itself sought commercial financing. Eventually the United Mexican States' (UMS) jumbo of $2.5 billion was clubbed together by the Bank of America, but terms stiffened to 1 percent over LIBOR for the first three years of the loan and 1 $1/2$ percent for the remaining seven years.[117] In the words of a Bank of America official, "syndication went like a stone,"[11];8 with regionals backing away and money-center lead banks being forced to "hold the baby." The natural question that lead bankers and Mexican authorities asked of the reluctant regionals was why they had participated in the PEMEX syndication and then shied away from the UMS loan a few weeks later. "Country exposure ceilings" was the most common answer to this inquiry, many regionals asserting that the PEMEX participation effectively disallowed additional loans to any Mexican borrower.[119] It was apparent, though, that the regionals had altered their perception of Mexican public loans as a credit risk, and the scales had tipped to Mexico's disfavor. De Larosière realized that this change had taken place, and knowing that "a radical cut-off of funds," from banks to Mexico "could produce an uncontrollable social reaction,"[120] he forced banks with substantial Mexican loans to continue providing credits. Some conservative European bankers had eluded the Fund's grip by previously limiting their Mexican exposures, the Germans and Swiss being particularly pessimistic about Mexico's immediate prospects.[121] Whether sovereign Mexican borrowers can obtain more jumbos from private creditors beyond the $5 billion extended as a result of the IMF squeeze is problematical. If they are able to negotiate fresh commercial funds, however, there is no doubt that a high price will be paid, with spreads of 2 $1/2$ percent to 3 percent above LIBOR being mentioned as minima for future borrowings.[122]

As a major LDC borrower, Mexico is one of the developing countries in which a few banks have a great deal at stake. In 1982, American banks were reported to hold around 70 percent of the country's total external debt,[123] with Japanese banks running second among Mexico's creditors. The Bank of America, for example, had a total of $3 billion in its Mexican portfolio,[124] and of the $13 billion in Mexican Euroloans in 1981, 37 percent were led or co-led by the Bank of America.[125] Among the Japanese, the Bank of Tokyo, Fuji Bank, Dai-Ichi Kangyo Bank and Sumitomo Bank each have more than $1 billion in Mexican loans, with the Bank of Tokyo having 80 percent of its equity at risk in Mexico.[126]

There are two facets of Mexico's debt profile that intensify commercial risk in Mexican loans. First, the accumulation of purely private debt has been largely uncontrolled,[127] with ballpark estimates of private external debt running at $35 billion to $40 billion.[128] More substantially, Mexico's government-guaranteed foreign debt is concentrated in short-term credits, shorter maturities being one risk reduction tactic adopted by commercial lenders since mid–1981. "Loans maturing in less than one year increased from 5 percent of Mexico's public debt in 1980 to 22 percent at the end of 1982," [129] with banks extending loans of six and three months to sovereign borrowers for balance of payments purposes. [130] Astoundingly, as of November, 1982 (the time of rescheduling), the country's debt-service ratio was calculated at 1:110 to 1:130, [131] making it impossible for Mexico to meet its foreign loan obligations without debt restructuring. The very policies that lenders adopted to limit risks in Mexican loans, (e.g., hard terms and short maturities) have placed inordinate pressures on the nation's debt-service schedule.

Whenever Mexican officials have been asked about the overrapid pace of national economic development, they have invariably pointed to Mexico's most essential natural resource, its people. How can development be slowed, they ask, when growth is necessary to accommodate rapid increases in Mexico's population? Strides have been made in decelerating the rate of population expansion by inhibiting fertility rates. "The population policy adopted in 1973–1974 has been successful. . . . the rate of population increase, which reached 3.6 percent, dropped to 2.6 percent in 1980; the goal for 1990 is an annual growth rate of 1.0 percent." [132] Fertility rates have been reduced, but Mexico's total populace, now numbering some 70 million, will nonetheless reach 100 million by the year 2000, and all of these people must be housed, fed, clothed, educated and put to work. [133] The country's age demography makes these needs all the more immediate. Between 1950 and 1970 the median age in Mexico declined by two years to 16.6 years, and by 1970 "about 47 percent of the population was below 15 years of age." [134] This bunching in population growth has swelled the Mexican labor force to an all-time high. Lacking expansion of economic opportunities through rapid development, two interrelated phenomena would be likely to occur. First, while there are no satisfactory unemployment figures for Mexico, it is apparent from the flow of illegal immigrants into the United States that jobs have not kept pace with the growth of the workforce. This is true of both unskilled and skilled labor, for "growth in private employment opportunities during the Echeverria period did not match the rapid increase in university graduates." [135] Mexico's jobless graduates represent a hotbed for revolutionary sentiment, their frustrations bearing latent extremism. Second, without more economic opportunities through expansionary policies, existing income disparities will be exacerbated. As of 1980, "nearly 10 percent of [Mexico's] population enjoyed 40 percent of the national income, while the lowest 40 percent of the population earned barely 10 percent of the national income." [136] This figure for the bottom rung is lower than the "expected" 11.5 percent figure, and is less than that of every other Latin American country with the exceptions of Honduras, Peru and Brazil. [137] Once again, these inequalities represent a potential powderkeg, and Mexican officials must think several times over before taking a deflationary approach to adjustment, whether or not the Fund, industrial governments and the banks insist upon it.

The current President, Miguel de la Madrid, was the former Budget and

Planning Secretary and was hand-picked by Lopez-Portillo to be his successor, according to the modern Mexican custom "to ensure the survival of the party to which they [both] belong," the PRI.[138] This mode of presidential succession is vulnerable to radical swings in executive policy and style, for having watched quietly from the wings, the PRI's selected candidate is more than "ready to play his own game" when his turn comes.[139] The power structure of the Mexican government certainly affords him the means to do so: government power in Mexico is centered in the executive branch, and power within the executive branch is concentrated in the Presidency. Elected for a six-year term, with no re-election being permitted, the Mexican President has unlimited powers of appointment and removal over federal, state and local offices as well as those in the military. He is in complete control of foreign policy, and the instrumentality of executive decree allows him to take extra-constitutional measures in dictating domestic affairs. The Mexican legislature is virtually a "rubber stamp" organ; the judiciary is chosen by executive appointment.[140]

Along with being President, Mexico's Chief Executive functions as the leader of the largest and most important political group in Mexico, the Institutional Revolutionary Party (PRI). In its five decades of existence, the PRI has always maintained control of the federal government and has never lost a state election. Described as more of an "octopus" than a political party, the PRI's membership encompasses all shades of ideological opinion, from right-wing neo-Fascism to left-wing neo-Marxism. The Party has four pillars of support: the National Campensinos representing the peasants, the Mexican Workers Federation, the middle-class National Federation of Popular Organizations, and the military.[141] Of late, however, fractures have begun to appear in the PRI's monolithic hold over the Mexican polity. Conflicts between industrialists and workers have emerged,[142] as have antagonisms between rural and urban regions.[143] "In 1978, in a move designed to ease social pressures and democratize the process, Lopez-Portillo legalized opposition parties, among them the Partido Communista de Mexico (PCM) and the Partido Democrata Mexicano (PDM)."[144] Legalization of opposition parties was seen as a way of enhancing the PRI's own legitimacy and of fragmenting ideologically diverse opponents. However, the recent merger of four left-wing parties has strengthened resistance to the PRI's supremacy,[145] and whether it will maintain its record of uninterrupted electoral victories is now very much in doubt.

Foreign policy has also influenced Mexico's handling of development and external debt. The overarching reality of Mexican foreign policy is its "special relationship" with the United States. Mexico lives in the shadow of the giant to the north, the relationship between the two nations often being cynically compared to that of a rider and his horse.[146] Mexico has attempted to gradually get out from under the sway of the United States. It has limited oil exports to "no more than half of the total going to any single country,"[147] and no nation may acquire more than 20 percent of its oil and gas supplies from PEMEX.[148] These provisions were intended to prevent overdependence on a single export market, to reduce the rationale for American interference in Mexican policy and to show the Americans that Mexico is a country, not an oil well. Both Lopez-Portillo and de la Madrid have rejected President Reagan's call for the establishment of a North American Common Market, having no doubts about just who would be the majority partner in such an arrangement.[149] The Mexican government has taken a strong stand against "dangerous" American interventionism in Central America,[150] and has supported Nicaragua's Sandinista government.[151] Despite its prior "count-me-out" posture on generalized debt relief, Mexico has assumed an active role as a leader of the Third World, co-chairing the October, 1981, North/South summit meeting in Cancun and endorsing the concept of a New International Economic Order.[152] The country's ties to the United States remain necessarily strong. The United States government has acknowledged its interest in the resolution of Mexico's debt crisis, extending emergency credits, easing monetary policy and prodding American banks to continue their Mexican lending. Mexico, paradoxically, has tried to use American bank money and oil export receipts from U.S. markets to finance its development plans, one objective of which is increased independence from American economic and political influence.

Notes

1. Alan Robinson, "Will Mexico's New President Match Lopez Portillo?" *Euromoney*, April 1982 (Latin American Survey), p.27.

2. B. Cohen, p.204.

3. A. Robinson, "Mexico's New President," p.27.

4. Richard S. Weinert, "The State and Foreign Capital," in *Authoritarianism in Mexico*, ed. Jose Luis Reyna and Richard S. Weinert (Philadelphia: Institute for the Study of Human Issues, 1977), p.126.

5. B. Cohen, p.204.

6. Victor L. Urquidi, "Not by Oil Alone: The Outlook for Mexico," *Current History*, February, 1982, p.79.

7. B. Cohen, p.204.

8. James H. Street, "Mexico's Economic Development Plan," *Current History*, November, 1981, p.375.

9. Ibid.

10. Ibid.

11. B. Cohen, p.205.

12. Street, p.375.

13. B. Cohen, p.205.

14. A. Robinson, "Mexico's New President," p.27.

15. Urquidi, p.79.

16. B. Cohen, p.206.

17. Urquidi, p.79.

18. B. Cohen, p.205.

19. Urquidi, p.79.

20. B. Cohen, p.207.

21. Ibid., pp.208–209.

22. Street, p.374.

23. Alexander Stuart, "Opportunity Knocks in Troubled Mexico," *Fortune*, 23 August, 1982, p.151.

24. A. Robinson, "End of Illusion," p.86.

25. Stuart, p.151.

26. Nicholas Asheshov, "What's Ahead for Mexican Borrowing," *Institutional Investor*, November, 1981, p.308.

27. A. Robinson, "Latin America's Economies," p.16.

28. George W. Grayson, "Oil and Politics in Mexico," *Current History*, November, 1981, p.380.

29. A. Robinson, "End of Illusion," p.80.

30. IBRD, *Annual Report: 1982*, p.90.

31. OECD, pp.46–47.

32. Donal Curtin, "The Mexican Shokku," *Euromoney*, November, 1982, p.116.

33. Alan Robinson, "Portillo Pockets the Banks," *Euromoney*, October, 1982, p.48.

34. A. Robinson, "End of Illusion," p.96.

35. Stuart, p.151.

36. Alan Robinson, "The Position of ALFA is Delicate, Delicate, Delicate," *Euromoney*, June, 1982, p.47.

37. Ibid., p.44.

38. Stuart, pp.148–152.

39. A. Robinson, "End of Illusion," p.82.

40. Ibid., p.78.

41. Stuart, p.148.

42. A. Robinson, "End of Illusion," p.77.

43. Kenneth N. Gilpin, "The Maze of Latin America's Debt," *The New York Times*, 13 March, 1983, p.D–1.

44. A. Robinson, "Portillo Pockets," p.47.

45. Ibid.

46. Ibid., p.48.

47. A. Robinson, "End of Illusion," p.82.

48. Ibid., p.80.

49. A. Robinson, "Portillo Pockets," pp.50–51.

50. Asheshov, p.310.

51. A. Robinson, "End of Illusion," p.82.

52. A. Robinson, "Portillo Pockets," p.51.

53. Ibid., p.53.

54. Field, Shirref and Ollard, p.40.

55. Stephen D. Cohen, p.65.

56. Egan, p.29.

57. Pine, p.56.

58. Field, Shirref and Ollard, p.38.

59. Ibid.

60. Pine, p.56.

61. Stuart, p.146.

62. Ibid., p.148.

63. Grayson, p.379.

64. Stuart, p.150.

65. A. Robinson, "End of Illusion," p.80.

66. Urquidi, p.80.

67. Ibid., p.78.

68. A. Robinson, "Portillo Pockets," p.53.

69. Francisco Carrada-Bravo, *Oil, Money, and the Mexican Economy: A Macro-econometric Analysis* (Boulder: Westview, 1982).

70. Street, p.376.

71. Stuart, p.148.

72. Dod, p.104.

73. Gilpin, p.D-2.

74. Street, p.374.

75. Ibid., p.377.

76. Grayson, p.379.

77. Street, p. 374.

78. Grayson, p.379.

79. Urquidi, p.81.

80. Street, p.389.

81. Robert E. Looney, *Development Alternatives of Mexico: Beyond the 1980s* (New York: Praeger, 1982), pp.242–243.

82. Street, p.390.

83. Weinert, p.110.

84. Ibid., p.124.

85. Adriaan ten Kate and Robert Bruce Wallace, *Protection and Economic Development in Mexico* (New York: St. Martin's, 1980), p.261.

86. Stuart, p.153.

87. Looney, p.210.

88. Stuart, p.154.

89. A. Robinson, "Portillo Pockets," p.48.

90. Stuart, p.146.

91. A. Robinson, "Latin American's Economics," p.15.

92. Weinert, p.115.

93. Ibid., p.109.

94. Ibid., p.120.

95. Stuart, p.150.

96. Weinert, p.125.

97. Joel Bergsman, *Income Distribution and Poverty in Mexico.* World Bank Staff Paper No. 395 (Washington: IBRD, 1980), p.39.

98. Looney, p.239.

99. Street, p.376.

100. Ibid.

101. Urquidi, p.90.

102. Street, p.376.

103. Urquidi, p.78.

104. Street, p.376.

105. Urquidi, p.76.

106. Looney, p.235.

107. Ibid., pp.236–237.

108. Street, p.375.

109. Bergsman, p.32.

110. B. Cohen, p.204.

111. Stuart, p.151.

112. Ibid., p.148.

113. A. Robinson, "End of Illusion," p.84.

114. "As Debt Grows, the Economy Grows Faster," *Euromoney*, March, 1981, p.22.

115. Ibid., p.21.

116. A. Robinson, "End of Illusion," p.82.

117. Ibid., p.84.

118. "Vintage Deals of the Year," *Euromoney*, September, 1982, p.299.

119. Ibid., p.300.

120. Grant, "Stuffees Have Left," p.35.

121. A. Robinson, "End of Illusion," p.78.

122. Gilpin, p.D-1.

123. Stuart, p.148.

124. Ibid., p.150.

125. "Lead Managers of Loans to Latin America," *Euromoney*, April, 1982 (Latin American Survey), p.5.

126. Curtin, p.113.

127. Asheshov, p.30.

128. Lim, "The Big Shift," p.21.

129. Stuart, p.152.

130. A. Robinson, "End of Illusion," p.84.

131. Grant "Stuffees Have Left," p.36.

132. Urquidi, p.81.

133. Ibid., p.90.

134. Bergsman, p.31.

135. Street, p.388.

136. Urquidi, p.78.

137. Bergsman, p.17.

138. A. Robinson, "Mexico's New President," p.27.

139. Ibid.

140. Ibid., p.30.

141. Ibid.

142. Ibid., p.29.

143. Looney, p. 239.

144. James L. Schlagheck, *The Political, Economic and Labor Climate in Mexico* (Philadelphia: Wharton School of Economics, 1979), p.152.

145. Robinson, "Mexico's New President," p.27.

146. Susan Kaufman Purcell, "Mexico-U.S. Relations: Big Initiatives Can Cause Big Problems," *Foreign Affairs*, Winter, 1981–1982, p.383.

147. Street, p.390.

148. Grayson, p.380.

149. Street, p.391.

150. A. Robinson, "Mexico's New President," p.29.

151. Carlos A. Astiz, "Changing United States Policy in Latin America," *Current History*, February, 1982, p.49.

152. Grayson, p.393.

Chapter 7

CASE 3: BRAZIL

Chronology

The much-heralded "Brazilian miracle" of the late 1960s and early 1970s had its origin in the 1964 military overthrow of the João Goulart Administration and the replacement of civilian government by a series of military-backed regimes. The combination of high inflation rates and stagnating economic growth was a principal factor motivating the army's coup,[1] and when the Humberto de Aloncar Branco government came to power, the appointment of Roberto Campos as Brazil's chief economic policy-maker signaled a marked change from the past. Campos went immediately to work at combating inflationary forces, indexing worker's wages to price rises on consumer goods.[2] His prescription to cure inadequate economic growth was based on a highly defensive import-substitution strategy. From 1960 to 1966, imported inputs as a share of manufactured goods declined from 10.8 percent to 7.5 percent.[3] The so-called Law of Similars practically eliminated imports by public sector and subsidized private sector firms.[4] The approach had the acknowledged side-effect of raising input costs for the production of tradeables, thereby inhibiting the growth of Brazilian exports. In conjunction with tax disincentives on exports, this strategy led to rapid internal growth, but then encountered an intractable barrier as domestic markets could no longer absorb the expanded production from the nation's protected enterprises.[5]

Lacking popular support, the Brazilian government was under profound pressure to use economic performance as a legitimizing device.[6] The Branco Administration was retired by Brazil's "real" political leadership, i.e., the military and intelligence communities. Artur Costa e Silva was selected as the nation's nominal President, while Campos was succeeded by his former protégé, Brazil's "Great Planner," Delfim Neto.[7] It was under Neto's direction that the Brazilian economy achieved its "miracle," the phenomenon of expansionary stabilization.[8] Neto maintained the protectionist edifice erected by Campos, but his approach to national economic development was two-pronged. In Neto's plan, import-substitution would be used in conjunction with export-promotion. The economy would be opened up to foreign direct investment and autonomous flows of external capital, and the state would play a central activist role in the orchestration of economic growth. Export-promotion would be implemented through the elimination of tax discrimination against exports, relaxation of trade barriers on imports required as inputs for export production, and direct subsidies to exporters. This fiscal thrust would be accompanied by the unification of the Brazilian exchange rate and a series of gradual mini-devaluations.[9]

Judged purely from the standpoint of economic growth, Neto's program worked wonders. According to one estimate, economic growth in Brazil over the period 1967 to 1973 averaged 10 percent annually,[10] while another calculation sets the pace of growth at 14 percent a year.[11] Even as the "miracle" unfolded, however, the vulnerabilities of Neto's approach became evident. Heavy investment was made by the state in capital-intensive manufacturing, e.g., automotive and agrarian technology production.[12] This intensive pattern of industrial development created an ongoing reliance upon imported energy, materials and capital goods, and, of course, the foreign exchange requisite for their purchase.[13] Moreover, as Neto was to inform IBRD President Robert S. McNamara, his intention for Brazil's economy was to "take off or bust," emphasizing pure growth over social welfare, and plainly stating that "when that is achieved we can worry about fairer shares."[14]

The year 1974 marked the end of Brazil's first "miracle," a hiatus in Neto's career, and the impact of the first oil shock on the country's energy-intensive industrialization program. Under the new military-supported President, Ernesto Geisel, Neto was pushed aside, and a new economic overlord, Mario Henrique Simonsen, was put in charge of the nation's development policy.[15] Inflation had risen from 13 percent in 1972–1973 to 28 percent in 1974, with the cost of oil imports growing by one-third and that of chemical, metal and capital goods imports increasing by two-thirds.[16] Simonsen began a modest stabilization program, accelerating the crawling peg (a "managed" floating exchange rate, pegged to market values of a country's currency through a series of frequent, gradual changes in the "official" exchange rate of the currency), raising tariffs on non-essential consumer imports and imposing a 100 percent duty on imported petroleum. These belt-tightening exercises soon lapsed as government candidates in the November, 1974, senatorial elections won by unexpectedly slim margins.[17] Chafing under Simonsen's brand of adjustment, the Brazilian polity expressed its displeasure in such limited fashion as was allowed. Simonsen's program took on a stop-and-go pattern, as adjustment alternated with more popular expansionist policies.[18]

Simonsen's Second Five Year Development Plan (1975–1979), issued in 1974, contained measures designed to balance economic development, including a call for greater diversification of agricultural exports.[19] The Plan still focused on aggregate growth through industrial modernization, targets of 10 percent yearly GDP growth and 12 percent annual increases in manufacturing being set as its chief priorities. Actual growth of GDP fell far below these expectations, running at 5.7 percent in 1975, 9. percent in 1976, 4.7 percent in 1977 and 6. percent in 1978.[20] Simultaneously, monetary and fiscal discipline by the Brazilian government was relegated to secondary status. "The money base grew by 27 percent between June, 1975 and June, 1976, while Federal government expenditures in the first half of 1976 were 81 percent higher than in the first half of 1975."[21]

Not only was the Brazilian government spending and printing more money; it was borrowing greater sums of external capital to finance structural adjustments and maintain current levels of consumption.[22] Much of the international banking community remained leery of Brazil's unorthodox expansion, but some venturesome bankers, like Citibank's Walter Wriston, expressed their enthusiasm by enlarging their Brazilian loan portfolios. Table 6 illustrates the growth of Brazil's public external debt, debt service and the amounts of debt and debt service owing to commercial lenders over the period 1975–1980.

Three points of paramount importance are revealed in these figures: while total debt was growing, total debt service was increasing even faster; commercial debt was increasing as a share of total debt; and debt service on commercial loans reached an extremely high proportion of total annual external debt obligations.[23] Brazil was borrowing more from foreigners, and floating-rate bank loans were becoming the predominant form of external credit.

In 1979, Geisel's "term" as Brazil's President came to an end and João Baptista Figueiredo was selected by the military/intelligence cadre as the country's new chief executive. Figueiredo immediately called Delfim Neto back to government.[24] Neto's return led to an inevitable showdown between the Great Planner, with his go for broke strategy, and Simonsen, with his stop-and-go hedging approach.[25] Neto dismissed his rival's call for credit and fiscal restrictions, propounding that the country's annual 2.7 percent population growth rate demanded abandonment of the go-slow tactics advocated by Simonsen.[26] In-

Table 6
Brazilian External Debt and Debt Service, 1975–1980
(in $ million)

Year	Total Debt	Total Debt Service	Commercial Debt	Commercial Debt Service
1975	22,750	3,988.5	15,076	2,684.9
1976	27,620	5,009.1	17,774	3,529.4
1977	33,480	6,357.3	22,135	4,721.9
1978	45,266	8,375.1	31,421	6,098.3
1979	50,786	11,415.2	35,276	8,853.7
1980	56,980	13,739.9	39,139	11,009.6

Source: OECD, p. 58.

stead, Neto proposed a highly unconventional expansionary program, combining cheap credit with strict government control over exchange rates and internal pricing.[27] Figueiredo and his backstage masters were impressed by Neto's ambitious plans, and in mid–1979 they shelved Simonsen and returned Neto to power.[28] Indeed, Neto would have far greater control than Simonsen had wielded, virtually all development planning being concentrated in the office of this single economic czar.[29]

Neto's primary concern was the downturn in Brazil's balance of trade and the corresponding rise in its debt-service ratio. As of 1979, three-fourths of the nation's foreign exchange export receipts were required to service external debt,[30] and even greater export volumes were needed to compensate for a worsening in terms of trade between Brazil, on the one hand, and the industrialized and OPEC nations, on the other.[31] He set into motion a concerted export drive in late 1979, resulting in a 33 percent growth of exports for 1980 and a further increase of 20 percent in 1981.[32] The Brazilian government linked this latest assault on world markets with Neto's first miracle, noting that in ten years Brazil's exports had risen by 500 percent, while manufactured exports had grown by 1,000 percent.[33] With imports running at 3.8 percent below the previous year,[34] the nation's export campaign led to a remarkable reversal in its trade position, moving from a current account deficit of $2.8 billion in 1980 to a surplus of $1.2 billion in 1981. Equally impressive, the export drive was carried out on a broad front, with manufactured goods accounting for one-half of total export revenues, and with capital goods,[35] automotive products and technological exports posting enormous gains.[36] The Brazilians also diversified their export markets, shifting away from North America and Western Europe and toward the developing Third World.[37] In fact, by 1981 fully 40 percent of all Brazil's exports were destined for markets in Latin America, Africa and the Middle East.[38] Neto used an entire arsenal of export-promotion measures,[39] direct subsidies to exporters, tax breaks and frequent mini-devaluations to enhance competitiveness while minimizing exchange rate uncertainty.[40]

As Brazil's external economy boomed, the internal sector languished. The year 1981 was the first in three decades in which GDP did not increase at all.[41] Indeed, industrial production declined by 9.3 percent, and, in contrast to manufactured tradeables, world demand for Brazil's export commodities plunged. The government was forced into a radical drawdown on its reserves, foreign exchange stockpiles plummeting in year 1980 from $12 billion to $6.9 billion.[42] The growth at any cost development strategy had also fueled inflationary fires, with rates growing far faster than those forecast by Neto. Consumer inflation rose from 40.8 percent in 1978 to 72.2 percent in 1979 and to 110.2 percent in 1980 before "stabilizing" at just below 100 percent in 1981.[43]

The course taken by Brazil's economy piqued the interest of international commercial creditors. Neto's reincarnation proved a seminal event in the massive expansion of commercial loans to Brazil. He may have been an unorthodox capitalist, but his maverick style was highly compatible with that of competitive bankers seeking to recycle the great quantities of OPEC petrodollars flowing into their treasuries. Neto's liberalization of the Brazilian economy and his specific call for increased external capital flows was irresistible for the bankers.[44] In 1979, American and Western European bankers extended a twelve-year, $1.2 billion commercial loan to finance Neto's energy-substitution Proalcool project at a margin of less than 1 percent over LIBOR.[45] The Brazilians encouraged skeptical German and Japanese bankers to join their fellows, offering high spreads for medium-term loans,[46] margins reaching a record 2 percent above LIBOR in 1980–1981.[47] As base interest continued near 20 percent, sporadic efforts were made to curb new borrowings, but floating-interest loans affected the country's entire stock of accumulated commercial debt. Table 7 provides an accounting of the rise of Brazil's sovereign net floating-interest debt as a percentage of total public net debt and as a percentage of GNP over the period 1978–1982. Interest payments alone had risen from a yearly average of $437 million in 1972–1973 to $6.3 billion in 1980 and $9.2 billion in 1981, interest charges coming to exceed amortization payments as a component of Brazil's yearly debt service.[48]

The year 1981 was a milestone in the course of the country's economic and political evolution. In August, 1981, General Golbery Costo e Silva was ousted by his junta comrades as head of the Casa Civil, Figueiredo's presidential advisory staff. Golbery was a "king-maker," a "gray eminence" whose reputation for pulling the strings of civilian government had led many to believe that it was he who actually ran the country. Golbery's removal represented a victory for Figueiredo and, of equal significance, a triumph for Delfim Neto. The éminence grise and the Great Planner had come to loggerheads over Golbery's demand for an increase in social welfare expenditures as a means of placating popular unrest. Neto, with his investment-first, consumption-later orientation, had set about "deliberately trimming the Administration's Social Benefits Package."[49] Golbery's departure paved the way for Neto's new approach: austere deflationary adjustment to external shocks. Attempting to circumvent IMF conditionality, Neto formulated an adjustment package virtually identical to the

Table 7
Estimated Total Net Floating-Interest Debt for Brazil, 1978–1982, as a Percentage of (1) Total Net Debt, and (2) GNP

Year	Total ($ billion)	(1)	(2)
1978	18.5	50	10
1980	30.9	57	13
1982	45.5	62	18

Source: OECD, p. 19.

one the Fund would have required for an upper-tranche quota loan.[50] Going to the Fund would have offered new monies at a discount below those available to Brazil on the Euromarket, but it would have limited the government's flexibility in executing adjustment, especially its capacity to relax quickly as conditions improved, and, in Neto's view, it would do more harm than good for the country's commercial credit standing, regardless of the IMF's seal of approval argument.

The outcome was a recessionary program as orthodox as any approved by the Fund. Indeed, as John Williamson evaluates it, the "clearest case of overkill—a deflationary policy pushing output below internal balance—is Brazil's deflation in 1981 to avoid having to borrow from the Fund."[51] This severe retrenchment generated zero growth in GNP for 1981,[52] a drop of 4 percent in total GDP,[53] and a capital goods sector operating at 50 percent of capacity.[54] The dissipation of Brazil's aborted second miracle had a greater impact on lender policies than Neto's embrace of orthodox stabilization, estimated new flows from the banks to Brazil ebbing to $1.5 billion for all of 1981.

Where had the nation's economic development program gone astray? Part of the answer surely lies in the disastrous influence of increased oil-import costs, rising dollar interest rates and worsening of terms of trade on the Brazilian economy from 1979 to 1981. The second oil shock was the first major externality of the late 1970s that the country encountered. Brazil was, and remains, the largest LDC importer of oil. Consequently, "a $5 increase in the price per barrel" for imported oil "translates into $1.5 billion in added foreign exchange requirements," for Brazil.[55] The country's yearly oil-import bill rose from $4.5 billion in 1974 to $11.3 billion in 1980.[56] Government policy-makers were certainly aware of the subversive effects of these costs on the nation's balance of payments. Crude-oil imports were slashed in 1981 to their lowest levels since 1977 (some 20 percent below the 1979 peak),[57] while efforts to speed the Proalcool scheme were intensified.[58] Unfortunately, for a government which had spent more than a decade implementing energy-intensive industrialization, strict conservation of energy and cuts in oil imports meant underutilization of industrial capacity. As Central Bank President Ernane Galveas observed, from 1974 to 1980 Brazilians had invested a total of $60 billion in "non-ferrous metals, steel, fertilizers, petro-chemicals, paper production, capital goods, electric power, alcohol, fuel and oil" production, all material-, energy- and oil-intensive activities.[59]

The capital-intensive character of Brazil's development also made it vulnerable to the second hammer blow of the 1980s, high dollar interest rates. Interest charges alone on external debt in 1981 totaled $9.6 billion, equivalent to 41 percent of export exchange earnings and leading to a current account deficit of $10.6 billion,[60] a figure which would have been far worse if it had not been for the country's spectacular success in manufactured exports for the year. As of 1981, one study reports that "each percentage point in [international] interest rates means about $500 million in net costs"[61] to the Brazilian economy. The impact of high dollar interest rates on Brazil's balance of payments and debt-service capacity was on the order of the oil price hike, for "an increase of one point on [Brazil's] foreign debt has the same effect as an increase of 4 percent on the price of petroleum."[62] OPEC may have scuttled Brazil's second miracle, but the U.S. Federal Reserve's monetary policy had clearly played its part as well.

Rising oil prices and the appreciation of American imports resulting from a strong dollar both contributed to a deterioration of Brazil's terms of trade in the early 1980s. Recession in OECD countries forced the price of Brazilian commodity exports down while protectionist measures constrained their volume. The price of Brazilian coffee on North American and Western Euopean markets, for example, dropped by 40 percent in 1981, as other mainstay commodities experienced similar downturns.[63] Brazil responded to overdependence on commodity exports in industrialized nations by increasing sales to Third World and COMECON countries, and by increasing the share of consumer durables exported abroad. Diversification in the Brazilian export structure had been achieved, but its new markets were mainly in developing countries which had suffered from the same externalities as Brazil. Moreover, while the cruzeiro maintained its competitiveness vis-à-vis the dollar, it did not remain competitive against the deutsche mark, yen and French franc, West Germany, Japan and France collectively accounting for 15 percent of Brazil's export trade.[64] To make Brazilian exports more attractive on world markets, the government interspersed substantial devaluations with a series of mini-devaluations—a 23 percent official depreciation of the cruzeiro occurring in March, 1981—but devaluation had an inflationary impact on the domestic economy and stimulated popular unrest as real wages, welfare expenditures and employment declined.[65]

In the first six months of 1982, the Brazilian economy continued on the recessionary course initiated by the austerity program of the previous year. It became more apparent that the deflation of the economy had been too drastic and too sudden as 1982 went on. Having forecast a 1982 trade surplus of $3 billion, Brazil's economists were deeply disappointed with the year's actual surplus of barely $500 million.[66] In 1982, service of external debt consumed all of the country's export revenues,[67] restrictions on imported inputs holding down export production. With their impossible debt-service ratio, the Brazilians found themselves needing "about $330 million a week to pay [their] international obligations,"[68] and foreign exchange earnings falling far short of this mark. At the same time, the 1981 adjustment program did little to stem the tide of domestic inflation, yearly price rises on consumer goods remaining near 100 percent from January to June, 1982.[69]

How could Brazil meet its external public debt repayment schedule without a large-scale debt reorganization pivoting around the IMF? Throughout 1982, the government tried to roll over existing debt by using new loans to repay old ones. Spreads on Euroloans to Brazil's sovereign borrowers climbed rapidly as Neto and his team scrambled across the globe conferring with commercial lend-

ers on the topic of fresh credits. "In the first week of September, some Brazilian bank agencies in New York found themselves without money to honour their
obligations of the day,"[70] emergency interbank lines being made available only
at the eleventh hour. In mid–1982, Neto had calculated that Brazil needed only
$3.6 billion in new monies to avoid rescheduling, having already raised $13.4
billion in commercial funds during the year. But bankers had their own set of
figures on Brazil's debt burden, and they did not like what they saw. The figures showed a total foreign indebtedness of $84 billion, with $19 billion due
over the short term and $20.5 billion owed to U.S. banks alone.[71] The situation
was plain: even with massive new borrowings, Brazil would not be able to finance any new investment or even to support domestic production at near-full
capacity.[72]

In September, 1982, the Brazilians tried one last-ditch effort to convince international creditors that their nation would soon be back on the right track and
thereby avoid dreaded Fund conditionality. In Neto's own words, the September, 1982, stabilization program was intended to "show that Brazil is capable
of rowing against the stream."[73] The new austerity package targeted a slice in
the government deficit from 4.9 percent of GDP to 2.5 percent within twelve
months, and a reduction in total investment of 3 percent to 4 percent. Credit
was curbed through a 25 percent tax on domestic loans,[74] and the pace of mini-
devaluations was intensified.[75] Again, the medicine proved too potent for the
patient: "In the space of three days, private companies found themselves unable to get credits in the domestic market, dollars were unattainable, the legal
reserve rate jumped from 35 percent to 45 percent, and the banks were told to
place 5 percent of their time deposits with the Central Bank."[76] There were
sweeping cuts in dollar allowances for private sector firms in Brazil, only companies with large export volumes being permitted to purchase American imports without paying a 25 percent surcharge duty.[77] Neto's combination of exchange and bank credit restrictions closely resembled Lopez-Portillo's
simultaneous decrees in Mexico. The international banking community heartily
applauded these new Draconian measures, but none was willing to hand over fresh
monies to Brazil's public borrowers.

Since the country's last rescheduling in 1964, Brazil's leaders had consis-
tently rejected the idea of going to the IMF for a conditional drawing. In September, 1982, Carlos Langoni, a governor of Brazil's Central Bank, reiterated
two primary objections to any Fund-sponsored rescheduling of the nation's external debt: (1) "The scale of the IMF is not compatible with the scale of the
Brazilian economy, nor with the scale of the international economic crisis" and
(2) "There is no truth in the idea that going to the IMF constitutes an essential
guarantee for continued access to resources from the private banks."[78] The lending
resources of the IMF were indeed limited in the context of Brazil's debt burden;
its seal of approval was merely an informal certification of creditworthiness which
would supplement lender analyses; and the IMF's conditions were too inflexible
in form, even if their basic intent was identical to that of Brazil's own adjust-

ment programs. Brazil, like Mexico, was a "de facto dropout" from the Third World "chorus demanding generalized debt relief,"[79] so that going to the Fund represented a confession of serious debt problems and a further erosion of lender confidence.

Unable to avoid the Fund in the long run, the Brazilian government followed what it considered to be the next best alternative, delaying application to the Fund until after the November, 1982, senatorial elections. It was on 15 December, 1982 that the IMF and Brazil announced agreement on a $4.5 billion credit to be disbursed over three years, possibly including an additional $2.2 billion loan within the period. IMF conditions included a minimum 23 percent devaluation of the cruzeiro, cuts in public deficits similar to those of the September program, and a highly ambitious $6 billion trade surplus goal for 1983.[80] The signing of the accord was preceded by President Reagan's carefully timed visit to Brazil in early December, Reagan greeting his hosts with a $1.2 billion emergency short-term loan, and it was accompanied by a $600 million stop-gap credit from the money-center banks.[81]

With official creditors providing Brazil with new loans, the focus of the restructuring process shifted to Brazil's commercial debt, by far the largest and most worrisome component of its debt stock. In October, 1982, a Brazilian mission headed by Langoni met with representatives of Citibank and Morgan Guaranty in New York. The bankers expressed a willingness to enter rescheduling discussions, but not without a prior IMF conditional loan. Five days after the IMF agreement was concluded, Brazilian and Fund representatives met again with major banks and designed a four-part package of commercial debt rescheduling and refinancing. Project One was a fresh, eight-year $4.4 billion club loan led by Morgan Guaranty. Project Two involved a rescheduling of $4 billion in debt service due to major money-center banks in 1983, with Citibank in charge of negotiations. The third project was a $9 billion standby credit in support of Brazil's targeted export expansion and trade surplus, Chase Manhattan leading the syndication. The fourth, and most critical, element was the arrangement of $10 billion in interbank credit lines between Brazil's banks and hundreds of foreign institutions, with Banco do Brazil assigned to arrange these credits. The package was an integrated one, with all four projects needed to coherently address Brazil's immediate debt problems, but the fourth component, the interbank lines, was the most crucial, because Brazil's leaders "were counting on interbank loans to make up the difference between the $4.4 billion in Project One and [their] real liquidity needs."[82]

Projects One and Two were completed in two months, with only the big banks participating, and thus a minimum of wrangling among creditors who had already "bought in" through their high levels of exposure in Brazil. Regional banks oversubscribed by $1 billion to the trade-related Project Three, seeing it as entailing minimum risk and functioning to improve bank relations with American exporters. The entire reorganization, however, fell apart on the matter of the interbank credit lines. The regionals would not commit themselves to increased interbank credit lines for Brazil's banks. Indeed, American regional banks reduced these credit lines throughout late 1982 and early 1983, and since they had previously provided about 20 percent of Brazil's interbank financing, the money-center banks were faced with a $1.5 billion shortfall on Project Four, this deficit jeopardizing the entire commercial rescheduling package.[83] Having voluntarily participated in short-term roll-overs of loans to Brazil, the regionals were well acquainted with the transformation of short-term credits into medium- and long-term loans by the borrower. They feared that the Brazilian government would suspend repayments from the nation's banks to commercial lenders, thereby "forcibly transmuting the regionals' short-term money into long-term loans."[84] Grounds for such objections became more substantial in January, 1983, when Brazil's government announced that it was temporarily holding back "the publication of reserve figures altogether until tension in international financial markets eased,"[85] causing the possibility of an imminent liquidity crisis to loom still larger. The money-center banks attempted to enlist the regionals through a campaign of peer pressure and moral suasion, but having been given no part in the steering committee negotiations which had led to the rescue package, the smaller banks were not about to alter their attitudes on the interbank project.

In May, 1983, Federal Reserve Chairman Volcker and representatives of the Bank of England met in New York with money-center personnel. The government officials urged a reformulation of the initial four-part plan amid rumors that the Brazilians were about to freeze all interbank funds in their possession. Unable to resurrect Project Four as originally designed, the money-center banks formed a committee to keep lines of communication open with the regionals and to try to attract the latter's funds into short-term syndicated loans to Brazil's Central Bank. One month later, the entire restructuring process was brought to an abrupt halt when IMF monitors declared that Brazil "wasn't complying with some of the provisions" incorporated into the Fund's adjustment loan and stopped disbursement of all IMF monies to Brazil until a new conditional loan agreement could be negotiated.[86] With the country already $1 billion in arrears on trade obligations,[87] the need for a reorganization of external public debts was even more pressing, but when and how a successful restructuring would occur was still far from clear.

Commentary

Brazil's approach to national economic development has been broadly similar to that of Mexico. To be sure, there are differences between them, e.g., Mexico enjoys energy resources that Brazil does not possess, and Brazil boasts a diversified industrial export capacity which the Mexicans have not yet attained. Both, however, adopted the basic "engine of growth" development model, concentrating investment in capital-intensive, energy-intensive industrialization. As their debt profiles reveal, both Brazil and Mexico tapped commercial credit markets when the vulnerabilities of this approach resulted in balance of payments deficits, although the Mexicans resorted to more short-term credits than the Brazilians. The most prominent shared characteristic of the Mexican and Brazilian developmental strategies resides in the central role assigned to the state in the ownership and regulation of economic activity.

Brazil's central government has had a comparatively modest role in the actual ownership of the country's productive facilities. The government's part as an investor in industry expanded after 1974 in the wake of Simonsen's import-substitution strategy. As a consequence of this enlargement of the public sector, "state enterprises became more important for the economy," and direct investment by MNCs declined in relative significance.[88] Delfim Neto, however, was much more liberal in his treatment of the private sector than were Echeverria and Lopez-Portillo, and a much greater proportion of Brazil's industry remains in private hands than is the case with Mexico. It is through monetary and fiscal policy that Brazilian officials effectively control both the public and private sectors, with the planning ministry orchestrating the course of the economy as a whole. The history of Brazil's exchange rate policy illustrates government intervention in private sector activity through monetary mechanisms. Since 1968, Brazil has utilized the crawling peg as a means of keeping its exports competitive while minimizing the exchange rate uncertainty accompanying the alternative pattern of infrequent, massive devaluations.[89] Campos's "belt-tightening law" of 1964, indexing wages with consumer inflation, provides another example of the comprehensive regulatory powers of the state.[90] Successive administrations have extended generous subsidies to private industry (especially export-production), agriculture and social welfare programs.[91] Apart from their relatively ineffective results, the 1981 and 1982 adjustment programs demonstrate the central government's power to control virtually all economic and financial processes in the country. Critics have charged that this omnipotence has led to a stop-and-go development course, the government frequently reversing its policy and compelling the private sector to switch back and forth between expansion and retrenchment. In Albert Fishlow's opinion, the decline of the nation's international commercial credit standing in the early 1980s can be largely attributed to the "exaggerated and unfulfilled claims made by Delfim after taking office."[92] Nonetheless, the fact that these claims could be believed at all is a rough index of the perceived power of the central government in formulating and implementing broad economic policy.

As in Mexico, the expansion of the state's regulatory apparatus over private enterprise was partially a response to increased multinational investment in the country during the 1960s. The foreign share of fixed assets in Brazil is about 15 percent of the total,[93] but, again, MNCs have concentrated their investments in industries with oligopolistic structures, giving them heightened leverage relative to their portion of total investment. MNCs have large holdings in transport equipment, electrical machinery and appliances, mechanical industry, rubber, etc.,[94] so that "the most dynamic modern sectors of the economy are predominantly under the majority contol of multinational capital."[95]

The Brazilian government has been far less restrictive than its Mexican counterpart in regulating direct investment within Brazil. According to Maria Alves, Brazil's economic leaders have purposely sought to establish "a secure and attractive environment for foreign capital."[96] To this end, the argument runs, Brazil's development plans have been biased toward the production of durable consumer goods, "adapting the pattern of domestic final demand to the expansion needs of the MNCs,"[97] consciously favoring upper- and middle-class consumers of these goods to the detriment of low-income consumers without funds for their purchase. Finally, "Delfim's industrialization policies of the late–1960s and early–1970s failed to develop domestic capital goods industries, allowing the multinationals to establish a monopoly in this area,"[98] leading to semipermanent dependence on MNC and foreign suppliers to Brazil's industrial sector.

As for agriculture, Brazil's planners have tended to bypass the agrarian sector in their development programs. Although the nation's full granary potential remains dormant, Brazilian agriculture has shown some buoyancy in the early 1980s, despite the general downturn in global prices and demand for commodity exports.[99] Not only have development programs placed agriculture below industry/infrastructure in their priority hierarchies, "increases in agricultural output have come from the extension of the frontier rather than an intensification of production."[100] The familiar Latin American land tenure pattern of many small owners occupying a minuscule percentage of the land while latifundia take up the bulk of viable agrarian property is firmly embedded in Brazil. Currently, "72 percent of all rural properties (minfundios) are too small to be economically productive," accounting for a total of less than 13 percent of all registered land holdings.[101] Under such conditions, the government's attempts to boost agricultural productivity have necessarily focused on the needs of the large property holders. The government has shown reluctance to tackle the volatile issue of land reform, and has been content with passively reinforcing the status quo. Agriculture as a whole, however, is not a favored part of the Brazilian economy, and, indeed, unlike manufactures, all agrarian exports are subject to export taxes. Such state assistance as is provided to Brazil's farmers accrues to only a small fraction of the rank and file, i.e., those in the "front."

"Brazil—The Land of the Future," reads the investment literature; "and it always will be," add skeptics of Brazilian development. The enormous potential of the Brazilian economy is apparent when we contemplate the possible future of the nation's largest project, the development of the Amazon's Carajas mineral region. At an estimated total investment cost of $60 billion, the Amazon's natural wealth has a latent earning potential of $11 billion a year.[102] The promises and problems of the Amazon project are reflected on a more modest scale in the country's long-range planning horizon as a whole. Projects which were begun in the mid–1970s are not due to come on line until the early 1990s,[103] and additional capital will be required before they become fully operational.[104] When Ernane Galveas proclaimed that "in the near future, these projects will form the launching pad for a new period of accelerated growth," [105] it was difficult to refute this contention. The only catch in Galveas's assertion is precisely when the "near future" will arise.

Given Brazil's diversified potential and long-range planning orientation, it is not surprising to find that major money-center banks, willing to grant long-term project financing, have been the primary source of external flows into Brazil. Among American banks with the most extensive Brazilian portfolios and most critical exposure levels are the giant "name" banks, including Citibank, Chase Manhattan, the Bank of America, Chemical Bank, Banker's Trust, Morgan Guaranty, Manufacturer's Hanover, First Chicago and Continental Illinois.[106] Individually, none of these lenders can simply opt out of Brazil, all being effectively locked in. Collectively, these nine banks alone "have loaned more than $16.6 billion to Brazil, a sum that represents about 57 percent of their entire capital base." [107] This high degree of exposure on the part of the money-center banks contrasts sharply with the more prudent approach of the regionals in their Brazilian lending, for "few of these banks have more than 20 percent of their capital base invested in Brazilian loans." [108] Furthermore, the money-center institutions have extended long-term project loans directly to the central government, while the regionals have confined their lending to short-term, trade-related credits. The bank with the most to lose in Brazil is undoubtedly Citibank of New York. While others shied away from Neto's aggressive expansionism, Citibank, under the direction of Walter Wriston, increased loan volumes to Brazil throughout the 1980s, Brazilian loans accounting for 20 percent of Citibank's global profits in 1976.[109] The bank maintains a staff of 5,000 manning its Brazilian branches, having lent $4.6 billion to Brazilian public borrowers from its U.S. headquarters and an additional $1 billion from its branches in Brazil.[110] In 1982, these investments generated 22 percent of Citibank's total profits, but they also amounted to 83 percent of its capital.[111] The going joke is that worries over Brazilian exposure are the real reason why the "City never sleeps."

Unlike Mexico, Brazil's external debt maturity structure is not concentrated in short-term credits and displays none of the bunching effect that plagues the Mexican debt profile. In mid–1982, Galveas calculated that only $8 billion of Brazil's net $72.5 billion external debt was short-term, although considerable latitude in the definition of short-term credit must be used to arrive at such a figure.[112] The country's favorable external debt repayment schedule is an outcome of the government's strategy of offering higher spreads in return for longer maturities. Public sector borrowers have used the basic rule of thumb that all commercial foreign loans must carry at least an eight-year maturity with three years' grace. In fact, the government has occasionally prohibited private borrowers from accepting any external credit with shorter maturities and/or grace periods.[113] Aside from stretching out amortization payments and thus "smoothing" annual debt service, this borrowing approach has two important advantages for the debtor. First, during times of high international interest rates, when the debtor must nevertheless borrow at an initially unattractive floating rate, any future downward trend in LIBOR/U.S. prime means a substantial real cost reduction. Second, as Anthony Sampson suspects, by insisting on large, long-term loans, the Brazilians have forged a lasting bond with their commercial creditors, deliberately laying the "trap" that locks in the money-center banks.[114] However, as is invariably the case, there are gaping loopholes in the Brazilian government's restriction on short-term credit and treatment of short-term credit for national accounting purposes. As a prime example, interbank loans are largely unregistered in Brazil, and Brazilian banks have employed their overseas branches as sources of funding for domestic operations. These debts are not reflected in Brazil's national account ledgers, but the Bank for International Settlements has estimated a total of $17 billion in such credits.[115] Moreover, the government's definition of short-term loans does not encompass credits owed in the current fiscal year, these being treated as part of the nation's current trade account rather than as external debt obligations.[116]

The pace of Brazilian economic development and its reliance upon massive infusions of external capital are both partially derivative of the country's rapidly expanding population. The rate of Brazil's population growth has been reduced from 2.9 percent a year at the outset of the 1970s to 2.4 percent annually at the end of the decade.[117] Nevertheless, "Brazil needs about 1.5 million new jobs a year to keep pace with its expanding labor force."[118] This need is most urgent among the urban residents who inhabit the slums surrounding Brazil's metropolitan and industrial centers. The capital-intensive mode of development is not congruous with these employment pressures. Modern industrial production entails comparatively small labor inputs, with only skilled and semi-skilled workers being in demand. Expenditures on vocational training have never been a high priority in the country's development budgets. In fact, "two-thirds of all Brazilians still reach adulthood without completing primary schooling."[119] The development path that Brazil has followed over the past twenty years has led to an increase in average per capita income, but income disparities within Brazil have widened and the distribution of wealth has become even less equitable. From 1970 to 1980 the nation's GDP grew more lopsided in its distribution, as "the share of the bottom 50 percent of the population fell from 17.4 percent to 12.6 percent while that of the top 1 percent rose from 11.9 percent to 16.9 percent."[120] The inflationary forces accompanying accelerated development, deficit spending and external indebtedness have effectively nullified any benefits which the process may have brought to those at the bottom of Brazilian society, making development more of a handicap than a boon for the nation's low-income citizens.

The widening of income and wealth gaps as a result of selective development investment has produced waves of popular unrest throughout Brazil.[121] Social discontent intensified in the wake of the 1981 and 1982 austerity programs, which have had a disproportionately harsh effect upon the country's poorest. Spontaneous *querba-querba* anti-property riots have broken out in Brazil's ghettoes,[122] marked by widespread vandalism and looting. Organized protest has taken the form of labor movement strikes, with 113 strikes involving 3 million workers occurring in 1979.[123] São Paulo, with its large numbers of industrial workers, clerks, students and university intellectuals, is the geographic nexus of Brazil's union activities,[124] and Luis Inacio da Silva (Lula) and his Worker's Party (PT) is its vanguard.[125] The Worker's Party has sought informal alliances with the Popular Party and the Party of the Brazilian Democratic Movement, with the austerity measures of the early 1980s creating a common bond among the country's disaffected.

The Brazilian government has responded to growing social unrest with the "velvet glove," using both repression and concession to quell popular outrage. The pervasive social control apparatus that has been erected in Brazil has prompted Alves to call Brazil the first national security state. Both "legal" and extralegal means are employed by the government to stifle militant social reform. "The military governments of the national-security state launched in Brazil in 1964 have passed a total of 17 institutional acts, nearly 80 complementary acts and hundreds of decree-laws based on these acts,"[126] using pure fiat with no reference to the wants or needs of the masses. The darker side of the government's duress against the alienated has been the province of the National Information Service (SNI), this agency operating without any system of legal restraint. The SNI has become so powerful in its clandestine activities that it may have become "an uncontrollable beast," answering to no one, including the country's public leadership.[127] The centrality of the SNI within the Brazilian political structure is evident when it is noted that General Golbery was its founding father and President Figueiredo a member of its staff.[128]

Unable to contain social unrest through simple, but costly, force, the Brazilian government has embarked upon a process of relaxing these strictures to placate democratic and social reform forces. Termed *abertura* (literally, "opening"), this process had its birth in the mid–1970s as *distensao* (relaxation), a conservative, limited and managed democratization,"[129] with Golbery himself serving as its midwife. As *distensao* gained momentum, it was modified by the Figueiredo Administration into the broader *abertura*, which has been depicted by official sources as a "genuine opening to broader participation" by the public in legal, political, social and economic policy-making.[130] The current administration has pledged that it will gradually extend power to the Brazilian people, offering substantive proof of this intention by repealing some of the infamous Institutional Acts.

From the government's standpoint, *abertura* performs a number of important functions. "Lacking balanced economic growth," the promise of democratization can be used by the state "as a legitimation device,"[131] providing a "safety valve" through which pent-up discontent can be diffused.[132] At a time when Brazil seeks greater integration with the outside world, *abertura* enhances the regime's image abroad.[133] *Abertura* was also intended to fragment political opposition to the government, dividing those willing to wait for further reform from more radical elements. Finally, *abertura* is "a strategy against the military hard-liners *and* the perceived civil opposition,"[134] counterbalancing the unrestrained power of the military's right wing and the SNI.

Once the idea of *abertura* had been implanted in the minds of the Brazilian people it became an animate force in "the arena of public expectations."[135] Lagging economic performance amplified the call for more direct popular participation in the decisions confronting the country, and broader popular involvement "transformed the political opening from a paternal dispensation to a semi-autonomous process."[136] Having taken on a life of its own, the promise of *abertura* now carries its own sanctions for non-fulfillment. Gaps between the government's endorsement of greater democratization and the actual enfranchisements extended could engender deep frustrations within the Brazilian polity and set off total civil disorder. *Abertura* has also had inadvertent effects on the political Right. In the 1980s, there has been a "steady rise of violent right-wing resistance to political and social liberalization," taking its most deadly form in a "surge of right-wing terrorist activity in major urban areas."[137] In one of his last public addresses, Golbery warned reactionaries that once *abertura* had been set in motion, it could not be simply abandoned; the response was a bomb explosion killing an army intelligence officer at the rally.[138] Golbery's departure from government has given hard-liners within the military/intelligence corps greater influence, and the fate of *abertura* in Brazil is by no means certain.[139]

A critical test of *abertura* took place in November, 1982, when, for the first time since 1965, free elections were held in Brazil. The immediate issue was the selection of congressional representatives, but the government's cardinal concern was with shaping political support for the 1986 presidential election, when Figueiredo is scheduled to step down and thereby end twenty-two consecutive years of military rule.[140] Both *abertura* and the November ballot were part of Golbery's master plan to restore civilian government, and the gerrymandering of electoral districts was meant to ensure victories for government-backed candidates. As the election drew near, the Brazilian government was under severe pressure to reflate the adjusted economy, and the Figueiredo Administration purposely postponed application to the IMF until after the election. The results for the government were disappointing, but not disastrous. The bulk of the votes went to opposition parties, but the government party did receive a 30 percent plurality, enough to control the electoral college and choose Figueiredo's successor in 1986.

The lack of free elections in Brazil was a major point of conflict between the Brazilian government and the Carter Administration's human rights campaign.[141] The Brazilians have opposed some American hemispheric policies, notably by developing nuclear energy for civilian purposes in a manner deemed unsafe by U.S. authorities.[142] On the other side, the Reagan Administration's Caribbean focus and its longstanding opposition to increased multilateral flows to the Third World have cooled relations between Brazil and the United States.[143]

As the diversification of its export markets indicates, Brazil has been tilting away from the American/Western European orbit and toward its own independent course.[144] Whether this bodes ill or well for the nation's foreign creditors is clearly a matter of conjecture. Greater independence may upgrade the country's capacity to repay external debt, but it may also mean increased willingness to take unilateral action on its debt problem through a declared moratorium on repayment.

Notes

1. B. Cohen, p.191.
2. Sampson, p.259.
3. Bela Balassa, *Incentive Policies in Brazil.* World Bank Staff Working Paper No. 133 (Washington: World Bank, 1981), p.1024.
4. Ibid., p.1023.
5. Ibid.
6. Edmar L. Bacha, "Selected Issues in Post–1964 Brazilian Economic Growth," in *Models of Growth and Distribution for Brazil* ed. Lance Taylor et al. (New York: Oxford University Press, 1980), p.44.
7. Sampson, p.259.
8. Williamson, p.30.
9. Balassa, *Incentive Policies,* p.1024.
10. B. Cohen, p.191.
11. Sampson, p.259.
12. IBRD, *Annual Report: 1982,* p.92.
13. B. Cohen, p.191
14. Clark, p.175.
15. Sampson, p.260.
16. B. Cohen, p.193.
17. Bacha, "Selected Issues," p.44.
18. Ibid., pp.41–42.
19. B. Cohen, p.193.
20. Ibid., p.194.
21. Bacha, *Incentive Policies,* p.43.
22. B. Cohen, p.193.
23. Basil Caplan, "Brazil's Delicate Balancing Act," *The Banker,* December, 1981, p.20.
24. Sampson, p.260.
25. Albert Fishlow, "The United States and Brazil: The Case of the Missing Relationship," *Foreign Affairs,* Spring, 1982, p.909.
26. Eul-Soo Pang, "Abertura in Brazil: A Road to Chaos?" *Current History,* February, 1981, p.59.
27. Fishlow, "United States and Brazil," p.909.
28. Pang, p.59.
29. Thomas G. Sanders, "Brazil in the 1980s: The Emerging Political Model," in *Authoritarian Capitalism: Brazil's Contemporary Economic and Political Development,* ed. Thomas C. Bruneau and Philippe Faucher (Boulder, Colorado: Westview, 1981), pp.216–217.

30. Sampson, p.259.
31. A. Robinson, "End of Illusion," p.90.
32. Caplan, p.21.
33. A. Robinson, "Latin America's Economies," p.10.
34. Ibid.
35. Alan Robinson, "Can Brazil Make It?" *Euromoney*, November, 1982, p.111.
36. IBRD, *Annual Report: 1982*, p.91.
37. IBRD, *World Development Report*, p.111.
38. A. Robinson "End of Illusion" p.90.
39. "Brazil: Having to Run Harder," *The Banker*, March, 1982, p.91.
40. Donald V. Coes, *The Impact of Price Uncertainty: A Study of Brazilian Exchange Rate Policy* (New York: Garland, 1979), p.207.
41. "A Nightmare" p.55.
42. Caplan, p.19.
43. Fishlow, "United States and Brazil," p.909.
44. Fishlow, "Latin American External Debt," p.162.
45. Sampson, p.260.
46. Guth, p.28.
47. Caplan, p.19.
48. A. Robinson, "Can Brazil Make It?", p.109.
49. Robert M. Levine, "Brazil: The Dimensions of Democratization," *Current History*, February, 1982, p.61.
50. Williamson, p.19.
51. Ibid.
52. Caplan, p.20.
53. IBRD, *Annual Report: 1982*, p.88.
54. Caplan, p.20.
55. Fishlow, "Latin American External Debt," p.161.
56. A. Robinson, "Can Brazil Make It?" p.109.
57. Thomas J. Trebat, "Brazil's Balancing Act: Austerity Versus Social Stability," *Euromoney*, April, 1982, p.55.
58. Pang, p.88.
59. A. Robinson, "End of Illusion," p.109.
60. Trebat, p.55.
61. Fishlow, "Latin American External Debt," p.161.
62. A. Robinson, "End of Illusion," p.12.
63. Trebat, p.55.
64. Hughes, p.109.
65. Gilpin, p.D–1.
66. Hughes, p.109.
67. David B. Tinnin, "The War Among Brazil's Bankers," *Fortune*, 11 July, 1983, p.50.
68. A. Robinson, "Can Brazil Make It?" p.109.
69. A. Robinson, "End of Illusion," p.90.
70. A. Robinson, "Can Brazil Make It?" p.111.
71. Gilpin, p.D–1.
72. A. Robinson, "Can Brazil Make It?" p.109.
73. Ibid., p.104.

74. Ibid.
75. Hughes, p.109.
76. A. Robinson, "Can Brazil Make It?" pp.103–104.
77. Ibid., p.104.
78. Ibid., p.106.
79. S. Cohen, p.65.
80. Tinnin, p.50.
81. Field, Shirref and Ollard, p.41.
82. Tinnin, p.52.
83. Ibid., p.153.
84. Ibid., p.154.
85. Hughes, p.108.
86. Tinnin, p.50.
87. Ibid., p.55.
88. Bacha, p.32.
89. Coes, pp.208–215.
90. Maria Helena Moreira Alves, "Mechanisms of Social Control of the Military Governments in Brazil, 1964–1980," in *Latin American Prospects for the 1980s: Equity, Democratization and Development*, ed. Archibald R.M. Ritter and David H. Pollock (New York: Praeger, 1983), p.272.
91. Trebat, p.57.
92. Fishlow, "United States and Brazil," p.909.
93. Bacha, p.28.
94. Ibid., p.26.
95. Alves, p.284.
96. Ibid., p.242.
97. Bacha, p.28.
98. Pang, pp.60–61.
99. Caplan, p.21.
100. John P. Dickenson, *Brazil* (Kent: William Dawson, 1978), pp.22.
101. Pang, p.61.
102. Caplan, p.22.
103. Trebat, p.59.
104. "Nightmare", p.56.
105. A. Robinson, "Can Brazil Make It?" p.109.
106. Tinnin, p.50.
107. Ibid., p.51.
108. Ibid., p.52.
109. Sampson, p.259.
110. Joe Asher, "Is a Global Debt Crisis Looming?" *ABA Banking Journal,* June, 1981, p.50.
111. Tinnin, p.52.
112. A. Robinson, "Can Brazil Make It?" p.106.
113. Caplan, p.20
114. Sampson, p.319.
115. A. Robinson, "Can Brazil Make It?" p.109.
116. "Serrano Guides the World's Biggest Borrowings," *Euromoney,* November, 1981, p.29.

117. Caplan, p.23.

118. Trebat, p.55.

119. Thomas W. Merrick and Douglas H. Graham, *Population and Economic Development in Brazil: 1800 to the Present* (Baltimore: Johns Hopkins, 1979), p.237.

120. Caplan, p.23.

121. "Nightmare," p.56.

122. Levine, p.63.

123. Alves, p.288.

124. Pang, p.60.

125. Levine, p.62.

126. Alves, p.243.

127. Ibid., p.250.

128. Fishlow "United States and Brazil," p.914.

129. Levine, p.60.

130. Fishlow, "United States and Brazil," p.915.

131. Bacha, p.245.

132. Levine, p.62.

133. Pang, p.67.

134. Fishlow "United States and Brazil," p.914.

135. Levine, p.60.

136. Fishlow "United States and Brazil," p.916.

137. Pang, p.57.

138. Ibid., p.58.

139. Levine, p.62.

140. A. Robinson, "Can Brazil Make It?" p.103.

141. Fishlow "United States and Brazil," p.908.

142. Astiz, p.49.

143. Fishlow "United States and Brazil," pp.905, 922.

144. William G. Tyler, *Advanced Developinq Countries as Export Competitors in Third World Markets: The Brazilian Experience* (Washington: The Center for Strategic and International Studies, 1980), p.vi.

Chapter 8

CASE 4: ARGENTINA

Chronology

Argentina entered the 1970s against a backdrop of political turmoil and economic crisis. In its final two years (1968–1970), the Juan Carlos Ongania regime adopted an orthodox stabilization program which led to moderate growth in GDP and a reduction of the inflation rate to 10 percent, in sharp relief from an average yearly increase of 25 percent from 1955 to 1965.[1] In 1970, the government's austerity program collapsed as restrictive economic and financial policies gave way to political violence. The nation's military executed a coup in 1971, setting the stage for the return of Juan Perón from his exile in Spain. Peron's triumph proved short-lived, as the aging dictator died in July, 1974. Following his death, "administrative chaos, policy confusion, internal struggles for power, opposition attacks and escalating urban guerilla warfare against the regime destroyed the illusion that Argentina was being governed at all."[2] Señora Isabel Perón was unable to restore civil order, and on 24 March, 1976, a three-man military junta headed by Lt. General Jorge Videla took over the government. Videla moved swiftly to crush all political opposition to his rule. "Political parties were banned, labor and other active interest groups were banned and all conventional political activity was suspended indefinitely."[3] Some 10,000 to 15,000 Argentine citizens were imprisoned by the military, as the Prussian-model armed forces once again intervened in the country's civil affairs. After years of protracted disorder, the nation's middle class welcomed the stern reign imposed by Videla.[4]

Social unrest was not the only danger facing the junta in the mid–1970s. The Argentine economy suffered from several chronic ailments, among them:

1. Excessive dependence on unreliable international commodity markets
2. Similarly excessive reliance on foreign capital
3. Ineffective government interventionism in domesticmarkets
4. Antiquated industry and technological stagnation in agriculture

5. A highly-mobilized labor movement

6. A bloated public sector, featuring high levels of deficit spending[5]

Amidst these conditions, Argentina's sovereign borrowers found themselves unable to roll over foreign commercial credits, as the country's external debt climbed to $7 billion in 1976.[6] The man charged with restoring economic stability to Argentina was the newly appointed Minister of the Economy, José Martines de Hoz. In April, 1976, de Hoz took the most expedient course available to him in meeting the nation's imminent debt-service crisis, cooling off the situation by informally requesting a six-month deferral on foreign loan repayments to Argentina's major official and commercial creditors. In the same year, de Hoz brought forward a comprehensive plan to cure the country of its economic problems. The de Hoz program, or "process," as it came to be called, was a sharp departure from prior government policies. It included the customary targets of balancing the budget and curbing monetary growth, but it also contained new measures to develop a flexible financial sector, and, most significant, to dismantle the excessive protectionist barriers which had closed off the economy from the world, to "transform a highly regulated economy into an ecomony in which the market would decide most economic gains and losses."[7] By opening the nation to imports, decreasing state regulation and transferring state production to the private sector, the core of de Hoz's liberalization process was to "make Argentines live by the rules of the market place, internally and externally."[8] Following decades of self-imposed economic isolationism, de Hoz's ambitious scheme aimed at a renewed role for Argentina as a first-rate international commercial power.

The freeing of the Argentine economy was to be accomplished through a combination of changes in fiscal, monetary and regulatory policies. Previous state controls over wages, prices and deposit interest rates would be terminated. Tariffs on imports would be slashed, those on exports eliminated altogether.[9] The Argentine peso would be allowed to float freely, unimpaired by preset official exchange rates.[10] The growth of the money supply would be halved, and the percentage of government deficit to GDP was also to be cut in two. De Hoz's program called for 300,000 jobs to be cut from the public payroll and the replacement of these jobs by the private sector.[11]

The initial results of the de Hoz process comprised a modest miracle, with gradual but substantial improvements in several key areas. After a 1.7 percent decline in GDP for 1976, the Argentine economy expanded at a rate of 5.2 percent in the following year.[12] The pace of inflation slowed to a mere 276 percent annually, down from the mind-boggling rate of 543 percent for 1976. There was a notable upturn in the current balance of payments account, with the 1976 surplus of $655 million growing to $1.287 billion in 1977, and central bank reserves being built up from $1.445 billion in 1976 to $3.154 billion in 1977.[13] After a time lag, these aggregate advances began to trickle down to the nation's workforce. "Although real wages dropped substantially in 1977 and

1978, near-full employment prevailed and wages rose again in 1979 and 1980." [14]
On the basis of these performance indicators, de Hoz's purge of the Argentine
economy appeared to clear the ground for continued, balanced economic development.

There were, however, some unexpected victims of the economy's liberalization. Reduced import costs necessarily meant that small, inefficient domestic
producers would be driven out of business. Because the peso remained overvalued and domestic credit markets sere, several larger, modernized firms were
unable to compete under de Hoz's new set of open market rules. In 1980–1981,
a number of established manufacturers went bankrupt and sixty financial institutions closed their doors for good. [15] The extent of government intervention in
response to private sector failures was a simple 10 percent devaluation of the
peso.

By the beginning of the 1980s, Argentina's external debt had already assumed worrisome dimensions. De Hoz's liberalization process was undertaken
at a time when Argentina's guaranteed borrowers faced severe liquidity strains
on repayment of foreign loans. Shortly after Peron's death, international bankers lent considerable sums to the Argentine government, justifying the risk of
such investment by pointing forward to competitive advantages gained through
an "early" relationship with the new, open market National Administration. [16]
De Hoz's adjustment measures enabled the government to renegotiate the bulk
of its 1976 commercial debt service, a four-year refinancing being granted at a
margin of 2 percent above LIBOR. [17] By 1978, the improvement of the country's balance of payments position permitted the total amortization of the refinancing package, two years ahead of schedule. This, in turn, encouraged the
banks to offer sovereign loans with ten- to twelve-year maturities, and allowed
the borrowers to garner spreads of less than 1 percent. Table 8 provides a running account of Argentina's external public debt and debt service over the years

Table 8
Argentine External Debt and Debt Service,
1975–1980
(in $ million)

Year	Total ($ million)	Annual Debt Service
1975	4,314	992
1976	5,852	1,456
1977	6,915	1,575
1978	8,793	2,572
1979	12,627	2,082
1980	15,643	2,810

Source: OECD, p. 52.

Table 9
Estimated Total Net Floating-Interest Debt
for Argentina, 1978–1982, as a Percentage of
(1) Total Net Debt, and (2) GNP

Year	Total ($ billion)	(1)	(2)
1978	0.8	12	1
1980	9.4	58	7
1982	20.5	66	10

Source: OECD, p. 19.

1975 to 1980, while Table 9 records the growth of total public net floating-interest debt as a percentage of total debt and as a percentage of GNP for the years 1978, 1980 and 1982. These figures demonstrate a sharp increase in commercial credit flowing into Argentina, with total floating-interest debt growing from virtually nothing in 1978 to nearly $10 billion in 1980, and doubling again by 1982. Bankers who gladly extended credit during the infancy of the process were more and more reluctant to provide financing as its adolescent growing pains became more pronounced, among them increased external indebtedness itself.[18]

In March, 1981, the characteristic instability of the Argentinian government structure became manifest again. A combination of flagging economic performance and heavy-handed political repression altered middle-class attitudes toward the Videla regime, prompting another military coup placing Roberto Viola in power. Three-digit inflation, a 1981 trade deficit of $1.6 billion and accumulated external public debts of $27 billion greeted Viola upon taking office.[19] Lacking the full support of the military, Viola's grip on the reins of Argentina's government was far more tenuous than that of his predecessor. Understandably, Viola took a cautious approach to economic adjustment. For instance, "instead of placing all economic activity in one individual as Videla had done, [Viola] divided it among several ministers."[20] He replaced de Hoz as head of the Ministry of the Economy with Lorenzo Sigaut, and the latter immediately adopted a more conciliatory attitude toward the private sector. Videla and de Hoz had alienated the country's business interests with their "sink or swim" decrees, but Viola and Sigaut consulted actively with the leaders of the private sector. A brief harmonizing of public policy and private sector wants occurred, but this modus vivendi led to a decided watering down of de Hoz's process, as businessmen advanced their special claims on government. Sigaut had originally begun a new comprehensive program to succeed "the process," but as the summer of 1981 wore on, no such plan was forthcoming. Most disturbing of all, the government's target figure of 2 percent of GDP for public deficit expenditure, set at the start of 1981, proved too ambitious, the actual figure approaching 5.7 percent.[21] The fiscal and monetary discipline intrinsic to the de Hoz process was noticeably absent in Sigaut's piecemeal and compromising policies.

In 1981, Argentina's key economic indicators worsened across the board. GDP for 1981 fell 4.5 percent, "bringing per capita GDP and per capita income down below 1974 levels."[22] Inflation remained at three-digit levels,[23] consumer prices rising 130 percent in 1981, wholesale prices increasing 180 percent for the year.[24] The balance of trade was lackluster, a rough parity between imports and exports being achieved, but reserves dipped from five-months of import cover to only three months' cover.[25] In April, 1981, the peso was devalued by 30 percent, followed by another official depreciation of 30 percent in June.[26] By the end of 1981, total foreign indebtedness had reached \$32 billion, the country's debt-service ratio stood at 27 percent, and spreads on commercial loans worsened, moving from an average 13/16 percent over LIBOR in mid–1981 to $1^1/_4$ percent at the beginning of 1982.[27]

Viola was hospitalized in November, 1981. His illness provided the military with yet another opportunity to change the nation's leadership. On 11 December, 1981, a three-man military junta assumed power, with Commander-in-Chief Leopoldo Galtieri taking the lead. Galtieri firmed his position by declaring himself Argentina's President until March, 1984, while retaining his command status over the armed forces. He removed the "moderate" Sigaut from government and put Roberto Alemann in charge of the Ministry of the Economy. An admirer of de Hoz, Alemann switched the direction of the Argentine economy back toward that of "the process." Like his mentor's program, Alemann's Process of National Reorganization was imbued with a "thorough-going liberal orthodoxy."[28] As Alemann saw it, the twin culprits holding down the Argentina economy were inflation and its closely associated cohort, public deficit spending. Inflation would be contained by curbs on the growth of the money supply and a severe slashing of government deficits, from the current 7 percent of GDP to 2 percent.[29] Alemann adopted stern monetary discipline, but he characterized his approach as a "fiscalist" remedy, pointing out that "all questions of importance with the Argentine economy are in some way related to public expenditure which because of its size, nature and composition gives rise to all the real economic problems."[30]

Having undergone "liberalization" before, the Argentine public was even less keen on Alemann's version than they had been on the de Hoz program. The freezing of public sector wages (public employment accounting for 70 percent of government expenditures) alienated a broad cross-section of Argentina's labor force. Alemann eliminated the preferred exchange rate enjoyed by business interests, reunifying the exchange market and again freeing the peso to float on its own. He also contemplated eliminating government guarantees on private bank deposits, and while this measure was never enacted, some Argentinian bankers voluntarily gave up the guarantees in anticipation of such an action.[31] In a country in which nationalist sentiments have always been high-pitched,

Alemann's proposal to sell off state-owned enterprises to private buyers created a political uproar, opposition leaders promising a re-nationalization of these industries following a return to civilian government. In retrospect, Alemann would have had extreme difficulty in convincing private businessmen to purchase flabby state entities. As recent history has repeatedly shown, nationalization can be accomplished by pointing to or with the ''gun'' of state power; short of slavery, even a dictator cannot force his citizens to buy businesses and then run them at a profit.

In April, 1982, the debate over the process was overshadowed by Galtieri's ill-fated invasion of the Falkland Islands.[32] Whether Galtieri tried to divert public attention from domestic economic problems or found a national consensus based on territorial aggression cannot be answered. What is certain about the Falklands debacle is that foreign creditors to Argentina's sovereign borrowers were caught completely off guard by the attack. As one of Citibank's top country risk analysts would later comment, the Falklands invasion was ''completely unforeseen,'' no country risk model being capable of predicting Galtieri's brash action.[33]

The Falklands defeat led to Galtieri's demise and the ascension of General Reynaldo Bignone. Unlike Viola's, Bignone's reversal of ''the process'' was sudden and virtually complete. Bignone fired Alemann on the spot, putting the economy under Dagnino Pastore, a staunch advocate of state interventionism in Argentina's domestic and external economies. Along with a 27 percent devaluation of the peso and export-promotion subsidies, Pastore again split the exchange rate, imposed import barriers and fixed the rate paid on bank deposits.[34] As to the state-owned enterprises, Pastore moved them further away from the influence of market mechanisms, prohibiting any borrowings by them from private banks and compelling them to cover their perennial deficits by going directly to the Argentine Treasury. In the course of eighteen months, Argentina had witnessed four presidents, five ministers of the economy and one war, with political instability causing inflation to skyrocket above 200 percent a year.[35] Since his assumption of power, Bignone repeatedly claimed that national elections would be held in November, 1983, in preparation for a return to civilian government on 30 January, 1984. His promises, however, did not appease the active national labor movement. Large-scale strikes continued as a protest against political oppression.

On 10 December, 1983, the Argentine Republic achieved a political miracle with a civilian government headed by President Raul Ricardo Alfonsín returning to power after a protracted period of military rule. Alfonsín, a political ''liberal,'' defeated a Peronist coalition by linking Peronist leaders to the repressive policies of the military executed during the 1970s. Alfonsín moved quickly to arrest Galtieri, Viola and Videla for crimes committed in the ''dirty war'' against the political opposition during the 1970s. General Bignone was spared arrest on these grounds, but was later arrested for his involvement in cadet deaths at an Argentine military academy. In a conciliatory gesture, Alfonsín allowed Isabel Perón to return from exile in Spain. The central thrust of Alfonsín's policy to date has come in the area of labor reform, the government removing from power labor leaders who had collaborated with the junta governments of the 1970s in repressing the labor movements that they were supposed to represent.

While Alfonsín's ascension is a most welcome event politically, in terms of the country's external debt (now estimated at between $42 billion and $45 billion), the return to civilian government is a mixed blessing. While a civilian government may afford Argentina increased political stability, Alfonsín's preliminary statements concerning debt and development certainly do not assuage the fears of its creditors. He has announced that Argentina will follow an unorthodox, non-monetarist policy, seeking an expansion of economic activity *and* a reduction of inflation, while the IMF and the nation's creditors continue to urge restraint and deflationary policies as a means of improving the country's debt-service capacity. With inflation hovering at 500 percent a year, Alfonsín may achieve his promised 100 percent reduction in inflation (down to 350 or 400 percent annual inflation), but expansionary policies of the type contemplated by Alfonsín are likely to lead to a further deterioration in Argentina's debt profile. The consensus is that Alfonsín will continue to advocate expansionary policies and to build up the nation's foreign exhange reserves until his political support has firmed, but that he will eventually knuckle under to IMF demands for an austerity program by mid–1984.

As Argentina suffered through 1982 under conditions of runaway inflation, the nation's debt profile and debt-service burdens went totally out of control.[36] According to data assembled by Morgan Guaranty, Argentina's total public external debt came to $38.5 billion by December, 1982, with nearly half ($19 billion) due within one year and $8.8 billion owed to U.S. banks alone as of June, 1982.[37] Annual debt service on foreign borrowings amounted to $7.8 billion for 1982,[38] giving the country an unsupportable debt-service ratio of 1:179.[39] Non-guaranteed private external debt, also involving a foreign exchange burden, has been estimated at about one-half of the public stock ($15 billion),[40] most of it due in the extremely near term, private borrowers having relied on foreign creditors to roll over thirty- to ninety-day credits.[41]

Any synopsis of Argentina's rescheduling in the early 1980s must remain murky and incomplete. The country's reorganization of its debt in late 1982 occurred among confusing circumstances and with none of the participants confident of its success in meeting existing debt problems. Owing some $25 billion to American, Western European and Japanese bankers, Argentina's government simply stalled for time in the summer of 1982. In July, the Bignone regime added further uncertainty to the proceedings by announcing that it was not planning to refinance its external debt, causing the specter of outright repudiation to haunt Argentina's creditors. Days later, the government reversed its position and declared its intention to reschedule official and commercial loans, but by October, 1982, the nation was making only minimal interest payments, halting amortization altogether.[42] Approaching Fund representatives at the Toronto meeting in September, 1982, Pastore and the IMF began negotiations which would eventually lead to an agreement on an emergency three-year quota loan totaling $2.15 billion in December, 1982.[43] Conditions were attached to the December credit, but the Fund took a realistic view of the country's dire circumstances in assessing just how much remedial action could be taken in the near future. For instance, one condition of the accord was a targeted inflation rate of 150 percent for 1983, down from the 200 plus percent pace of 1982 but still far from acceptable. In December, 1982, an *ad hoc* cartel of commercial creditors agreed to allow a stretching-out of maturities on $4.7 billion due in 1982, again under the urging of the IMF and official creditor governments.[44] Curiously, Great Britain, Argentina's mortal enemy in April, was highly instrumental in arranging the commercial rescheduling, with Lloyd's International leading British bankers in a bridging loan to help support the Argentinians in the fall of 1982, the Bank of England exercising its considerable influence in this matter.[45] Nineteen eighty-three was predicted to be a record year for Argentine grain harvests and commodity export receipts, but the political situation is so unstable that few analysts could express any faith that the current junta will comply with even the lenient IMF conditions attached to the December agreement.[46]

Commentary

There are four essential features of Argentina's development policy that have handicapped its economic performance and impaired its capacity to service the external debts used directly or indirectly to delay the adjustment of these inefficiencies. Bela Kadar's study of the Argentine economy provides a cogent account of the first intrinsic source of stagnation and mounting indebtedness, the inward-oriented, protectionist policy which has inhibited competitive integration of the domestic and external sectors. Economic growth in Argentina proceeded apace until the early 1950s, but thereafter stagnated and reversed itself. Kadar locates the cause of this cessation in the "import-substituting and protectionist economic development launched in the thirties and gaining momentum in the forties, [which] were able to uphold the traditional rate of progress until the early fifties," when GNP growth began to decelerate.[47] Under the first Perón regime, the Argentine government extended higher effective rates of protectionism to its domestic industry than any other country in Latin America, favoring state-run, capital-intensive production (e.g., Perón's "empire of steel") and setting a pattern maintained by special interests in the 1970s. One result of this protectionist regime was the "permanent narrowing down of contacts with the world economy"[48] as domestic production remained too inefficient to compete on global markets and imports were all but disallowed by trade barriers. As the capacity of domestic markets to absorb the production of hothouse industry reached its limit, productivity gains for industry declined. The ultimate paradox of this defensive, nationalist approach was "the increasing de-nation-alization of economic life in Argentina."[49] Import-substitution industry was heavily financed by foreign investors, MNCs bought up the remnants of poorly managed enterprises, and, later, external loans substituted for foreign exchange receipts as exports continued to labor under restrictive policies. Since the 1960s, there have been periodic efforts to expand and diversify Argentine exports,[50] but protectionism and exchange rate interventionism have offset any export-promotion measures.

The second impediment to balanced economic growth in Argentina has al-ready been highlighted in the discussion of Alemann's plans for revitalizing the economy. The size of the public sector and its high levels of deficit expenditure have been persistent obstacles to genuine economic development in Argen-tina.[51] The Argentine government has made distorted concessions to domestic producers in subsidizing and protecting industry, and it has sought to purchase the allegiance of its citizens by creating employment, fixing internal prices and underwriting vast social welfare programs. The IBRD calculates that public consumption as a percentage of GDP in Argentina grew from 9 percent in 1960 to 24 percent in 1980, a figure contrasting sharply with a 12 percent share for Mexico and a 10 percent share for Brazil.[52] The same political factors that have influenced the size of the public budget have worked against any increase in tax levies. Faced with chronic budget deficits, the Argentine government has resorted to the tandem measures of borrowing abroad and expanding the money supply.[53] During the Perón interim of the mid–1970s, the public deficit rose from 2 percent of GDP (1970–1972) to 6 percent in 1974 and 12 percent in 1975.[54] The record-breaking domestic inflation rates of the mid–1970s were the immediate outcome of this fiscal profligacy, and this same legacy has been passed down to the 1980s along with its attendant effects.

Public sector employment is the main source of government deficit spending in Argentina. Wages to workers in the public's employ comprise more than one-half of the public budget, a more precise figure being hard to deduce because data on military expenditures are not published by the Argentine government.[55] The government is not only responsive to the demands of its workers; it helps to organize them by running the country's largest union, an interest group which successfully pressured the Perón government into enlarging jobs for public ad-ministration workers from 283,000 in 1973 to 407,000 in 1975.[56] Subsidies to state-run industry are part and parcel of this syndrome.[57] The Argentine gov-ernment owns or controls the nation's "oil, transportation, airlines, shipping lines, all of the railroads, all of the underground, steel,"[58] half of the banks and nearly half of the insurance industry. These state enterprises are woefully inefficient in comparison to private entities, their prices are kept competitive only through government subsidies, and, since the advent of the Bignone re-gime, their deficits are made good by direct drawings on the Argentine Treas-ury.

The third aspect of Argentina's development strategy that has had a negative impact on its balance of payments and external debt positions is the disregard shown by the government toward the private sector. To be sure, Argentina's business community has benefitted from projects and programs designed to assist publicly owned enterprises, e.g., improvements in the infrastructure, financial institutions and the educational system.[59] During the brief Viola Administration the government initiated the semblance of a dialogue with entrepreneurial critics. Private business, however, has been forced to operate at a competitive disadvantage vis-à-vis subsidized, state-owned producers, and such openings as the government has extended for private inputs into economic policy-making have been quickly shut.[60] The extreme nationalism of the Argentine government has led to the promulgation of laws restricting joint domestic and foreign investment, the most sweeping being the Foreign Investment Act of 1973.[61] The de Hoz/Alemann reorganization programs evoked strong reaction from the private sector, opposition to tariff liberalization being especially avid.[62] Commenting on the effect of Alemann's process, Raul Prebisch complained that, "the policy followed here has suffocated private enterprise instead of promoting it."[63] Government favoritism toward the financial sector has also worked against the interests of private producers. Interest rates on domestic loans have been kept artificially high through government fixing; capital formation has been inhibited; and financial intermediation has become "more attractive than work,"[64] resulting in less productive employment.

The country's private agricultural producers have suffered from similar neglect. Over the decades, agricultural surplus has been systematically skimmed off to support industrialization, the government buying agrarian produce at 30 to 40 percent of its world market value and diverting the profits to investment in industrial modernization.[65] Occasionally, the Argentine government has indirectly promoted agrarian exports through devaluation of the peso,[66] but, more commonly, the peso's chronic overvaluation has hurt the nation's farmers in foreign markets.[67] In 1981, the country's export-oriented farmers were enraged by the government's decision "to hold up the inevitable devaluations until the end of the harvest,"[68] after grain exports had been marketed.

This brings the analysis to the final facet of government policy that has hindered development and undermined debt-service capacity: the rapid shifts in policy which have come about as successive governments have risen and been toppled. The exchange rate uncertainty which Argentina's exporters confront as a result of unexpected, massive devaluations is symptomatic of the insecure position of domestic investors in general. As Laura Randall finds, "The rapid shifts in Argentine economic policy led investors . . . to concentrate on projects that had a maximum pay back period of three years, and, when inflation was severe, of one year."[69] Reversals in the economic policy of the Argentine government create uncertainties among investors regarding future profit opportunities. These doubts predispose investors to go short, spread risks and hedge their bets, contrary to the needs of development for long-term, concentrated project capital. The consequence is that only the public sector has played a role in financing large-scale development projects, Argentine businessmen avoiding long-term commitments during which government policy may change many times over.

Stop-and-go shifts are part of the country's political life as well. Upon taking office, Videla promised to consult with civilians on matters of economic policy, but very little communication actually occurred.[70] In March, 1980, Videla proclaimed a Political Basis for National Reconstruction as a companion to de Hoz's process. The program included no reference to national elections, but simply the "identification of fundamental political values and democratic institutions around which a new national consensus could be constructed,"[71] in effect, a lower-case *abertura*. Billed as a gradual approach to democratization, political reconstruction in Argentina proceeded in a spasmodic stop-and-go pattern, with more "take" than "give."[72] The government repeatedly granted political concessions and then rescinded them in response to reactionary fears. The material basis for social discontent in Argentina is evident. Living conditions of the nation's working classes have decayed since 1950, giving Argentina the dubious distinction of being the only nation on earth "where the real wages of the workers have been stagnating for more than four decades."[73] The characteristic government solution for expressions of disaffection has been wholesale imprisonment, former President Ongania being a recent victim of political jailings due to his criticism of "the process" during the Galtieri regime.[74]

The willingness of the Argentine government to repay external debts to Western creditors has become more questionable in light of the downturn in relations between Argentina and its most prominent source of foreign borrowings, the U.S. government and its commercial lenders. Videla fulminated over Jimmy Carter's human rights campaign, weakened the U.S. embargo on grain deliveries to the Soviet Union, and supported anti-U.S. regimes in Latin America.[75] The Carter Administration responded in 1978 by cutting military aid and blocking credits to Argentina from the U.S. Export-Import Bank, but two years later $1 billion in trade credits were granted to Argentina through the lobbying efforts of American MNCs with subsidiaries in Argentina.[76] In the aftermath of American support for Great Britain during the Falklands War, U.S.-Argentine relations have reached their historical nadir. President Bignone refused to meet with Reagan during the latter's South American tour of December, 1982. Equally worrisome for the Western governments and their commercial lenders, the Argentinians have expanded contacts with the communist world, establishing relations with Cuba, East Germany, North Korea and the People's Republic of China, and exporting automobiles to Cuba and grain to the Soviet Union. "In the last few years, the Soviet Union has become one of the country's best customers,"[77] a telling indicator of the direction of Argentine foreign policy. As was the case with Mexico, Brazil, and, to a lesser extent, Turkey, the Argentines now eschew a special relationship with the United States. The erosion of

American-Argentine affairs adds further concern over the possibility of a unilaterally declared moratorium on the repayment of foreign debt and the more remote prospect of complete repudiation.

Notes

1. Bela Kadar, *Problems of Economic Growth in Latin America* (New York: St. Martin's 1980), p.178.
2. B. Cohen, p.186.
3. Gary Wynia, "Illusion and Reality in Argentina," *Current History,* February, 1981, p.62.
4. Ibid., p.64.
5. Ibid., p.62.
6. B. Cohen, p.186.
7. Gary Wynia, "The Argentine Revolution Falters," *Current History,* February, 1982, p.74.
8. Wynia, "Illusion and Reality", p.63.
9. Ibid.
10. B. Cohen, p.188.
11. Kadar, p.175.
12. Wynia, "Illusion and Reality", p.63.
13. B. Cohen, p.190.
14. Wynia, "Argentine Revolution", p.77.
15. Ibid., p.74.
16. Korth, "Country-Risk Analysis," p.57.
17. B. Cohen, p.188.
18. Lim, "Big Shift," pp.19–20.
19. Alan Robinson, "Roberto Alemann Treats Inflation as a Personal Enemy," *Euromoney,* April, 1982, p.17.
20. Wynia "Argentine Revolution," p.75.
21. Ibid.
22. A. Robinson, "Roberto Alemann," p.17–19.
23. Grant, "Carnival Is Over," p.3.
24. A. Robinson, "Roberto Alemann," p.17.
25. A. Robinson, "Latin America's Economies," p.10.
26. A. Robinson, "Roberto Alemann," p.17.
27. Grant, "Carnival Is Over," p.3.
28. A. Robinson, "Roberto Alemann," p.17.
29. Ibid., p.18.
30. Ibid., p.20.
31. Ibid., p.21.
32. Anderson "More Models," p.41.
33. Ibid.
34. A. Robinson, "End of Illusion," p.92.
35. Hughes, p.109.
36. A. Robinson, "End of Illusion," p.77.
37. Gilpin, p.D–1.
38. A. Robinson, "End of Illusion," p.92.

39. Grant, "Stuffees Have Left," p.36.

40. Lim, "Big Shift," p.31.

41. A. Robinson, "End of Illusion," p.92.

42. Egan, p.29; A. Robinson, "End of Illusion," p.92.

43. Gilpin, p.D–4.

44. Quek Peck Lim, "LBI Gets Caught in the Crossfire," *Euromoney,* February, 1983, pp.29–30.

45. Ibid., p.29.

46. Gilpin, p.D–4.

47. Kadar, p.173.

48. Ibid., p.181.

49. Ibid., p.182.

50. IBRD, *Annual Report: 1982,* p.13.

51. Wynia, "Argentine Revolution," p.75.

52. Ibid.

53. A. Robinson, "Roberto Alemann," p.20.

54. B. Cohen, p.187.

55. A. Robinson, "Roberto Alemann," p.20.

56. Kadar, p.190.

57. A. Robinson, "Roberto Alemann," p.20.

58. Ibid., p.22.

59. Laura Randall, *An Economic History of Argentina in the Twentieth Century* (New York: Columbia University, 1978), p.20.

60. Wynia "Argentine Revolution," p.76.

61. Kadar, p.187.

62. Wynia "Argentine Revolution," p.75.

63. A. Robinson, "Roberto Alemann," p.23.

64. Ibid.

65. Kadar, p.174.

66. Randall, p.23.

67. Wynia, "Illusion and Reality," p.63.

68. Wynia, "Argentine Revolution," p.75.

69. Randall, pp.18–19.

70. Wynia, "Illusion and Reality," p.65.

71. Ibid., p.64.

72. Wynia, "Argentine Revolution," p.76.

73. Kadar, p.182.

74. A. Robinson, "Roberto Alemann," p.22.

75. Astiz, p.49.

76. Wynia, "Illusion and Reality," p.85.

77. Astiz, p.89.

Chapter 9

CASE 5: POLAND

The External Setting

Much to the chagrin of Western bankers and official creditors, lending to Eastern European Council of Mutual Economic Assistance (CMEA/COMECON) nations has indeed proved different. Unlike the relatively comprehensive data supplied by most Hi-Income LDCs, communist-bloc countries do not provide full disclosure of their national accounts, and what they do publish is difficult to compare with figures from countries outside the Soviet sphere. Estimates of CMEA indebtedness are necessarily guesswork,[1] with the Soviets themselves setting the general pattern of withholding information on "sensitive" debt-related matters.[2] As important, most of the COMECON nations (including Poland at this writing) are not members of the International Monetary Fund. The Fund does not collect data on its non-members, it has no authority to furnish them with emergency loans, and it cannot mandate adjustment programs in these countries. To lend to a nation like Poland is to enter into uncharted waters without the conventional lifeboats on board.

For Poland, the central political reality is the pervasive dominance of the Soviet Union over national affairs. The "Poland that re-emerged after World War II was a product of Soviet thinking,"[3] the Russians conceptualizing Poland as both a bridge to and a buffer from the West. As the "majority" member of the COMECON economic alliance, the Soviet Union "can step in at any time and dramatically alter terms of trade" with and among its minority satellites, or it can "fail to supply the usual cheap energy and raw materials,"[4] using its economic leverage to keep dependent Eastern European nations in line. It is, then, Moscow, not the IMF, that functions as the "ultimate disciplinarian" over Polish economic policy, including the Poles' accumulation and handling of foreign debt.[5]

U.S. and Western European bankers were well aware of this arrangement as they considered expanding loan flows to Poland. Country risk analysts discovered a way of looking at loans to Poland that gave the impression of orthodox prudence, the vague "umbrella theory." [6] This notion "assumed that the Soviet Union would give its economic support to any [Soviet-bloc] country in trouble, like the IMF and the Central Banks in the West." [7] The Russians' interest in maintaining the stability and reputation of the COMECON pact would compel them to intervene if the domestic economies of their minions encountered significant difficulties, especially if Western creditors were involved. The history of Soviet lending policy to Eastern Europe gave additional force to the umbrella theory. "The Soviets underpinned and supervised their lending more strictly than the IMF, with all the rigours of the IMF, with no misgivings about usury, and with large supplies of gold to fortify reserves." [8]

The two main holes in the umbrella theory were the capacity of the Soviet Union to rescue communist-bloc countries with debt problems and its willingness to do so. By 1981, it was estimated that downturns in the balance of payments position of COMECON nations had led to a build-up of $80 billion in external debt for the alliance as a whole. [9] The Soviet's chief concern was rightfully with Poland, but other Eastern nations, e.g., Hungary and Romania, experienced similar debt crises in the early 1980s. [10] The Soviet Union did try to assist the Poles in 1981–1982, [11] much of this support financed by Soviet sales of gas and gold. [12] But the Russians soon began to feel their own liquidity strains as their domestic economy worsened and more "Polands" emerged. Even if the Soviet Union's ability to prop up communist economies was unlimited, whether it would want to exert unrestrained expenditure to this end is problematical. COMECON borrowings from the West formed a link between Soviet-bloc nations and capitalist creditors which ran directly across one of Russia's long-time goals, the greater economic integration of Eastern Europe. [13] As the dominant trading partner of all CMEA nations, the Soviet Union has the power to alter intra-bloc terms of trade at will. After World War II, the Soviets set prices on their exports to Eastern Europe at levels favorable to themselves. In the mid–1970s, Eastern Europe enjoyed a huge subsidy from the Soviets as a result of more favorable pricing to the buyers, with official U.S. estimates of net transfer amounting to $5–6 billion a year from Russia to its allies. In the 1980s, the Soviets have again reversed pricing arrangements, particularly through their charges on oil and gas exports at near-market rates. [14] If saving COMECON nations from declarations of default by Western creditors is at all a priority for the Soviet Union, it does not appear to rank very high on the list.

Western lending to Poland and other Eastern-bloc nations took on significant volumes in the mid–1970s. The flow of Eurocurrency bank credits to Eastern European and COMECON institutions increased from $38 million in 1970 to $3,394 million in 1977. [15] As the political thaw of detente took hold in the mid–1970s, "American business was increasingly reluctant to forego opportunities," [16] even in Marxist markets, and their export agencies and bankers were eager to support them with trade-related credits. The COMECON nations wanted Western technology to boost the productivity of their economies. This, in turn, would allow for increased exports to the West, which would generate the receipts necessary to pay for the debts assumed in the purchase of advanced capital goods.[17] Surveying the prospects among potential CMEA borrowers, Western bankers saw Poland as an outstanding investment opportunity, partially because Poland "had the richest resources of minerals of any of the six countries of Eastern Europe,"[18] including coal, sulfur, copper, zinc, silver and lignite.

While full accounting of Polish debt accumulation during the 1970s must remain sketchy, it is clear that the Poles entered the 1970s with less than $1 billion in foreign obligations and amassed over $30 billion in external debt by 1982.[19] As petrodollars from the banks and trade credits from Western export agencies poured into the country between 1976 and 1980, Poland's external debt more than doubled.[20] Some nations, like the United States, began to slow their Polish lending in the late 1970s, but others, like the Western Europeans and the Japanese, took up the slack. As of August, 1981, 17.3 percent of sovereign Polish debt was owed to official and commercial West German creditors, 13.1 percent to the United States, 11 percent to France, 7.8 percent to Austria, 7.6 percent to Britain, 4.5 percent to Japan, and, curiously enough, 6.5 percent to Brazil.[21] As late as March, 1979, a $500 million syndicated loan led by the Bank of America was not only marshalled: it was oversubscribed by $50 million,[22] as regional banks sought relationship business with the Poles and the money-center loan leaders.

One year later, in 1980, the appetite of Western bankers for Polish loans had been more than sated.[23] The Polish government's projected current account deficit for 1979 "proved wildly inaccurate," the actual figure being more than double that of the forecast.[24] When the Bank of America attempted syndication of another $500 million loan to the Polish government itself, it could raise only $375 million, including $80 million from Moscow's Bank Narodny and Poland's own Pekao Bank. West German bankers were able to raise a similar $500 million credit, but only after the West German Finance Ministry guaranteed 40 percent of the loan.[25] At the beginning of 1981, Poland's public external debt stood at $24 billion, evenly divided between commercial loans and official Western government credits.[26] During 1980, Poland was obligated to repay $5.2 billion in debt principal and $1.9 billion in interest—a sum equivalent to 68 percent of the nation's estimated exports.[27] As data on the situation trickled to the West, regional bankers followed their instincts and began to retreat from Polish lending en masse. Hence, when Bank Handlowy's Jan Woloszyn informed money-center bankers that the Polish government needed a new $1 billion jumbo in January, 1981, he drew a complete blank.[28]

Much of the change in bank attitudes toward Polish lending can be attributed to alterations in the foreign policies of their home governments. In the early 1970s, Western governments, particularly the West German Brandt Administration, saw social discontent in Poland as an opening for expanded relations with Poland via trade and credit, leading, perhaps, to a loosening of ties between Poland and the Soviet Union.[29] As Jerry Hough relates, Western governments reinforced the influence they had exerted on their bankers to lend to Poland by extending substantial trade credits themselves: "In June, 1977 Poland had $200 million of Commodity Credit Corporation credits outstanding and $143 million from the Export-Import Bank. In 1978 and 1979 Poland was granted an average of over $450 million of CCC credits a year, and the unpaid credits rose to $800 million in December, 1979. In 1980, 37 percent of the world-wide CCC outstanding credits were held by Poland."[30] Like other Western regimes, the Carter Administration would not decrease its flow of official trade credits to Poland because of the perception "that a U.S. refusal of loans would be a signal to the entire Western banking community of the precarious nature of the Polish situation," and the American President "did not want to be the one to bring down the house of cards."[31]

In Ronald Reagan the American people selected a President with no such qualms about upsetting the Polish applecart. Reagan's policy toward the Soviet Union was built on the self-fulfilling assumption that East/West detente had long since died, the Soviet invasion of Afghanistan being only a belated funeral. Within the Reagan Administration two distinct policy lines toward the Soviet bloc emerged. The Department of State's view, expressed by Secretary Alexander Haig and his staff, was multilateralist with regard to the iron curtain countries of Eastern Europe. The United States had legitimate interests in cooling relations with the Soviets, but as to the captive nations under its hegemony, sanctions against them would only punish the victims and alienate the United States from its Western European allies. The alternative unilateralist stance, professed by Secretary Caspar Weinberger and the Department of Defense, viewed Russia and its COMECON subordinates as being all of the same red cloth. By placing economic pressure on the already heavily burdened economies of Eastern Europe, the unilateralists maintained that the Soviets would be forced to divert resources to assist Poland, Romania, Hungary, etc., thereby lessening Russian defense expenditures.[32] The oil and gas pipeline and grain embargo issues demonstrated the hard-nosed approach of the Reagan Administration toward communism, and the American government became more averse to rescuing a totalitarian Poland from its debt crisis. Washington risk became as worrisome for Poland's commercial creditors as the downhill trend of the Polish economy. The bankers feared that the Reagan Administration might pressure American and foreign banks to cease loan flows to Poland, that the Commodity Credit Corporation might not honor its guarantees on U.S. bank loans to Poland, and that the American government, as one of Poland's principal creditors, might call the Poles into default, initiating the entire cross-default mechanism.[33]

The changed position of the United States government on East European debt brought the Americans into sharp conflict with their West European allies, especially the West Germans. The Europeans had a comparatively greater stake in resolving the Polish debt quandary than the Americans. West Germany, France, Austria, Italy and Great Britain had all increased their trade flows to Poland,

and the Germans, Austrians and French had been particularly heavy lenders to Poland relative to the size of their economies.[34] The Europeans interpreted the U.S. position as a disintegrative force within the Western alliance, and they pragmatically remarked that continued contacts with the East European nations would eventually indoctrinate the Poles with Western consumerism. An outright break in the ranks of Western governments on the Polish debt issue arose in December, 1979, when, "in defiance of the gentleman's agreement between Western export credit agencies," France's CoFace (the French equivalent of the U.S. Import/Export Agency) agreed to a bilateral rescheduling of $208 million in Polish loans. Western debt was burdening the borrowers, but it was threatening the stability of relationships among the lenders as well.

The Internal Setting

Why had Poland borrowed so heavily from Western official and commercial sources, and why was it unable to repay these obligations as originally contracted? Assuming power from Wladislaw Gomulka after the 1970 food riots, the regime of Edward Gierek sought a redirection of the course that national economic development had taken in Poland. As part of the 1971–1976 five-year plan, the new Polish leadership altered the path of economic growth from an "extensive to an intensive development pattern."[35] The new strategy rested on two planks. First, Poland would undertake the modernization of its industry by importing Western technology and contracting Western credit. These inputs would eventually pay for themselves in the form of increased production of tradeables, resulting in growth of export receipts from Western Europe and the United States. Second, foreign credit would also be used to support higher levels of current consumption. Bread and butter would be offered by the government to link the Polish people to the current regime and to encourage them to work the new industrial machinery without protests, strikes or riots. Official emphasis was placed on the first agenda item, the purchase of the most modern capital goods available from the West, but the ongoing need to satiate the Polish workforce had a powerful tacit part in Poland's enlargement of external borrowings.

From the standpoint of aggregate growth and productivity gains, Gierek's strategy produced extremely impressive results. Between 1971 and 1976, there was a 130 percent increase in industrial production and an 85 percent rise in national income,[36] so that "not only did the rate of industrial growth accelerate rapidly but real income rose 40 percent from 1971 to 1976."[37] Poland had accomplished the first part of its development process successfully by enlarging and enhancing industrial production, but the acid test of the strategy remained ahead. The essential premise of the 1976–1980 development program was that modernized and increased productive capacity would "permit an increase in export and a limitation of the expansion of import,"[38] converting the Poles' negative trade balance into positive terms. Raising exports more rapidly than imports would lead to a slowing of growth and current consumption increases, but once the foreign exchange burden of Western credit had been overcome, authentic, balanced development would again proceed apace.

By 1979, the shortcomings of this approach manifested themselves in a yearly growth rate of only 2.6 percent and a decline in national income of 2 percent.[39] More important, in this second stage of the Polish modernization scheme the planned 16.6 percent yearly rate of export growth did not materialize as exports increased at a 7.1 percent pace. Because of the disappointing export performance, the Gierek regime adjusted its balance of trade by reducing the annual rate of import growth from 14.4 percent to 10.6 percent.[40] Restricting imports further slowed the production increases in both tradeables and non-tradeables. Plants built under the optimistic assumptions of the early 1970s stood idle as capacity utilization plummeted.[41] By 1980, it was clear that Gierek's two-step approach to national economic development would mean one step forward followed by one step backward rather than a coordinated advance.

Why did the Polish development strategy falter over the financial obstacle of insufficient foreign exchange receipts to service external debt? The timing of Poland's planned entrance into the modern industrial world was unfortunate, the country having begun "developing its heavy industries at a time when the decline of steel production in the West had already reached crisis proportions."[42] Stagflation in the West, accompanied by heightened protectionism, dampened demand for Polish exports in Western European and American markets, while inflation in these countries caused the price of imported inputs to rise.[43] Raw materials and petroleum were necessary to run Poland's material- and energy-intensive production facilities, and the cost of these goods was increasing quickly, especially as the Soviet Union raised the price of its energy exports to world market levels.[44]

As suggested above, many of the main projects which the Poles had undertaken relied heavily on imported inputs. Activities like the production of steel and iron, nonferrous metals, chemicals and building materials required a 30 percent increase in costly fuel consumption,[45] the bulk of these needs being met from abroad. Moreover, it was in precisely the industries earmarked for export growth that this squeeze on foreign inputs was greatest.[46] The consequences were exacerbated by the focus of Poland's industrial program on finished manufactured goods, with "little effort . . . to develop domestic suppliers of raw materials,"[47] and, thus, a semi-permanent dependence on outside suppliers, primarily the Soviet Union and Western creditor nations. As a Polish journalist recalls, the fate of the Polish match industry was emblematic of this failure in the nation's industrial strategy.[48] Poland's small "match power" industry had served as a modest source of export revenues for decades. Gierek seized upon this performance and constructed gigantic match factories with the use of foreign technology and capital. The outcome was that "the import of certain components that were not needed for the old methods of production became necessary,"[49] these items being costly and limited by import tariffs. The lack of these essential inputs resulted in enormous factories with huge spare capacity where a few small and efficient producers had once stood. Poland is now a net importer of matches.

Then there is the debatable question, "Can Eastern manufactured goods really compete successfully with Western manufactured goods?"[50] The Poles had purchased capital goods of recent vintage from the West, but Western manufacturers still retained a technological edge in their even more recent improvements in plant. Quality control and marketing techniques did not meet the standards of Western production, and centralized planning and management lacked the flexibility to meet volatile fluctuations in world demand pricing.

Finally, as Zbigniew Fallenbuchl relates, Gierek's development approach proceeded on the "mistaken assumption that the transfer of technology on a large scale with the help of foreign borrowing was a viable alternative to economic reforms."[51] The Gierek regime had attempted to purchase popular support through economic performance and increased consumption in the first phase of the development program. When performance stumbled and consumption was constricted, there was no reciprocal compensation to the Polish people in meeting authoritarian demands. In the end, both planks of the first stage lacked the staying power needed for the second phase.

Even as Gierek and the Polish leadership exulted over the results of the first five-year plan, a storm was brewing among the Polish workforce. In June, 1976, a coalition of workers and intellectuals laid the groundwork for Solidarity with the establishment of the Committee for the Defense of the Workers (KOR).[52] This alliance between Poland's laborers and intelligentsia was an innovation in the opposition's organization against the country's authorities, the first time in which the two groups had actively collaborated. The intellectuals included a "second generation" of the learned elite, "less beholden" to the communists for their privileged status in Polish society.[53] It was KOR that provided the nucleus for the Solidarity movement which surfaced in the summer of 1980.[54]

As the breadth of Solidarity's backing became evident to Gierek and his comrades, the government met the situation with promises of greater citizen participation in national decision-making and an upgrading of individual rights.[55] Whether Gierek actually intended to create an opening in the Polish power structure is doubtful, and, in retrospect, initial government concessions to Solidarity were obviously not meant to transform Poland to the degree envisioned by the movement.

One year later, the ultimate fate of Solidarity was determined within the institution of Poland's Communist Party. Those at the top of the Party's hierarchy were increasingly disturbed by Solidarity's growing influence on the lower echelons, many younger Party members showing signs of a divided loyalty.[56] It was at the July, 1981, Communist Party Congress that the repression of Solidarity was set into motion. The Congress "failed to introduce a system of 'contractual' democracy, which on the one hand would guarantee genuine political pluralism in Poland, and, on the other hand, would preclude the possibility of struggle for political survival,'' in effect, one acceptable to the Soviet Union.[57] Long before the declaration of martial law, Poland's old guard Communist Party leaders had formed their own coalition with the military and taken the upper hand. One inadvertent effect of the Solidarity movement was that initial decentralization of the power structure "weakened the ability of the central authorities to solve pressing national problems," including rapidly mounting foreign debts.[58]

It was with the Solidarity movement in full swing that the Polish government sought a restructuring of its external official and commercial borrowings. The reorganization of credits on bilateral government-to-government loans, mainly trade-related financing from Western export agencies, was begun in May, 1981.[59] With the promise of greater democratization in Poland before them, Paris Club members readily agreed to assist the Poles, renegotiating $1.5 billion in debt service on $6 billion of official loans, including some $300 million in accumulated arrears.[60] Negotiated on the standard year-by-year basis, the 1981 accord was to have been followed in 1982 by a similar treatment of the nation's 1982 debt service. However, when the party and the military ousted Gierek and imposed martial law in December, 1981, Western leaders refused to enter into a new round of negotiations with Warsaw, leaving commercial creditors to go it alone in 1982.

Bank lenders from various OECD nations had an obvious shared interest in the successful restructuring of Poland's commercial debt, but different shadings soon emerged within their ranks. In general, the European bankers, with higher relative levels of exposure in Poland, were more eager to put a solution in place and avoid a declaration of default than were their American counterparts.[61] With 501 Western banks holding claims against sovereign Polish debtors and no IMF to supervise negotiations and adjustment, the banks approached their task with trepidation. Their anxieties were not assuaged by the statements of the Polish government. In June, 1980, Woloszyn had assured assembled Western creditors that his nation would pay its obligations on time. By March, 1981, Woloszyn informed these same bankers that the country was illiquid and could not meet its repayment schedule.[62] The bankers established a twenty-bank multinational task force as the sole medium for commercial debt negotiations with Poland, the committee being staffed exclusively by major money-center personnel. The Poles insisted on an immediate deferral of all principal payments due between 27 March and 30 June, 1981. Quarreling among the bankers arose on this matter, the West Germans willing to accept the proposal, the Swiss rejecting it and the Americans calling for penal interest rates over the period. The Germans prevailed and the committee established its first common principle for the upcoming bargaining rounds: there would be no rescheduling of interest payments owed by Poland.[63] On 20 May, 1981, the bankers came to an accord among themselves on the terms of a rescheduling of Poland's current commercial debts. Ninety-five percent of the $2.1 billion due to the banks as amortization payments in the last nine months of 1981 would be rescheduled over seven and a half years, with a four-year grace period. Margins would be "hard," with interest charges set at 1 $^3/_4$ percent over LIBOR, a stiff additional penalty of 2 $^3/_4$ percent for late payments and an extra 1 percent renegotiation fee. The terms of rescheduling were especially harsh since no refinancing was to be extended. Hammering out these terms proved easier than coming to agreement among creditors on the issue of conditionality. Hard-line American banks, led by Banker's Trust, insisted on fuller disclosure of relevant national account data from the Poles, while the more liberal European banks pushed for a quick signing. Individual lenders began to press their own unique interests, with Chase Manhattan unsuccessfully arguing that its $525 million loans to a state-owned copper producer be treated separately since the entity received its own distinct foreign currency inflow. A schism among the bankers was averted at a 22 July meeting in Zurich. A steering committee would issue quarterly progress reports on Poland using official data, the debtor providing the necessary figures without revealing their sensitive sources. The banks also wrote a stipulation into the agreement which would ultimately rebound on them, that "all interest payments must be current by the deadline for the signing of a full agreement"[64] in December, 1981. Presenting this unified restructuring program to the Poles in late September, the bankers compelled Polish officials to sign at once, threatening an immediate declaration of default and the end of all commercial credit for Poland in this century.

By March, 1982, the 1981 rescheduling was already in trouble. The Poles had fallen short on the $500 million interest payment for the third quarter of 1981 by some $50 million.[65] The Polish economy was so illiquid in its foreign currency holdings that this final payment came in March only after strenuous national effort supported by Soviet gold sales. The bankers were ambivalent in their attitudes toward the declaration of martial law, hoping for increased economic stability but watching their own governments grow stern on the issue of official renegotiations with the new Polish regime. The next hurdle was faced by creditors and debtors alike on 10 September, 1982. Designated as "cross-default day" in the 1981 accord, the provision stated that if the Poles were not meeting their 1982 repayments on commercial debt as scheduled, and had not agreed upon an acceptable rescheduling package for 1982's debt service by 10 September, the bankers could unravel the 1981 agreement, call in all their Polish loans and begin seizing such Polish assets as they could grasp. The day came and went without a ripple. Treasury Secretary Donald Regan commented in October, 1982, that the U.S. government's refusal to reschedule its Polish loans had little real effect on America's banks, noting that "the 1982 principal and interest [on commercial loans] are not yet rescheduled, but the banks of the world are still getting along."[66] On 3 November, 1982, 503 Western banks announced an agreement with Bank Handlowy to defer 95 percent of the nation's $2.4 billion principal payments owed in 1982. Repayment was stretched out over seven and a half years with a four-year grace period, and, identical to the 1981 terms, interest rates were set at 1 $^3/_4$ percent over LIBOR with a 1 percent rescheduling surcharge. Poland's sovereign borrowers were given until March, 1983, to repay $1.1 billion owed on interest for 1982, but the bankers effectively violated their own rule of no rescheduling on interest, rolling over 50 percent of interest due and providing $600 million in new, short-term hard currency credits.[67] As 1982 drew to a close, official lenders remained staunch in their refusal to deal with Poland's martial law government, and the banks faced the prospect of a long series of year-by-year reschedulings, without the benefit of IMF participation and, temporarily, without a parallel renegotiation of official credits. Once again, lending to the communist world had indeed proved different.

Commentary

The shortcomings of pervasive government control over national economic development are most fully illustrated in a centrally planned economy's performance when it interacts with open market forces. The distortions of information that occur as the characteristic result of subordinates attempting to meet iron-clad quotas[68] are merely a part of a broader set of problems endemic to centrally planned economies. The Polish government had undertaken the modernization of the national economy "by *a priori* decision from the center," i.e., the regime's top economic and planning offices, rather than "as an outcome of micro-decisions at the level of production and foreign trade enterprise."[69] Poland suffered doubly on this score. It had diffused the concentration of authority at the top without allowing free-market forces at the bottom to control costs and prices.[70] Exercising their power in regulating production and distribution, the central authorities lacked "an internal pricing system that properly reflects scarcity," meaning that the conduct of foreign trade based on artificially set prices was irrational.[71] Increased cross-border trade and capital movements functioned to open "traditionally closed Soviet bloc economies to outside economic forces, like rising interest rates and sagging markets."[72] The centralized decision-making format lacked the flexibility to respond to volatile shifts in global prices for factors of production, and therefore could not compete against fluid open market enterprises.[73] Moreover, "Soviet-style central planning is more effective in promoting quantity than quality; at encouraging risk-avoidance than innovation,"[74] giving products from these economies competitive disadvantages against capitalist goods of high standard and wide variety. The outcome for Poland was that internal economic growth proved feasible via credit and technology from the West, but external economic growth in competitive world markets was not achieved.

The Gierek government avoided a hard choice faced by LDCs in general— the tradeoff between using resources for productive investment or supporting higher levels of consumption—by simply borrowing more from the West. Productivity gains in the early 1970s appeared to confirm the validity of this approach in the short term, but Polish authorities were forced to re-examine this strategy after the first oil shock of 1973–1974. Some East European countries lowered their growth targets in response to this externality. The Poles elected to continue their import-led approach, using foreign capital and capital goods to attain further increases in domestic production *and* consumption.[75] In the early 1970s, Polish workers and peasants did enjoy a temporary rise in living standards, amounting to a 17 percent yearly increase in real household expenditures from 1970 to 1978.[76] These improvements were not perceived as significant and lasting by many Polish workers. In a secret poll of manual laborers taken in 1979, workers were asked: "Did living conditions for you and your family improve during 1970–1978?" A full 40 percent of the respondents answered "no change" or "deterioration" to this inquiry.[77] While the Western media emphasized the political and human rights aspects of the Solidarity movement, the opposition's grievances against the Polish government have usually taken the form of complaints about bread and butter issues, i.e., wage and price policies.[78] During the early and mid–1970s, Gierek avoided widespread popular disruption by increasing real purchasing power, using foreign money to foot a portion of the bill. When the second stage was reached in 1976 and exports did not approach their growth targets, imports were restricted, consumption was curbed, real wages went down and food riots erupted.[79] Whenever the Gierek regime contemplated adjusting its development course by cutting Western inputs, raising domestic prices and suppressing demand, it was deterred by the potential for renewed riots and strikes, and a re-enactment of the fall of Gomulka.[80]

Like major Latin American debtor countries, Poland's development approach In the 1970s stressed industrial modernization over increases in agrarian productivity. During the period 1971–1975, industry's share of total Polish investment grew from 39.4 percent to 43.8 percent, as agriculture's portion of the total declined from 16.1 percent to 13.7 percent.[81] In 1981, it was reported that agricultural productivity in Poland had risen by a mere 30 percent throughout the entire decade of the 1970s.[82] Poor performance in this sector had created a Polish "food deficit" and the accompanying need to import foodstuffs on a scale that affected the nation's entire balance of payments position. The Polish regime tried to placate the urban workforce by freezing the price of meat, but this policy "interacted disastrously [with] the rise in excess purchasing power."[83] Polish workers found themselves with enough currency to buy meat at the fixed price, but the freeze discouraged increased meat production and led to empty butchers' shelves. The heightened expectations that Polish workers had entertained as their paychecks grew were dashed when essential items became more and more scarce.[84]

The central figure in the Polish debt drama was undoubtedly Edward Gierek. Gierek took charge in 1970 when Wladislaw Gomulka enacted measures which meant sacrifices in living standards, e.g., price hikes on food.[85] In contrast to his successor, Gomulka had taken an overly cautious approach to economic development, exhibiting "a morbid fear of inflation" which led to recessionary policies.[86] Gierek observed these events at first hand, and so it was natural for him to adopt expansionary investment and high consumption levels as remedial policies and to continue them as an alternative to the Gomulka past. Gierek was also well acquainted with the bureaucratic backstabbing that is such a salient feature of political life in totalitarian regimes. Gierek appointed his own brand of pragmatists and technocrats, the so-called Silesian Gang, selecting officials more on the basis of personal loyalty than merit. Western observers watched as Gierek's "team changed posts in a totally irrational manner,"[87] but there was a certain method to this madness, insofar as it limited the ability of subordinates to establish their own stable power bases, which could eventually be used against the current regime. Ironically, the same manifestations of popular discontent that caused the downfall of the wary Gomulka also acted to topple the ambitious and expansive Gierek. Currently, General Wojciech Jaruzelski holds the reins of Polish economy in a vise-like grip. For Western creditors Jaruzelski and martial law have led to Draconian discipline and order in economic affairs. In 1982, the Jaruzelski regime cut imports from the West by 40 percent, transforming a 1981 balance of payments current account deficit into a modest $1 billion current surplus for 1982, thereby improving Poland's debt-service capacity on paper.[88] However, despite the forceful resolution of the political crisis in Poland, the nation's external debt crisis is still very much in the air as Western official creditors shun the Poles' authoritarian rulers.

In the previous cases examined in this book, major LDC debtor nations accumulated debt from the industrialized West and treated the problems it brought within a foreign policy framework aimed at achieving greater economic and political independence. For Mexico, Brazil, Argentina and Turkey, this meant a shift in a foreign policy axis away from Western Europe and especially the United States, and toward Third World, OPEC and COMECON nations. Poland, then, represents a variation on this theme, for its debt was contracted and rescheduled within an aborted movement toward Western Europe and the United States and away from dependence on the Soviet Union. The major debt crises of the present historical era have almost invariably occurred against a backdrop of significant shifts in domestic and foreign policies, their ramifications being both economic and political.

Notes

1. Donald W. Green, "How the Dollar's Fall Distorted the Picture of COMECON Debt," *Euromoney*, June, 1980, p.47.

2. Angelini, Eng and Lees, p.65.

3. Arthur R. Rachwald, "Poland: Quo Vadis?" *Current History*, November, 1982, p.371.

4. Fallon and Shirref, p.28.

5. Sampson, p.264.

6. "Nightmare," p.38.

7. Sampson, p.263.

8. Ibid., p.262.

9. Dini, p.53.

10. Anderson and Field, p.20.

11. Fallon and Shirref, p.19.

12. Hans Haumer, "Technology Went Eastward, But Some of It Was Misdirected," *Euromoney,* September, 1982, p.337.

13. Roger Skurski, "Trade and Integration in East Europe," *Current History,* November, 1982, p.357.

14. Ibid., p.358.

15. Angelini, Eng and Lees, p.62.

16. Skurski, p.359.

17. Haumer, p.335.

18. Sampson, p.264.

19. "Nightmare," p.16.

20. Ibid., p.10.

21. Ibid.

22. Ibid.

23. Sampson, p.266.

24. "Nightmare," p.15.

25. Ibid.

26. Sampson, p.266.

27. Jerry F. Hough, *The Polish Crisis: American Policy Options* (Washington: Brookings Institution, 1982,) p.17.

28. "Nightmare," p.15.

29. Sampson, p.264.

30. Hough, pp.15–16.

31. Ibid., p.16.

32. Fallon and Shirref, p.25.

33. "A Case for Default?" *The Banker,* April, 1982, p.7.

34. Haumer, p.337.

35. Zbigniew M. Fallenbuchl, "Policy Alternatives in Polish Foreign Economic Relations," in *Background to Crisis: Policy and Politics in Gierek's Poland,* ed. Maurice D. Simon and Roger E. Kaner (Boulder, Colorado: Westview, 1981), p.349.

36. Maurice D. Simon, "Poland Enters the Eighties," in *Background to Crisis: Policy and Politics in Gierek's Poland,* ed. Maurice D. Simon and Roger E. Kaner (Boulder, Colorado: Westview, 1981) p.406.

37. Hough, p.12.

38. Fallenbuchl, p.353.

39. Simon, p.408.

40. Fallenbuchl, p.353.

41. Hough, p.13.

42. Haumer, p.337.

43. Fallenbuchl, p.362.

44. Simon, p.406.

45. Fallenbuchl, p.362.

46. Ibid.

47. Hough, p.13.

48. Andrzej Szczypiorski, *The Polish Ordeal: The View from Within,* trans. Celina Wieniewska (London: Croom Helm, 1982), p.138.

49. Ibid.

50. Angelini, Eng and Lees, p.64.

51. Fallenbuchl, p.351.

52. Szczypiorski, p.4.

53. Simon, p.410.

54. Rachwald, p.373.

55. Simon, pp.405–406.

56. Szczypiorski, p.135.

57. Rachwald, p.389.

58. Ibid.

59. "Another Year Older," p.87.

60. Ibid.

61. Sampson, p.266.

62. "Nightmare," pp.9–10.

63. Ibid., p.16.

64. Ibid., pp.15–21.

65. "Another Year Older", p.87.

66. Anderson and Field, p.19.

67. Paul Lewis, "Polish Debt Refinancing Said to Be Near Signing," *The New York Times,* 2 November, 1982, p.D–1.

68. Szczypiorski, p.94.

69. Fallenbuchl, p.363.

70. Hough, p.13.

71. Skurski, p.360.

72. Ibid., p.386.

73. Fallenbuchl, p.360.

74. Skurski, pp.360–361.

75. Hough, p.12.

76. Ibid., p.14.

77. Ibid., p.16.

78. Simon, p.409.

79. Skurski, p.386.

80. "Nightmare," p.10.

81. Fallenbuchl, p.352.

82. Simon, p.407.

83. Hough, p.14.

84. Ibid.

85. Ibid., p.11.

86. Szczypiorski, p.85.

87. Ibid., p.92.

88. Lewis, p.D–1.

Chapter **10**

CONCLUSION

Introduction

Broad conclusive statements concerning the present debt dilemma of developing nations cannot be constructed without the aid of a patchwork of assumptions and interpretive generalizations. The dimensions of the current crisis are too extensive, too complex and too changeable to allow for sweeping summaries, and the non-economic factors influencing LDC external debt undermine universal conclusions. The same protean characteristics of the LDC debt problem necessarily diminish the validity and accuracy of forecasts about the future evolution of Third World indebtedness. Near-term predictions are of limited usefulness given the volatile nature of the situation at present, and, primarily for the same reason, long-range predictions are more akin to augury or prognostication than scientific forecast. Moreover, in the absence of a worldwide, systemic model of world debt as a framework (and no such reliable model is extant to my knowledge), narrow speculations (e.g., those on a country-by-country basis), will fail to capture essential multilateral interactions, and, of course, global predictions will have no firm ground at all. Nevertheless, there are discernible directions in the development of LDC debt which can be identified and articulated in a fairly reasonable manner, with the ongoing proviso that such ''weathervane'' predictions are tentative and ultimately simplistic.

The Borrowers

Some major LDC debtors may have ''laid the trap'' for commercial lenders by borrowing amounts so large and in such a short space of time that the resulting high levels of bank exposures in these lands create a substantial, long-term stake for the bankers in their economic progress and, thus, the motive for continued lending. Paradoxically, in laying this trap, many of these same countries now find themselves locked into their relations with commercial lenders, having become dependent upon these flows to support development investment and current consumption. At the same time, with official credits tied to even tighter specific conditions by lender governments and the IMF, versatile-use bank loans remain highly appealing to LDC economic policy-makers. Hence, while the banks may reduce the growth of their sovereign lending to developing nations, demand for such credit will continue to be strong, and such transfers will increase in volume over the next five years, albeit at a more modest pace than was the case in the 1978–1982 period. Some developing nations, however, may seek to replace a portion of these costly credits by encouraging greater multinational corporate investment in their economies, thereby spreading out foreign exchange repayment burdens. As World Bank President Tom Clausen recently observed, "Constrained commercial bank lending, together with high interest rates, makes direct foreign investment more attractive and more important to developing countries."[1] In the long term, then, autonomous capital from commercial lenders may undergo a cut in its share of total external financing to major LDC debtors, with direct investment progressively taking up the slack.

Most principle sovereign debtors, and all of the case countries examined in this book, have been compelled to enter into restructurings of their official and commercial debts over the past five years. In the vast majority of cases, such reschedulings have been permitted only within the context of an adjustment program approved by the IMF. In the short term, therefore, the general thrust of economic policy in these nations will be toward fiscal and monetary discipline, deflation and austerity, simply because of clauses in official and bank workouts requiring conformity to IMF-monitored adjustment criteria. In the long term, pressures to reflate the economies of indebted LDCs, particularly population growth in Latin American countries, are likely to lead to a resumption of economic expansionism and ambitious development programs in the mid- and late 1980s.

How the externalities which impacted upon Third World borrowers in the 1970s and early 1980s will affect their economic and debt-service performance in the next few years is problematical. In light of the dissipation of OPEC unity, the cost of energy inputs should be less dear for LDC importers of petroleum, relieving constraints on many of their newly established, energy-intensive industries. The movement of international interest rates depends largely on the budgetary and monetary policies pursued in the industrialized nations, especially the United States. Recent expressions of concern about the effect of U.S. interest rates on LDC debt repayment made by the Reagan Administration and the Federal Reserve Board provided cause for optimism on this front, but unabated federal deficit spending in the United States runs contrary to LDC debt relief. Probably the most uncontrollable of the three main external blows that shocked debt-laden LDCs in the recent past is the combined impact of deterioration in terms of trade for LDC commodity exports and heightened protectionist walls erected around developed nation markets. As Clausen maintains, in order for developing countries as a group to attain a 5.5 percent GDP annual growth rate over the next decade, there must be a reversal in policy by the United

States, Western Europe and Japan away from defensive trade barriers, and there must be a depreciation of the dollar in relation to LDC currencies, primarily through U.S. budgetary restraint.[2]

The Lenders

Multilateral lenders to the developing world are likely to increase their loan volumes to heavily indebted LDCs, in effect delaying their "graduation" and extending their eligibility for discount credit. The World Bank, in anticipation of a large role in financing Third World development, has recently requested a Selective Capital Increase parallel to the IMF's Eighth General Review of Quotas, and it is again considering tapping commercial bank sources for funds to be re-lent to developing countries. The IBRD, moreover, is moving decisively in the direction of "general" or balance of payments financing and away from pure project lending as a means of aiding debt-troubled nations. As Ernest Stern, the Bank's Vice-President for Operations, recently commented with specific reference to IBRD efforts in Brazil and Mexico: "There is a very dramatic shift to financing activities which are relatively quick disbursing and focused on (1) more effective utilization of capacity rather than starting new investments, (2) maintenance and rehabilitation of existing capacity, and (3) energy, to reduce demand for energy through conservation and to help countries achieve greater self-sufficiency."[3] Having participated in first-stage building of productive capacity, the Bank is now clearly moving toward second-stage development tasks, and this shift in orientation is bringing the IBRD close to balance of payments financing and the traditional functional area of the Fund. However, there are, and will be, closely defined limits on innovative lending by the IBRD, as, for example, that contained in the current policy of restricting structural adjustment lending to 10 percent of the Bank's annual lending. While the volume of loans from the IBRD and other multilateral institutions will certainly grow, the movement into new types of lending will proceed in a cautious, measured and reversible manner.

Sovereign LDC lending by the governments of the United States, Western Europe and Japan is not likely to experience an appreciable change in the near future apart from some periodic short-term, emergency credits to counter liquidity crises. Lending to the Third World is not a particularly popular policy objective, development aid in general having long since lost its luster among Western legislators, and charges of "bank bailout" are now being heard from without and within developed nation governments in response to current official support for LDCs with heavy commercial debts. The economic recovery in the West is welcome news for LDC exporters, as is the modest decline in American interest rates, but deficit spending on the part of the Reagan Administration, with its influence on an overly strong dollar, continues to cloud LDC debt-service capacity. Over the next five years, then, official lender governments will exercise their power over LDC debt not through a radical expansion of lending or a branching out into new forms of credit, but through fiscal, monetary and commercial policies targeted at external and internal economies and heavily influenced by domestic politics.

The critical flow of commercial bank loans to LDCs has certainly undergone a retrenchment phase which will be apt to remain in force over the next two years. Indeed, according to Clausen, it must be acknowledged that "problems of some major borrowers *have* shaken confidence in international commercial lending and slowed its rate of growth."[4] The withdrawal of money-center banks from LDC lending (or, more accurately, continued acceleration of credits to LDC borrowers) has been partially determined by the reluctance of regional banks to participate in syndicated loans to these countries. However, substantial pressures for continued lending on the part of the larger banks are prevalent, not the least of which are existing levels of exposure and the newfound interventionism of the IMF. While the bankers may bemoan the presumptive and preemptive actions of the Fund following the Toronto meeting of 1982, as Managing Director de Larosière notes, "the banking operations recently organized for the three largest Latin American countries [Brazil, Mexico and Argentina] show a net increase in exposure of 7 to 8 percent in 1983, compared with an average of about 30 percent during 1978–1981."[5] The confluence of caution, regard for existing LDC assets and official prodding will probably result in a steadied pattern of growth for commercial loan flows to LDCs in the near term, followed by a period of reassessment once present exposures are brought under prudential control and pressing debtor problems are contained.

The Negotiators

Much the same course that has been suggested for the World Bank will hold true as a general direction for the International Monetary Fund: IMF resources will be increased, but the Fund's basic mission will remain unaltered. As part of its balance of payments adjustment lending program through the quota mechanism, the IMF has granted some $24.8 billion in standby and extended conditional credits at present, with $15.6 billion of this amount remaining to be disbursed from 1983 through 1985.[6] IMF assets in currencies and securities from member quota contributions reached $65 billion as of 31 July, 1983, with $1 billion in reserves and $3.5 billion in gold holdings contributing to a total of $75 billion in the assets of the General Department.[7] In March, 1983, the Fund's Board of Governors authorized an increase in quota levels from the current figure of approximately $65 billion to $90 billion, with members having until 30 November, 1983, to consent to this proposed increase.[8] Preliminary reports indicate that most of the major IMF quota contributors, i.e., the nations of the Development Assistance Committee, Group of Ten and OPEC alliances, will approve this raise in quota obligations, progressively bolstering Fund resources for conditional lending.

The biggest news in Fund activities over the past two years was undoubtedly its intervention into commercial reschedulings as part of its efforts on behalf of Mexico, Brazil and Argentina. According to one Fund spokesman, "These were situations in which a failure to act would have harmed not only members' own adjustment programs but possibly the functioning of the international monetary system as well."[9] In his own retrospective analysis of the Fund's pivotal activism in the Latin American reschedulings of 1982–1983, de Larosière emphasized the moderating function of the Fund while downplaying the dramatic and precedent-setting character of its actions:

If the Fund had not sought to catalyze additional resources from the banks and advocated large-scale rescheduling of repayments, the countries in question would have been forced to adjust to far lower levels of financing. This would have entailed extremely high economic, social and human costs. . . . After the explosion of bank exposure in several countries in the late 1970s, it was important for banks to participate in new financing for 1983 and beyond, but in such a way as to gradually scale down their funding.[10]

Somewhat ironically, it is possible to argue that the Fund's activism in recent Latin American commercial debt reorganizations was an innovation that will work against a further enlargement of the IMF's formal powers. It will probably be argued that existing formal powers gave the Fund sufficient leverage vis-à-vis the banks in the Latin American orchestrations, and that additional empowerments are consequently unwarranted and undesirable. The inherent conservatism of both major voting member nations and the IMF itself will also constrain the Fund's powers into the same form that they presently exhibit. Over the medium term, i.e., the next two to ten years, we can foresee no new multilateral institution created to treat international debt, no return to the gold standard, no replacement of national currencies by SDR-like instruments and very little loosening of the Fund's conditional lending criteria.

Both the Paris Club and the *ad hoc* bank cartels involved respectively in official and commercial debt restructurings will retain their flexible/makeshift form, their short-term orientation and their narrow approach to LDC debt apart from the context of national economic development. The Paris Club and the bankers value their current maneuverability and will continue to rely upon previously negotiated IMF adjustment programs as controlling frameworks for their own reschedulings without establishing stronger formal links with the Fund. Bankers may close ranks further in their stances on LDC rescheduling, particularly as regionals withdraw from the field and the number of players is reduced, and some standardization of commercial rescheduling principles and procedures may occur; but, on the whole, the commercial bank rescheduling format will continue without further codification, much to the displeasure of the debtor nations.

Case Countries

Moving from the realm of grandiose, worldwide predictions to the more provincial matter of forecasts for the individual countries examined in the case portion of this study, the same balance of ameliorating and aggravating factors appearing in the prospects for LDC debt as a whole is found in the case of each of the major debtor nations investigated here. Turkey has been repeatedly cited as a prime example of successful adjustment designed by multilateral bodies, primarily the IMF.[11] While the Turks have exhausted their reserve tranche position with the Fund,[12] they have overcome the hump in their debt service schedule and onerous commercial debt service obligations have been greatly reduced. The recent popular election of parliamentary candidates from Turgut Ozal's Motherland Party, followed by General Evren's request to form a civilian coalition government in Turkey, will undoubtedly be welcomed by the international lending community. Ozal's selection as head of the Turkish state bodes well in terms of Turkey's capacity and willingness to honor external debt commitments in a timely fashion. On the other side of the ledger, the Turks may become embroiled in the emerging dispute over Cyprus. This, in turn, could drive another wedge between Turkey and its OECD/NATO allies, and it could lead to deficit spending in support of increased defense budgets. In the absence of such misplaced nationalism, the Turks appear to have successfully surmounted their latest debt crisis, and the debt and economic performance of Turkey in the most recent past encourages an optimistic outlook for the future.

Both Mexico and Brazil have experienced difficulties in conforming to conditions attached to IMF adjustment loans extended in late 1982, the bulk of which remain undisbursed. In both cases, considerable popular discontent, especially among industrial workers and students, has followed in the wake of deflationary austerity measures "dictated" by the Fund. Moreover, population growth in both countries runs directly counter to such orthodox stabilization campaigns, while full democratization of the Brazilian and Mexican political systems would probably result in further reflationary pressures. Neither Mexico nor Brazil has a remaining tranche reserve with the Fund,[13] and this too bodes ill in the near term. In the final analysis, though, we must concur with the rosy assessment of the "maverick" Walter Wriston in viewing the debt-service and economic potential of these countries in a favorable light, and we would predict that within the next decade there will be renewed growth in these economies equal to that of their respective "miracle" years. Therefore, while liquidity problems may arise from time to time for Mexico and Brazil in their repayment of external debt, both nations have the ability to meet financial/economic burdens of accumulated debt in the long run, and both, being committed to expansion of international trade, have ample reason to keep their international credit records clean by avoiding moratoria, repudiations and declarations of default.

Argentina's external debt prospects are infinitely less certain than those of Mexico and Brazil. Having also used up their reserve tranche position with the Fund,[14] the Argentines face the same chronic difficulties of inflation, deficit spending and a bloated public sector that have afflicted their economy over the past three decades. The 1983 election of a civilian government in Argentina is a heartening sign from a political standpoint, the Bignone regime's acceptance of this result being somewhat surprising given its previous authoritarian tendencies. Unfortunately, in contrast to the Ozal Administration in Turkey, Argentina's new leaders have no explicit commitment to rational adjustment, external debt repayment or economic orthodoxy beyond those specified in their comparatively liberal IMF package. It would appear that the stop-and-go pattern of vacillating economic policies that has been the rule in Argentina over the past decade will continue, hampering economic performance and external debt-service capacity.

As for Poland, it remained a "pariah nation" in international lending, the United States government maintaining the cut-off of trade, aid and capital flows to Poland that it established as response to the imposition of martial law in December, 1981. Solidarity leader Lech Walesa has called for a resumption of American and Western European credit to Poland, and President Reagan promised to consider such a restoration. However, the Soviet Union's power over intra-bloc terms of trade within the COMECON alliance is an uncontrollable factor in the Polish debt situation. The Soviet "umbrella" is now closed to Western bankers and has taken on the form of a prod or skewer as worsening East/West relations predispose the Russians to undercut normalization of Poland's economic ties to the West.

The Polish debt picture improved somewhat since the Jaruzelski regime announced the suspension of martial law on 21 July, 1983. This announcement was greeted by Western commercial creditors as a positive sign, and on 18 August, 1983, a cartel of Western banks approved the rescheduling of $2.6 billion in commercial debts due in 1983. Subsequently, on 2 November, 1983, the Reagan Administration announced that it would rejoin discussions on the reorganization of the $11 billion owed by Poland to Western governments, and the thaw between the United States and Poland continued as Reagan lifted on 19 January, 1984, two sanctions previously imposed by the United States against the martial law government.

Politically, while martial law has been suspended, the Jaruzelski regime finds itself in much the same spot as the Gierek government. For example, on 30 December, 1983, the government postponed an increase in consumer food prices in response to anticipated civil disturbances, only to impose the 10 percent price hike on 30 January, 1984. The economic discontent of the Polish people is accompanied by political discontent, the latest centering on the government's efforts to remove crucifixes from public places, schools, for example. This campaign has brought the political leadership into a direct confrontation with the Catholic church, with even the cautious Jozef Cardinal Glemp disapproving the state's disestablishment campaign.

Notes

1. A.W. Clausen, *Address to the Board of Governors: 27 September, 1983* (Washington: International Bank for Reconstruction and Development, 1983), p.11.

2. Ibid., p.8.

3. "The Challenge of Development Today," *Finance and Development,* September, 1983, p.3.

4. Clausen, *Address,* p.11.

5. "Debt Rescheduling: What Does It Mean," *Finance and Development,* September, 1983, p.29.

6. International Monetary Fund, *Financial Statements of the General Department: Quarter Ended July 31, 1983* (Washington: International Monetary Fund, 1983), p.35.

7. Ibid., p.5.

8. Ibid., p.13.

9. "Debt Rescheduling," p.29.

10. Ibid.

11. "Challenge of Development," p.3.

12. International Monetary Fund, *Financial Statements,* p.29.

13. Ibid., pp.21–25.

14. Ibid., p.21.

BIBLIOGRAPHY

"Akturk: The Planner Who Longs to Plan Less." *Euromoney,* February, 1982, pp.16–19.

Alves, Maria Helena Moreira. "Mechanisms of Social Control of the Military Governments in Brazil, 1964–1980." In *Latin American Prospects for the 1980s: Equity, Democratization and Development.* Ed. Archibald R.M. Ritter and David H. Pollock. New York: Praeger, 1983, pp.240–304.

Anderson, Tim, "More Models Than Vogue Magazine." *Euromoney,* November, 1982, pp.41–46.

————. "The Year of Rescheduling." *Euromoney,* August, 1982, pp.19–22.

Anderson, Tim, and Field, Peter. "The Tremors That Threaten the Banking System." *Euromoney,* October 1982, pp.17–31.

Anderson, Tim, and Lim, Quek Peck. "Syndicated Lending—Out for the Count." *Euromoney,* February 1983, pp.36–40.

Angelini, Anthony; Eng, Maximo; and Lees, Francis A. *International Lending, Risk and the Euromarket.* New York: John Wiley, 1979.

"Another Year Older and Deeper in Debt." *The Economist,* 6 March, 1982, pp.87–88.

"As Debt Grows, the Economy Grows Faster." *Euromoney,* March, 1981, pp.20–22.

Asheshov, Nicholas. "What's Ahead for Mexican Borrowing." *Institutional Investor,* November, 1981, pp.307–310.

Astiz, Carlos A. "Changing United States Policy in Latin America." *Current History,* February, 1982, pp.49–51, 88–90.

"At Last the Foreign Investor Is Welcome." *Euromoney,* February, 1982, pp.31–32.

Baburogulu, O.N. "Toward A Theory of Stalemated Social Systems: The Turkish Case." In *Dependence and Inequality: A Systems Approach to the Problems of Mexico and Other Developing Countries.* Ed. R. Felix Geyer and Johannes van der Zouwen. New York: Pergamon, 1982, pp.89–105.

Bacha, Edmar L. "Selected Issues in Post–1964 Brazilian Economic Growth." In *Models of Growth and Distribution for Brazil.* Ed. Lance Taylor, Edmar L. Bacha, Eliana A. Cardoso, and Frank H. Lyst. New York: Oxford University Press, 1980, pp.17–48.

Balassa, Bela. *Adjustment to External Shocks in Developing Economies.* World Bank Staff Working Paper No. 472. Washington: IBRD, 1981.

————. *Incentive Policies in Brazil.* World Bank Staff Working Paper No. 133, 1981.

————. *The Process of Industrial Development and Alternative Development Strategies*. Essays in International Finance, No. 141. Princeton: Princeton University Press, 1981.

Bee, Robert N. "Syndication." In *Offshore Lending by U.S. Commercial Banks*. Ed. F. John Mathis. Washington: Banker's Association for Foreign Trade, 1981, pp.177–181.

Bell, Geoffrey, "Debt Rescheduling—Can the Banking System Cope?" *The Banker*, February, 1982, pp.17–24.

Bennett, Robert A. "Brazil's Bank Loan Bid Stirs Concern." *The New York Times*, 18 November, 1982.

Bergsman, Joel. *Income Distribution and Poverty in Mexico*. World Bank Staff Working Paper No. 395, 1980.

Bitterman, Henry J. *The Refunding of International Debt*. Durham, North Carolina: Duke University, 1973.

"Brazil: Crashing Through the Debt Barrier." *The Economist*, 6 September, 1980, pp.76–77.

"Brazil: Having to Run Harder." *The Banker*, March, 1982, pp.88–91.

Brown, James. "Turkey's Policy in Flux." *Current History*, January, 1982, pp.26–30, 37, 38.

Buchanan, Sherry. "Bedding down with the World Bank." *Euromoney*, April, 1982, pp.111–115.

Calverley, John. "How the Cash Flow Crisis Floored the LDCs." *Euromoney*, August, 1982, pp.23–31.

Caplan, Basil. "Brazil's Delicate Balancing Act." *The Banker*, December, 1981, pp.19–23.

Carrada-Bravo, Francisco. *Oil, Money and the Mexican Economy: A Macroeconometric Analysis*. Boulder, Colorado: Westview, 1982.

"A Case for Default?" *The Banker*, April, 1982, p.7.

"The Challenge of Development Today." *Finance and Development*, September, 1983, pp.2–5.

Chenery, Hollis B. *Interactions Between Industrialization and Exports*. World Bank Staff Working Paper No. 150, n.d.

Cizauskas, Albert C. *The Changing Nature of Export Credit Finance and Its Implications for Developing Countries*. World Bank Staff Working Paper No. 409, 1980.

Clark, William. "Robert McNamara at the World Bank." *Foreign Affairs*, Fall, 1981, pp.167–184.

Clausen, A.W. *Address to the Board of Governors: 27 September, 1983* (Washington: International Bank for Reconstruction and Development, 1983).

———— "The World Bank: Helping One Another" *Vital Speeches*, 1 October, 1982, pp.751–756.

Cline, William R. *International Monetary Reform and the Developing Countries*. Washington: Brookings Institution, 1976.

Coes, Donald V. *The Impact of Price Uncertainty: A Study of Brazilian Exchange Rate Policy*. New York: Garland, 1979.

Cohen, Benjamin J. *Banks and the Balance of Payments: Private Lending in the International Adjustment Process*. Montclair, New Jersey: Allan Held, Osmun, 1981.

Cohen, Stephen D. "Forgiving Poverty: The Political Economy of International Debt Relief Negotiations." *International Affairs*, Winter/Spring, 1981–1982, pp.59–77.

Curtin, Donal. "The Bank of Tokyo Counts the Cost of Leadership." *Euromoney*, February, 1983, pp.91–96.

———. "The Mexican Shokku." *Euromoney*, November 1982, pp.113–120.

———. "Muldoon: Why There Will Be a Crash." *Euromoney*, February, 1983, pp.69–72.

DaCosta, Michael. "How Bank Lending Helps the LDCs." *The Banker*, October 1980, pp.47–51.

Davis, Christopher. "A New Approach to Rescheduling." *The Banker*, January, 1980, pp.105–109.

Davis, Stephen I. "International Bank Expansion: Time for a Reassessment." *The Banker*, May, 1981, pp.63–66.

"Debt Rescheduling: What Does It Mean." *Finance and Development*, September 1983, pp.26–30.

Dell, Sidney, and Lawrence, Roger. *The Balance of Payments Adjustment Process in Developing Countries*. New York: Pergamon, 1980.

Dickenson, John P. *Brazil*. Kent: William Dawson, 1978.

Dini, Lamberto. "Financial Strains in the World Economy." *Banco Nazionale del Lavoro: Quarterly Review*. March, 1983, pp.51–69.

Dod, David P. "Bank Lending to Developing Countries: Recent Developments in Historical Perspective." *Federal Reserve Bulletin*, September, 1981, pp.647–656.

Dodd, C.H. *Democracy and Development in Turkey*. London: Euthen, 1979.

Egan, Jack. "Banks on the Brink: Flirting with Global Collapse." *New York*, 25 October, 1982, pp.28–31.

Einzig, Paul, and Quinn, Brian Scott. *The Euro-Dollar System: Practice and Theory of International Interest Rates*. New York: St. Martin's, 1977.

"Energy? The Answer Is the Dam on the Euphrates." *Euromoney*, February, 1982, pp.24–25.

Fallenbuchl, Zbigniew M. "Policy Alternatives in Polish Foreign Economic Relations." In *Background to Crisis: Policy and Politics in Gierek's Poland*. Ed. Maurice D. Simon and Roger E. Kaner. Boulder, Colorado: Westview, 1981, pp.329–371.

Fallon, Padraic, and Shirref, David. "The Betrayal of Eastern Europe." *Euromoney*, September, 1982, pp.19–30.

Field, Peter. "Meet the New Breed of Banker: The Political Risk Expert." *Euromoney*, July, 1980, pp.9–21.

———. "The Shunning of the Sovereign Borrower." *Euromoney*, May, 1982, pp.27–41.

Field, Peter; Shirref, David; and Ollard, William. "The IMF and Central Banks Flex Their Muscles." *Euromoney*, January 1983, pp.35–44.

Fishlow, Albert. "Latin American External Debt: The Case of Uncertain Development." In *Trade, Stability, Technology and Equity in Latin America*. Ed. Moshe Syrquin and Simon Teitel. New York: Academic Press, 1982, pp.143–165.

———. "The United States and Brazil: The Case of the Missing Relationship." *Foreign Affairs*, Spring, 1982, pp.904–924.

Flamson, Richard J. "How Structural Distortions Hamper World Recovery." *Euromoney*, September, 1982, p.167.

Frank, Isaiah. *Trade Policy Issues for the Developing Countries in the 1980s*. World Bank Staff Working Paper No. 478, 1981.

Ganoe, Charles S. "A Banker's View: Country Analysis." In *Developing Country Debt*.

Ed. Lawrence G. Franko and Marilyn J. Seiber. New York: Pergamon, 1979, pp.93–100.

Gilpin, Kenneth N. "The Maze of Latin America's Debt." *The New York Times,* 13 March, 1983.

Gisselquist, David. *The Political Economy of International Bank Lending.* New York: Praeger, 1981.

"Global Ripples from Turkey's Financial Crisis," *Businessweek,* 15 December, 1980, p.91.

Gonzales, Emmanuel. "Call a Country a Company and It Looks Better." *Euromoney,* February, 1983, pp.47–55.

Goodman, Laurie, and Worth, Nancy. "The Future of Commercial Banks in LDC Financing." *The Banker's Magazine,* November/December, 1981, pp.78–83.

Grant, Charles. "The Carnival Is over, but There's Always Next Year." *Euromoney,* April, 1982, p.3.

————."Don't Call the IMF: It's Running out of Quotas." *Euromoney,* August, 1982, pp.51–52.

————."The Stuffees Have Left, the Stuffers Remain." *Euromoney,* November, 1982, pp.33–37.

Grayson, George W. "Oil and Politics in Mexico." *Current History,* November, 1981, pp.379–383, 393.

Green, Donald W. "How the Dollar's Fall Distorted the Picture of Comecon Debt." *Euromoney,* June, 1980, pp.47–53.

Greene, James R. "Financing Foreign Governments and Official Entities." In *Offshore Lending by U.S. Commercial Banks.* Ed. F. John Mathis. Washington: Banker's Association for Foreign Trade, 1981, pp.213–249.

Group of Thirty. *Risks in International Bank Lending.* New York: Group of Thirty, 1982.

Grubel, Herbert G. *A Proposal for the Establishment of an International Deposit Insurance Company.* Essays in International Finance, No. 133. Princeton: Princeton University, 1979.

Guth, Wilfred. "International Banking: The Next Phase." *The Banker,* October, 1981, pp.27–34.

Haegle, Monroe. "The Behavior and Determination of Spreads in the Medium-Term Eurocurrency Market." *Business Economics,* September, 1980, pp.41–48.

Hagen, Everett E. *The Economics of Development.* 3rd ed. Homewood, Illinois: Richard D. Irwin, 1980.

Ul Haq, Mahbub. "Negotiating a New Bargain with the Rich Countries." In *From Dependency to Development: Strategies to Overcome Underdevelopment and Inequality.* Ed. Heraldo Munoz. Boulder, Colorado: Westview, 1981, pp.117–123.

Hardy, Chandra. "Rescheduling Developing Country Debts." *The Banker,* July, 1981, pp.33–38.

Haumer, Hans. "Technology Went Eastward, But Some of It Was Misdirected." *Euromoney,* September, 1982, pp.335–339.

Hope, Nicholas C. *Developments in and Prospects for the External Debt of Developing Countries: 1970–1980 and Beyond.* World Bank Staff Working Paper No. 488, 1981.

Hough, Jerry F. *The Polish Crisis: American Policy Options.* Washington: Brookings Institution, 1982.

"How to Sell Garlic, Tractors and Fish." *Euromoney*, February, 1982, pp.26–27.

Hughes, Jane Spivak. "The Countries of the Future Don't Look So Hot Today." *Euromoney*, January, 1983, pp. 108–109.

Hurni, Bettina S. *The Lending Policy of the World Bank in the 1970s: Analysis and Evaluation*. Boulder, Colorado: Westview, 1980.

IBRD. *See* International Bank for Reconstruction and Development.

International Bank for Reconstruction and Development (IBRD). *The World Bank Annual Report: 1982*. Washington: World Bank, 1982.

———. *World Development Report: 1982*. New York: Oxford University Press, 1982.

International Monetary Fund. *Financial Statements of the General Department: Quarter Ended July 31, 1983*. Washington: International Monetary Fund, 1983.

———. *Summary Proceedings: Annual Meeting, 1982*. Washington: International Monetary Fund, 1982.

Ipsen, Erik. "After Mexico, the Regionals Retreat." *Euromoney*, January, 1983, pp.58–65.

"It Was a Black Economy: Now at Least It Will Be Gray." *Euromoney*, February, 1982, p.22.

Kadar, Bela. *Problems of Economic Growth in Latin America*. New York: St. Martin's, 1980.

ten Kate, Adriaan, and Wallace, Robert Bruce. *Protection and Economic Development in Mexico*. New York: St. Martin's, 1980.

Killick, Tony. "Euromarket Recycling of OPEC Surpluses: Fact or Myth?" *The Banker*, January, 1981, pp.15–23.

Kincaid, G. Russell. "Inflation and the External Debt of Developing Countries." *Finance and Development*, December, 1981, pp.45–48.

Korth, Christopher M. "Developing a Country-Risk Analysis System." *The Journal of Commercial Bank Lending*, December, 1979, pp.53–68.

———. "The Management of International Lending Risks by Regional Banks." *The Journal of Commercial Bank Lending*, October, 1981, pp.27–36.

———. "Risk Minimization for International Lending in Regional Banks." *Columbia Journal of World Business*, Winter, 1981, pp.21–28.

Krueger, Anne O., and Tuncer, Baran. "An Empirical Test of the Infant Industry Argument." *American Economic Review*, December, 1982, pp.1142–1152.

Kuczynski, Pedro-Pablo. "Action Steps After Cancun." *Foreign Affairs*, Summer, 1982, pp.1022–1037.

Lal, Deepak. *A Liberal International Economic Order: The International Monetary System and Economic Development*. Essays in International Finance, No. 139. Princeton: Princeton University, 1980.

"Lead Managers of Loans to Latin America." *Euromoney*, April, 1982, pp.5–7.

Leeds, Roger S. "External Financing of Development—Challenges and Concerns." *Journal of International Affairs*, Spring/Summer, 1980, pp.19–39.

———. "Why We Need More Co-Financing." *The Banker*, August, 1980, pp.21–26.

Leff, Nathaniel H. *Underdevelopment and Development in Brazil: Reassessing the Obstacles to Economic Development*. London: George Allen & Unwin, 1982.

Levine, Robert H. "Brazil: The Dimensions of Democratization." *Current History*, February, 1982, pp.60–63, 86, 87.

Lewis, Paul. "Polish Debt Refinancing Said to Be Near Signing." *The New York Times*, 2 November 1982.

————. "$20 Billion Aid Accord for IMF," *The New York Times*, 17 January, 1983.

Lim, Quek Peck. "The Big Shift in Bank Strategies." *Euromoney*, November, 1982, pp.16–21.

————. "The Borrower's Trump Card Is His Weakness." *Euromoney*, October, 1982, pp.35–37.

————. "LBI Gets Caught in the Cross-Fire." *Euromoney*, February, 1983, pp.29–35.

Long, Millard, and Veneroso, Frank. "The Debt-Related Problems of Non-Oil Less Developed Countries." *Economic Development and Cultural Change*, April, 1981, pp.501–516.

Looney, Robert E. *Development Alternatives of Mexico: Beyond the 1980s*. New York: Praeger, 1982.

Lutz, Ernst, and Bale, Malcolm D. *Agricultural Protectionism in Industrialized Countries and Its Global Effects: A Survey of the Issues*. World Bank Reprint Series, No. 174, n.d.

Lutz, Ernst, and Scandizzo, Pasquale E. *Price Distortions in Developing Countries: A Bias Against Agriculture*. World Bank Reprint Series, No. 175, n.d.

McCauley, Robert N. "A Compendium of IMF Troubles: Turkey, Portugal, Peru, Egypt." In *Developing Country Debt*. Ed. Lawrence G. Franko and Marilyn J. Seiber. New York: Pergamon, 1979, pp.143–181.

Merrick, Thomas W., and Graham, Douglas H. *Population and Economic Development in Brazil: 1800 to the Present*. Baltimore: John Hopkins, 1979.

Mueller, P. Henry. "A Conspectus for Offshore Lenders." In *Offshore Lending by U.S. Commercial Banks*. Ed. F. John Mathis. Washington: Banker's Association for Foreign Trade, 1981, pp.1–35.

Nashashibi, Karim. "Devaluation in Developing Countries: Difficult Choices." *Finance and Development*, March, 1983, pp.14–17.

Neu, Carl R. "The International Monetary Fund and LDC Debt." In *Developing Country Debt*. Ed. Lawrence G. Franko and Marilyn J. Seiber. New York: Pergamon, 1979, pp.236–249.

"A Nightmare of Debt: A Survey of International Banking." *The Economist*, 20 March, 1982, pp.3–29.

Nowzad, Bahram. "Debt in Developing Countries: Some Issues for the 1980s." *Finance and Development*, March, 1982, pp.13–16.

————. *The IMF and Its Critics*. Essays in International Finance, No. 146. Princeton: Princeton University, 1981.

Nowzad, Bahram, and Williams, Richard C. *External Indebtedness of Developing Countries*. IMF Occasional Paper No. 3. Washington: International Monetary Fund, 1981.

OECD. *See* Organization for Economic Cooperation and Development.

Ollard, William, and Sington, Anne. "The Unique Club of Michel Camdessus." *Euromoney*, August, 1982, p.54.

Orfila, Alejandro. *The Americas in the 1980s: An Agenda for the Decade Ahead*. Lanham, Maryland: University Press of America, 1980.

Organization for Economic Cooperation and Development (OECD). *External Debt of Developing Countries: 1982 Survey*. New York: 1982.

Palmer, Robert B. "The Funding Risk in International Lending." In *Offshore Lending by U.S. Commercial Banks*. Ed. F. John Mathis. Washington: Banker's Association for Foreign Trade, 1981, pp.249–263.

Pang, Eul-Soo. "Abertura in Brazil: A Road to Chaos?" *Current History,* February, 1981, pp.57–62, 88.

Pastore, José. *Inequality and Social Mobility in Brazil.* Madison: University of Wisconsin, 1982.

"Phaseout of Credit Restraint Measures." *Federal Reserve Bulletin,* July, 1980, pp.559–561.

Pine, Art. "IMF Becomes a Leader in Rescuing Debtor Lands, but Its Austerity Measures Are Called Too Rigid." *The Wall Street Journal,* 11 January 1983.

"Praying for Redundancy." *Euromoney,* November, 1982, p.46.

"Preparing for the Day When Turkey Can Borrow Again." *Euromoney,* February, 1982, pp.14–15.

"A Programme to Make Capitalism Work." *Euromoney,* February, 1982, pp.5–10.

Purcell, Susan Kaufman. "Mexico-U.S. Relations: Big Initiatives Can Cause Big Problems." *Foreign Affairs,* Winter, 1981–1982, pp.379–392.

"Pushing the Banks into Export Financing." *Euromoney,* February, 1982, pp.29–30.

Putnam, Bluford H., and Thomas, Lee. "Oil Might Soon Be $25 a Barrel or Less." *Euromoney,* February, 1983, pp.103–104.

Rachwald, Arthur R. "Poland: Quo Vadis?" *Current History,* November, 1982, pp.371–376, 389–392.

Randall, Laura. *An Economic History of Argentina in the Twentieth Century.* New York: Columbia University, 1978.

Riding, Alan. "Credit for Mexico Is Reported." *The New York Times,* 18 November, 1982.

Riley, William H. "How Regional Banks Approach Country Exposure and Country Risk." *Journal of Commercial Bank Lending,* March, 1980, pp.33–44.

"The Road to Capitalism." *Euromoney,* February, 1982, pp.1–4.

Roberts, David. "The LDC Debt Burden." *Federal Reserve Bank of New York,* Spring, 1981, pp.33–41.

Robinson, Alan. "Can Brazil Make It?" *Euromoney,* November, 1982, pp.103–111.

———. "The Cousins Who Take Care of Mexico's Borrowing." *Euromoney,* April, 1982, pp.32–37.

———. "The End of Illusion in Latin America." *Euromoney,* September, 1982, pp.77–82.

———. "How Latin America's Economies Are Under Pressure." *Euromoney,* April, 1982, pp.9–16.

———. "Portillo Pockets the Banks." *Euromoney,* October, 1982, pp.47–49.

———. "The Position of ALFA Is Delicate, Delicate, Delicate." *Euromoney,* June, 1982, pp.43–49.

———. "Roberto Alemann Treats Inflation as a Personal Enemy." *Euromoney,* April, 1982, pp.17–25.

———. "Will Mexico's New President Match Lopez Portillo?" *Euromoney,* April, 1982, pp.27–30.

Robinson, J.N. "Is It Possible to Assess Country Risk?" *The Banker,* January, 1981, pp.71–81.

Roll, Lord. "End the Chaos and Build a New System." *Euromoney,* September, 1982, pp.119–123.

Roth, Terrence. "Poland, Banks Agree on Plan for 1982 Debt." *The Wall Street Journal,* 2 November, 1982.

Ruding, H.O. "Lenders Ought to Consult the IMF." *Euromoney*, February, 1980, pp.34–38.

Sampson, Anthony. *The Money Lenders: Bankers and a World of Turmoil*. New York: Viking Press, 1981.

Sanders, Thomas G. "Brazil in the 1980s: The Emerging Political Model." In *Authoritarian Capitalism: Brazil's Contemporary Economic and Political Development*. Ed. Thomas C. Bruneau and Philippe Faucher. Boulder, Colorado: Westview, 1981, pp.193–219.

Schlagheck, James L. *The Political, Economic and Labor Climate in Mexico*. Philadelphia: Wharton School of Economics, 1979.

Seiber, Marilyn J. "Alternative Proposals for Debt Relief." In *Developing Country Debt*. Ed. Lawrence G. Franko and Marilyn J. Seiber. New York: Pergamon, 1979, pp.185–214.

————. "Debt Escalation: Developing Countries in the Eurocurrency Market." In *Developing Country Debt*. Eds. Lawrence G. Franko and Marilyn J. Seiber. New York: Pergamon, 1979, pp.42–80.

————. *International Borrowing by Developing Countries*. New York: Pergamon, 1982.

Senkin, Roman I. "Using Country Risk Assessments in Decision Making." *Journal of Commercial Bank Lending*, August, 1980, pp.28–37.

"Serrano Guides the World's Biggest Borrowings." *Euromoney*, November, 1981, pp.27–29.

"Shrinking from Mexico." *Euromoney*, October, 1982, p.2.

Sigmund, Paul E., "Latin America: Change or Continuity?" *Foreign Affairs*, Spring/Summer, 1982, pp.629–657.

Simon, Maurice D. "Poland Enters the Eighties." In *Background to Crisis: Policy and Politics in Gierek's Poland*. Ed. Maurice D. Simon and Roger E. Kaner. Boulder, Colorado: Westview, 1981, pp.405–418.

Singer, Morris. "Turkey in Crisis." *Current History*, January, 1981, pp. 27–32,39, 40.

Skurski, Roger. "Trade and Integation in East Europe." *Current History*, November, 1982, pp.357–362, 386–388.

Southard, Frank A. *The Evolution of the International Monetary Fund*. Essays in International Finance No. 135. Princeton: Princeton University, 1979.

"The State Enterprises Can't Simply Be Handed Over." *Euromoney*, February, 1982, pp.24–25.

Street, James H. "Mexico's Economic Development Plan." *Current History*, November, 1981, pp.374–379.

Stuart, Alexander. "Opportunity Knocks in Troubled Mexico." *Fortune*, 23 August 1982, pp.146–154.

Szczypiorski, Andrzej. *The Polish Ordeal: The View from Within*. Trans. Celina Wieniewska. London: Croom Helm, 1982.

Tinnin, David B. "The War Among Brazil's Bankers." *Fortune*, 11 July, 1983, pp.50–55.

Trebat, Thomas J. "Brazil's Balancing Act: Austerity Versus Social Stability." *Euromoney*, April, 1982, pp.55–59.

"Turkey: Back Again." *The Banker*, February, 1981, pp.77–78.

"Turkish Banker's Delight." *Euromoney*, December, 1982, p.12.

"Turkish Tea and Sympathy in the Royal Garden." *The Economist*, 17 January, 1981, p.79.

"Two Statistical Approaches." *The Banker*, January, 1981, p.79.

Tyler, William G. *Advanced Developing Countries as Export Competitors in Third World Markets: The Brazilian Experience*. Washington: The Center for Strategic and International Studies, 1980.

Urquidi, Victor L. "Not by Oil Alone: The Outlook for Mexico." *Current History*, February, 1982, pp.78–81,90.

"Vintage Deals of the Year." *Euromoney*, September, 1982, pp.299–303.

Weinert, Richard S. "The State and Foreign Capital," In *Authoritarianism in Mexico*. Ed. José Luis Reyna and Richard S. Weinert. Philadelphia: Institute for the Study of Human Issues, 1977, pp.109–129.

Willet, Thomas D. *International Liquidity Issues*. Washington: American Enterprise Institute for Public Policy Research, 1980.

Williams, Charles M. "International Lending in the Decade Ahead." In *Lending Offshore by U.S. Commercial Banks*. Ed. F. John Mathis. Washington: Banker's Association for Foreign Trade, 1981, pp.263–286.

Williamson, John. *The Lending Policies of the International Monetary Fund*. Washington: Institute for International Economics, 1982.

Wolfe, Alexander McW. "International Lending Risks: Country Risk." In *Offshore Lending by U.S. Commercial Banks*. Ed. F. John Mathis. Washington: Banker's Association for Foreign Trade, 1981, pp.43–76.

Wynia, Gary. "The Argentine Revolution Falters." *Current History*, February, 1982, pp.74–77, 87.

———. "Illusion and Reality in Argentina." *Current History*, February, 1981, pp.62–65, 84–85.

Yohai, Samuel Alberto. "How the World Bank Might Recycle Assets." *Euromoney*, January, 1983, pp.46–49.

INDEX

About the Author

CHRIS C. CARVOUNIS is Associate Professor of Economics and Finance at St. John's University, New York. He serves as Chairman of the Board of Education of the Greek Archdiocese of North and South America and is a member of the New York State Legislative Commission on Science and Technology. He has contributed to the *Columbia Journal of World Business*, the *Journal of Finance*, the *American Economist*, and the *Review of Economic Literature*, among others.